SPES ALIT AGRICOLAS

BRILL 325 YEARS OF SCHOLARLY PUBLISHING

BRILL 325 YEARS OF SCHOLARLY PUBLISHING

Sytze van der Veen

Contributions by

Paul Dijstelberge
Mirte D. Groskamp
Kasper van Ommen

TUTA SUB AEGIDE PALLAS · 1683 ·

BRILL

LEIDEN • BOSTON
2008

TABLE OF CONTENTS

INTRODUCTION

Reaching the age of 325 is an occasion that deserves to be celebrated. Koninklijke Brill, "Royal Brill," is the oldest publishing house in the Netherlands, and the firm takes pleasure in showing that it is alive and kicking.

Twenty-five years—sometimes turbulent, but ultimately very successful years—have elapsed since the third centenary in 1983. Once again, the commemorative celebration is designed to place Brill in its historical context. The publishing house is acting as the chief sponsor of the splendid exhibition "Leiden, City of Books," which is being held this year in the Stedelijk Museum De Lakenhal. Furthermore, as part of Brill's 325th anniversary celebration, Brill's archive for the years 1848-1991 has been added to the Luchtmans archive, which was previously donated to the Royal Society of the Dutch Book Trade. The complete company archive, covering the period 1683-1991, is now carefully administered by the Department of Special Collections at the University of Amsterdam Library. This provides a better opportunity not only for the study of our firm, but also for the study of the history of the book trade in our country. We look forward to the appearance of some interesting monographs in the years to come.

What you are holding is an informal company history that has been compiled largely on the basis of this archive. We are very grateful to Sytze van der Veen for the enthusiastic and expert way in which he told our story. Along with him, we too are curious about the sequel!

During the past few years, many people have been working to organize the archive, compile a complete list of the firm's publications, and study the source materials. Our special thanks go to Laurens van Krevelen, who, as chairman of the Library of the Book Trade Foundation, supported us very much in pursuing this initiative. The staff of the Department of Special Collections of the University of Amsterdam, in particular Garrelt Verhoeven and Nico Kool, were always willing to advise and assist us. Mirte Groskamp prepared much of the material that has been used for the present publication; her perseverance in taming the many-headed monster of our archive must be recorded here. On the Brill side, we would like to single out Gerrie de Vries for mention. Berry Dongelmans of the Book History Section of the University of Leiden turned out to be a valuable critical reader of the text. Nynke Leistra did a fine job on the translation of the Dutch text, and Mike Mozina and the people of Brill USA kindly screened the English edition.

Looking back is especially useful if it offers inspiration for the future. We hope that we will play an increasingly important role as scholarly publishers and that we will prove ourselves to be worthy successors to all those who preceded us at Brill.

Herman Pabbruwe,

CEO

IN OLDEN TIMES
THE HOUSE OF LUCHTMANS AND THE HOUSE OF BRILL, 1683-1848

Continuity and Change

In 2008 Brill is a modern publishing house, but it is also the outcome of a development that began 325 years ago. Few companies in the Netherlands or elsewhere can boast such a long history. *Tuta sub aegide Pallas*, the firm's motto proclaims: "Safe behind the shield of Pallas." Indeed, the aegis of the goddess of wisdom has stood the test of time, serving as Brill's guardian to this day. Not only is the company's longevity remarkable, but so is the shelf life of its products: some current publications have their forerunners in the late seventeenth century. This continuity over a period of more than three centuries is noteworthy, and it is by no means something to be taken for granted. Over such a long period one would have expected the opposite, since the ravages of time had every opportunity to carry out their destructive work.

Just as the founder back in 1683 could not have envisioned a future in 2008, the Brill of 2008 cannot expect success based on its past. Indeed, the company has a high regard for its past, but continuity must constantly be won from the changeable present. From a historical perspective, durability proves to be more of an ongoing process of change rather than the eternal recurrence of the same thing. Continuity can only be achieved by attuning the present with the past, and by ignoring the hype of the day. In this regard, change is not an indiscriminate adaptation to the present, but a careful blending of the past and the present. In this unique alchemy lies the essence of Brill's history.

As mentioned, this history goes back to the year 1683, but for a better understanding of its course we need to begin our journey through time in 1848. The specter of revolution haunted Europe in those days, although this was hardly noticeable in the fair city of Leiden. On the first of May however, a printed circular letter appeared that conjures specters of its own: "Your obliging servants" S. and J. Luchtmans announce that the firm named after them will be dissolved. Customers and business relations are requested to address themselves henceforth to E. J. Brill, who has been employed in their business for eighteen years and "will replace us."[1] In this letter, we seem to hear voices speaking from beyond the grave: Samuel Luchtmans II had died in 1780, while his brother Johannes passed away in 1809. After Johannes's death the family business was run for three years by his nephew Samuel III, son of Samuel II, but when he passed away in 1812, there was no Luchtmans who could take the helm.

From that moment on, the actual management of the business lay in the hands of Johannes Brill, who had joined the Luchtmans firm ten years previously and who also maintained his own printing shop in Leiden. In 1821 the family eventually supplied a

Around 1750 Samuel Luchtmans I commissioned this allegorical mantelpiece painting from the artist Nicolaas Reyers. For many years it decorated the home of the Luchtmans family on the Rapenburg, and it now hangs in the offices of Brill. The painting shows Pallas Athena with her shield and lance, accompanied by Hermes with his winged helmet and herald's staff. In the foreground three naked little boys are playing with prints depicting periwigged gentlemen, presumably Leiden professors.

The explanation is obvious: learning and commerce had entered into a fruitful union in the house of Luchtmans. Tradition has it that the mythological figures are disguised portraits of Samuel Luchtmans, his wife Cornelia, and their small sons. It does require some imagination to discern the sixty-five-year-old Samuel in the young Greek god and the matron Cornelia in the graceful Pallas. The naked little boys were in fact in their twenties at that time.

For many years the painting hung in Brill's composing room on the Oude Rijn, where the typesetters used to amuse themselves by shooting pieces of type at the bare buttocks of the boys. A thorough restoration was necessary before all the holes were mended. The stylized representation of Pallas Athena and Hermes in Brill's modern logo derives from this painting. Brill Coll.

Circular letter in which S. & J. Luchtmans announce that their business will be continued by E. J. Brill. Proof with corrections. LA/ULA

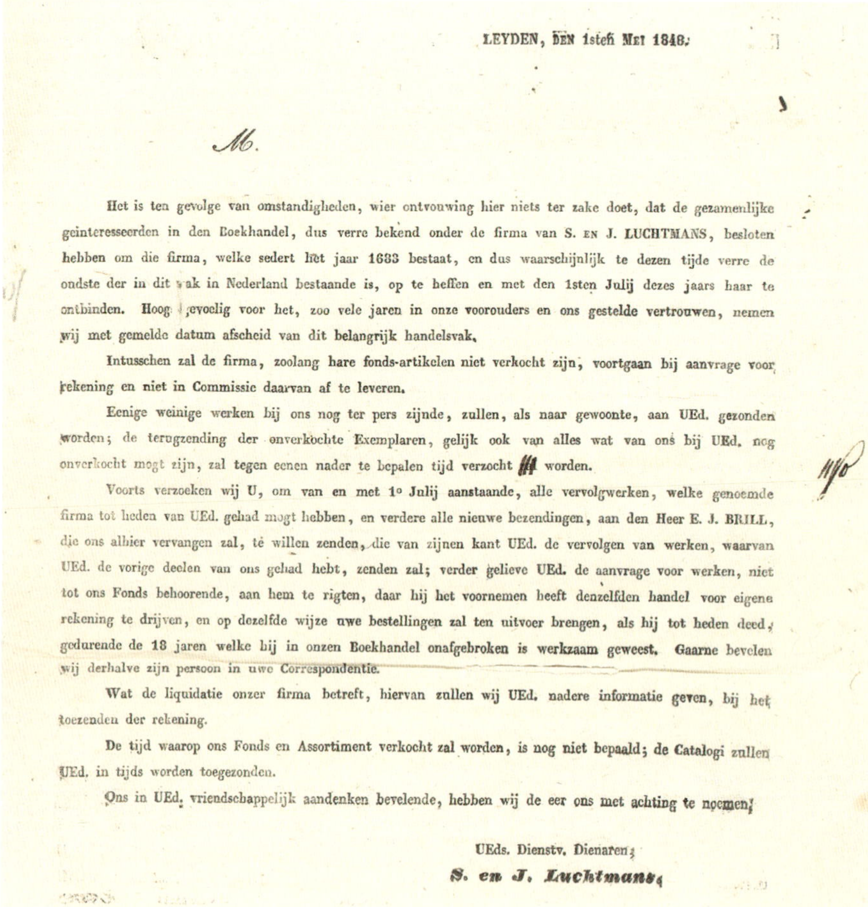

LEYDEN, DEN 1sten MEI 1848.

M.

Het is ten gevolge van omstandigheden, wier ontvouwing hier niets ter zake doet, dat de gezamenlijke geinteresseerden in den Boekhandel, dus verre bekend onder de firma van S. EN J. LUCHTMANS, besloten hebben om die firma, welke sedert het jaar 1683 bestaat, en dus waarschijnlijk te dezen tijde verre de oudste der in dit vak in Nederland bestaande is, op te heffen en met den 1sten Julij dezes jaars haar te ontbinden. Hoog gevoelig voor het, zoo vele jaren in onze voorouders en ons gestelde vertrouwen, nemen wij met gemelde datum afscheid van dit belangrijk handelsvak.

Intusschen zal de firma, zoolang hare fonds-artikelen niet verkocht zijn, voortgaan bij aanvrage voor rekening en niet in Commissie daarvan af te leveren.

Eenige weinige werken bij ons nog ter pers zijnde, zullen, als naar gewoonte, aan UEd. gezonden worden; de terugzending der onverkochte Exemplaren, gelijk ook van alles wat van ons bij UEd. nog onverkocht mogt zijn, zal tegen eenen nader te bepalen tijd verzocht worden.

Voorts verzoeken wij U, om van en met 1° Julij aanstaande, alle vervolgwerken, welke genoemde firma tot heden van UEd. gehad mogt hebben, en verdere alle nieuwe bezendingen, aan den Heer E. J. BRILL, die ons alhier vervangen zal, te willen zenden, die van zijnen kant UEd. de vervolgen van werken, waarvan UEd. de vorige deelen van ons gehad hebt, zenden zal; verder gelieve UEd. de aanvrage voor werken, niet tot ons Fonds behoorende, aan hem te rigten, daar hij het voornemen heeft denzelfden handel voor eigene rekening te drijven, en op dezelfde wijze uwe bestellingen zal ten uitvoer brengen, als hij tot heden deed, gedurende de 18 jaren welke hij in onzen Boekhandel onafgebroken is werkzaam geweest. Gaarne bevelen wij derhalve zijn persoon in uwe Correspondentie.

Wat de liquidatie onzer firma betreft, hiervan zullen wij UEd. nadere informatie geven, bij het toezenden der rekening.

De tijd waarop ons Fonds en Assortiment verkocht zal worden, is nog niet bepaald; de Catalogi zullen UEd. in tijds worden toegezonden.

Ons in UEd. vriendschappelijk aandenken bevelende, hebben wij de eer ons met achting te noemen,

UEds. Dienstv. Dienaren,

S. en J. Luchtmans.

new director, Johannes Tiberius Bodel Nijenhuis, grandson of Johannes Luchtmans. The erudite Bodel Nijenhuis was more of a scholar and a collector than a businessman; the splendid collection of maps and prints he built up during his lifetime is now housed in the library of Leiden University. He was the *auctor intellectualis* of the publishing house, while Brill took responsibility for its day-to-day management. On the basis of this fruitful distribution of labor, they ran the business together for more than twenty-five years.

In 1848 Johannes Brill had reached the ripe old age of eighty, and he had gradually come to the conclusion that it was time to step back. His son Evert Jan, who had been employed by the firm for many years, was his obvious successor. The fifty-year-old Bodel Nijenhuis could have gone on working with the younger Brill as he had with the elder, but he wished to devote himself to his intellectual pursuits without having to cope with business worries. In consultation with the other partners—male and female cousins who held an interest in the firm—the decision was made to liquidate the family business and transfer it to E. J. Brill.

Thus, S. and J. Luchtmans could still nominally be called upon to represent the firm in 1848, but the circular letter was of course drawn up by their "ghostwriter" Bodel

Nijenhuis. Judging from related documents in the company archive—including a note asking, "Don't you think this one's better?"—several versions of the letter were considered before Bodel and Brill Jr. settled on the final text. Bodel was fully entitled to sign the circular letter using the company name, but the absence of his own name creates an air of mystery: it seems as if the ancestral manes are being evoked to bestow their blessing on the metamorphosis of the firm. From the mists of the past, the Luchtmans brothers, born in 1725 and 1726 respectively, guaranteed the continuity between the old firm and the new firm. On the verso of the circular letter, E. J. Brill informs his esteemed business relations that the Luchtmans firm will be continued under his name, on the same footing as before, and at the old address. He promises "to continue to execute your orders within the shortest possible time and on the same terms." He lived up to this promise of continuity, which did not, however, prevent him from exploring new avenues.

Jordaan Luchtmans: The Early Years, 1683-1708

After this changing of the guard, the name of Brill would preside over 160 years of the company's history, but for the preceding 165 years the company had borne the name of Luchtmans. The actual beginning of the firm can be dated to May 17, 1683. On that day Jordaan Luchtmans (1652-1708), born in the village of Woudrichem, was registered as a bookseller with the Leiden book guild. The young man had previously been apprenticed to a bookseller in The Hague and had completed his apprenticeship with the Gaesbeek brothers in Leiden.

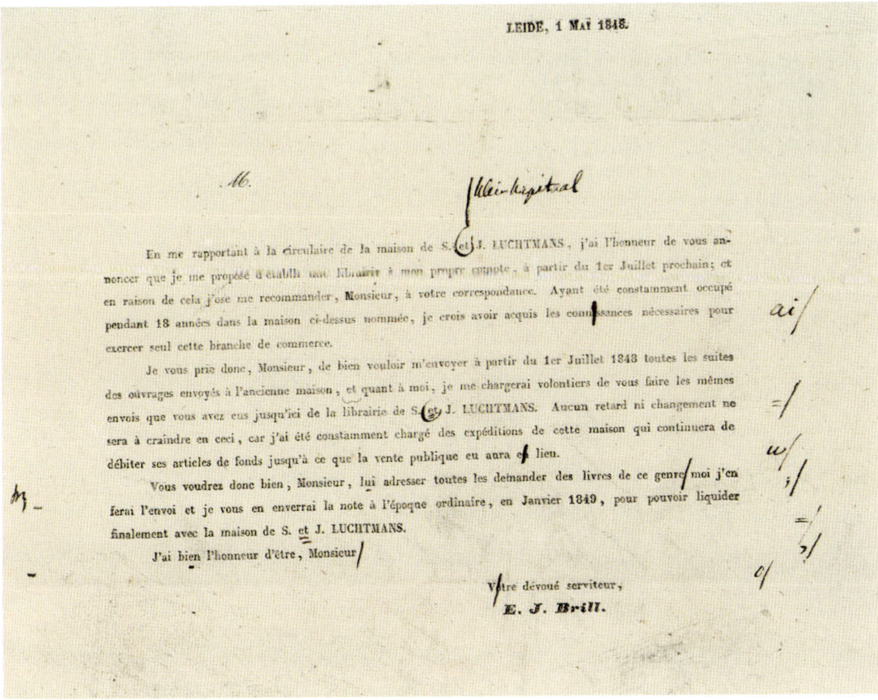
LEIDE, 1 MAI 1848.

M.

En me rapportant à la circulaire de la maison de S. et J. LUCHTMANS, j'ai l'honneur de vous annoncer que je me propose d'établir une librairie à mon propre compte, à partir du 1er Juillet prochain; et en raison de cela j'ose me recommander, Monsieur, à votre correspondance. Ayant été constamment occupé pendant 18 années dans la maison ci-dessus nommée, je crois avoir acquis les connaissances nécessaires pour exercer seul cette branche de commerce.

Je vous prie donc, Monsieur, de bien vouloir m'envoyer à partir du 1er Juillet 1848 toutes les suites des ouvrages envoyés à l'ancienne maison, et quant à moi, je me chargerai volontiers de vous faire les mêmes envois que vous avez eus jusqu'ici de la librairie de S. et J. LUCHTMANS. Aucun retard ni changement ne sera à craindre en ceci, car j'ai été constamment chargé des expéditions de cette maison qui continuera de débiter ses articles de fonds jusqu'à ce que la vente publique en aura et lieu.

Vous voudrez donc bien, Monsieur, lui adresser toutes les demander des livres de ce genre moi j'en ferai l'envoi et je vous en enverrai la note à l'époque ordinaire, en Janvier 1849, pour pouvoir liquider finalement avec la maison de S. et J. LUCHTMANS.

J'ai bien l'honneur d'être, Monsieur

Votre dévoué serviteur,

E. J. Brill.

In a French version of the circular letter E. J. Brill informed foreign business relations that he was taking over the Luchtmans firm. Proof with corrections. LA/ULA

A little under a week later, he took another important step: on May 23 he married Sara van Musschenbroek, who descended from a Leiden family with academic ties. Her father Samuel, who died in 1681, had been the respected instrument maker of the university, while her yet unborn nephew Petrus (1692-1761) would in time become the star of the new, Newtonian physics.[2] Moreover, as befitted the spouse of a bookseller, Sara had impressive credentials in the book trade: she was the great-granddaughter of Christoffel Plantijn, the famous sixteenth-century Antwerp printer, who had worked in Leiden for some time. Jordaan Luchtmans's in-laws provided him with a felicitous entrée into academic circles. Given the great number of competitors in the book-city of Leiden, an aspiring bookseller could take good advantage of such a connection.

Bibliopolis

In 1697 the Luchtmans couple moved into the premises at No. 69B on the Rapenburg, where the bookshop was also established. The patrician mansion was purchased for *f* 6,500, no mean sum in those days, and its renovation also cost a substantial amount.[3] Since 1683 Jordaan had established a reputation for himself with his publications, but this expensive relocation required a helping hand from his in-laws. The new residence was located on the section of the canal that featured the most renowned bookshops in Leiden. Through his choice of a new establishment, Luchtmans let it be known that he intended to compete with the best in the trade.

The stretch of the Rapenburg near the Academiegebouw, the main building of the university, was the book canal *par excellence*: sacred ground for bibliophiles and for buyers and sellers of books. The academic book trade was established in these houses along the canal, and as the university flourished it became a booming business.

The Rapenburg Canal in Leiden with the Academiegebouw, the main building of the University. Engraving by A. Delfos after a drawing by J. J. Bylaerdt. RAL

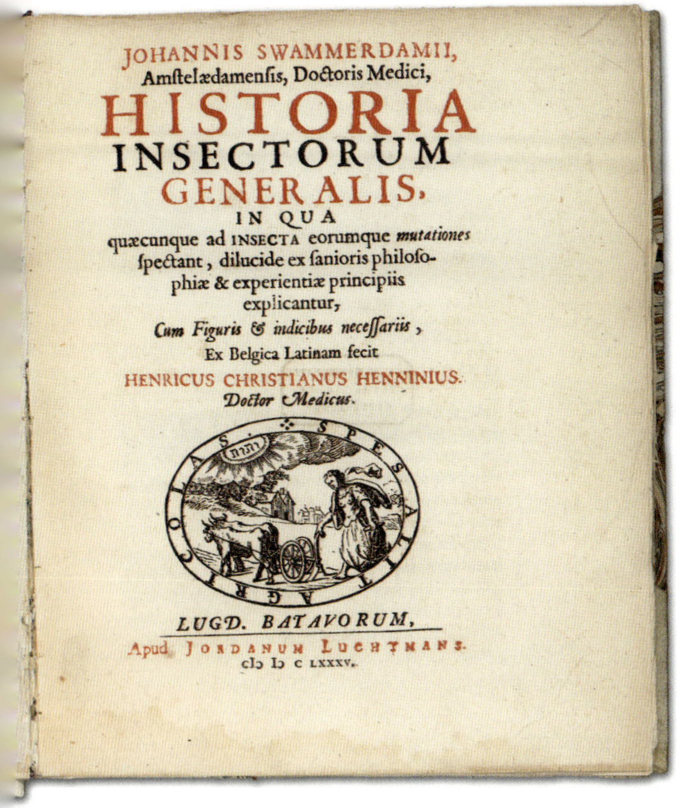
JOHANNIS SWAMMERDAMII,
Amstelædamensis, Doctoris Medici,
HISTORIA
INSECTORUM
GENERALIS,
IN QUA
quæcunque ad INSECTA eorumque *mutationes* spectant, dilucide ex sanioris philosophiæ & experientiæ principiis explicantur,
Cum Figuris & indicibus necessariis,
Ex Belgica Latinam fecit
HENRICUS CHRISTIANUS HENNINIUS.
Doctor Medicus.
LUGD. BATAVORUM,
Apud JORDANUM LUCHTMANS.
clɔ Iɔ c LXXXV.

The university and the adjacent bookshops formed the scholarly heart of the city. In a broader sense, this neighborhood also constituted the heart of the learned world in Europe: around 1700 Leiden still set the standard in scholarship and scholarly books. This section of the Rapenburg was rightly designated "the realm of Pallas," indicating that the goddess of knowledge resided there. Beginning in 1697, Luchtmans proudly indicated in the imprint of his Dutch books that his establishment was located "next to the Academie." His was not the only one. Fifteen of the forty bookshops operating in Leiden around 1700 were located in the immediate vicinity of the Academiegebouw.

Some of Luchtmans's neighbors on the Rapenburg had familiar names. At Nos. 71-73, just next to the Academiegebouw, stood the long-established firm of the Elzeviers. In Abraham, great-grandson of the patriarch Lodewijk, this dynasty of printers to the university and to the city had reached its fourth generation. But just as Abraham Elzevier himself was past his prime, so was his firm also in decline. Around 1700, the work of the academic printer had fallen so far below par that Leiden doctoral students regularly went to Utrecht to have their theses printed. Later on, after the death of the last Elzevier, the well-known bookshop of Pieter van der Aa would be established at the same address. Luchtmans's immediate neighbor at No. 69A was the *Gazette de Leyde*, a newspaper that enjoyed an international readership in the eighteenth century. The bookshop of Johannes Verbessel (later of Johannes van der Linden Jr.) was located at No. 54, and that of Cornelis Boutesteyn at No. 64. Quoting names from the directory of the Leiden book trade could be easily continued in this densely populated *bibliopolis*.[4] Around 1700 it could not be foreseen that of all those businesses, only that of Luchtmans would survive into the twenty-first century.

In 1685 Jordaan Luchtmans published the *Historia Generalis Insectorum* by Jan Swammerdam, who had died five years earlier. With the help of his microscope Swammerdam discovered the fascinating details of the insect world. The entomological study was the first illustrated publication offered by Luchtmans. As usual in those days, the printed sheets and engraved plates were sold in unbound state. The last page contains a notice for the binder indicating how the engraved plates should be bound into the text. ULA

A two-page spread from the *Opus* > *Aramaeum* of Carolus Schaaf, published by Jordaan Luchtmans in 1686. Because Aramaic is read from right to left, the pages are numbered from the back of the book to the front. ULA

mnes Angelos qui in cœlis *sunt*, & super omnes qui constituti sunt Primates in terra. 12 Quævis divitiæ divitum & quævis gloria Regum & Dominatorum à te data *sunt* ipsis, & tu potestatem habens in omnes eos, & manu tua potes magnificare & corroborare omnes. 13 Itaque nunc, Deus noster, confitemur nos tibi, & glorificamus nomen tuum gloriosum. 14 Et enim, quid ego, & quid populus meus, ut copiosi essemus opibus ad ultro erogandum hoc! quoniam à te datum *erat* omne istud, & ex benedictione manus tuæ

להון מלאכיא ד
מיא ועל כל ד
מנן לרישין ב
עא׃ 12 עתרא ד
ריא ויקרא ו
א דמלכיא ו
טיא מן קדמך ם
הב להון ואנת ש
ט בכלהון ובידך
יכילתא לרבאה ו
קפא לכלא׃
וכדון אלהנא מודין
לך ומשבחין לשום
שבחתך׃ 14 וארום
האנא ומה עמי דנסגי
ילא לאתנדבא כדא ארום מן קדמך מ
תיהב כלא ומן ברכת ידך יהבו לך׃

11. מתמנן B. מתמנן: *Vide Gram. pag.* 218.

gelorum, ad dan-
n legem populo
; & obtinuisti vi-
rias contra Amale-
, Sihonem, O-
n & Reges Cana-
orum; & splendo-
gloriæ tuæ stare fe-
solem supra Gi-
-nem, & lunam su-
vallem Ajjalonem;
ec vindicaretur
ulus domus Israel
osoribus suis; o-
ia enim opera ma-
um tuarum *sunt*,
a in cœlis quam in
terra, & tu Domi-
or *es* super eos, &
tas omnia ea quæ
cœlis & omnia ea
æ in terra *sunt*:
um ô Domine *est*
egnum in expanso,
evectus *es* super o-

ואתגליתא על טורא ד
דסיני בשבהורא עם
כתי מלאכיא למתן
אוריתא לעמך ו
ועבידתא נצחנין בעמלק
ובסיחון ובעוג ובמלכי
כנענאי ובזיו יקרך א
אקימתא שמשא בגבעון
וסיהרא במשר אילון
עד דיתפרעו עמא בית
ישראל מסנאיהון א
ארום כלהון עובדי ידך
בשמיא ובארעא ואת
שליט עליהון וסביל ב
כל מה די בשמיא וכל
ומתנ... מה די בארעא דילך יי מלכותא ברקיעא

11. עם כתי מלאכיא Cum turmis Angelorum.
vid. *Gal.* 3: 19. *Hebr.* 2: 2.

In those days the book trade was less specialized than it is now. Luchtmans was not only active as a publisher, he was also the manager of a shop in which he sold his own books as well as those of other publishers. Usually the merchandise was not a book in the proper sense of the word, but a pile of printed sheets. As a rule, the costs of finishing the book—folding, gathering, and binding the sheets—were covered by the customer. For that reason the bookshop had an attached bindery, where the citizens of Leiden could also have their old and tattered books rebound.[5] Some publishers had, in addition to their bookshop, their own printing shop, but Luchtmans outsourced his printing; only at a much later stage, in the days of Johannes Brill, was a printing establishment attached to the firm.

The stock in Luchtmans's shop consisted only in part of recent publications; the shelves were also filled with older and antiquarian works. The auctioning of private libraries was another important sideline. Thanks to the concentration of scholars and books within the walls of Leiden, such auctions took place regularly. On occasion a bookseller would auction the estate of an author who had published with him during his lifetime. Thus it happened that the theologian Jacob Trigland turned up in three different capacities on the publishing list of Jordaan Luchtmans: first as the author of a theological work (1701), then as the subject of a funeral oration (1705), and finally as the former owner of a library offered at auction (1706).

An Experiment with Type-Metal

Luchtmans would have had little time and attention to spare for the publishing house, if, in addition to his other responsibilities, he also had to manage a printing shop. In that case he would have had to keep the presses working with jobs supplied by a third party, and thus he would have become more of a printer than a publisher. Although the outsourcing of printing was a reasonable decision, Luchtmans nevertheless got involved in a remarkable typographic experiment. Around 1690 Johann Müller, a German-born Lutheran minister in Leiden, had invented a printing technique that would later be known as "stereotyping."[6] A plaster mold was made from the surface of a form of type, and then the mold was used to cast a solid plate of type-metal. Thus a duplicate impression of the original form of type was created. By means of such printing plates, a book could instantly be reprinted, without having to be typeset all over again. The innovation was time-consuming and only suitable for books with large print runs and regular reprints; in practice, it turned out that the minister's invention was particularly useful for the cheap reproduction of Bibles.

With this edifying purpose in mind, he founded a partnership with two booksellers, namely Jordaan Luchtmans and Cornelis Boutesteyn. The business associates set up a printing shop for stereotyping. The term "printing shop" in this case is slightly misleading, because its primary product were not books, but printing plates for books. After the printing shop had been shut down in 1716, the partnership continued to exist, although the lineup changed after the death of the original partners. Müller and Boutesteyn were replaced by their widows, and Luchtmans by his son Samuel. Over the course of the eighteenth century, these printing plates were used to produce several folio and quarto editions of the Bible; the only typesetting required was to alter the year of publication on the title page.

Stereotyping: printing plate for the New Testament in quarto size, used for several editions since 1711. SML

The third generation of the Luchtmans family still produced such Bibles, now in cooperation with the firm of Enschedé in Haarlem.[7] The mechanized reproduction of the Word must have been a tidy source of income for all parties concerned, but over time the printing plates wore out. The folio edition of 1791 proved to be so illegible that dissatisfied customers returned their Bibles to the publisher. After this failure, stereotyping came to an inglorious end, although it would be reinvented in France after its downfall in the Netherlands. The old printing plates were melted down, and only a few specimens were preserved as curiosities.

Competition and Cooperation

The gradual decline of Abraham Elzevier played into Jordaan Luchtmans's hands, but he was not the only entrepreneur starting up in Leiden. Already in 1677 Pieter van der Aa, Luchtmans's junior by seven years, had been admitted to the guild, and he had started his own bookshop a little earlier than Luchtmans. They had both been apprenticed to the Gaesbeek brothers and may have worked together in that firm. In 1708, Van der Aa purchased the premises at Rapenburg 32, previously the establishment of his master Gaesbeek. It was not until five years later that he would make it to the golden bend proper next to the Academiegebouw, where Luchtmans had been living since 1697.[8] Both booksellers concentrated on publishing scholarly works and thus were competitors in the acquisition of copy. In addition to their academic publishing lists, both also produced publications for a broader public. Van der Aa courted customers with travelogues, atlases, and magnificent books of plates. Luchtmans favored Bibles with large print runs, edifying works, and sermons: there was good money to be made in the virtuous segment of the market. Van der Aa had a more daring style of entrepreneurship than Luchtmans, and his scruples did not prevent him from publishing the occasional pirated edition.

Even competing booksellers worked together on occasion. In 1690 Luchtmans and Van der Aa jointly auctioned the library of the classicist Theodorus Rijcke, and in the same year they jointly published a book (*Strategematum libri octo*, a Latin translation of the *Military Stratagems* by the Greek author Polyainos). Evidently their collaboration was not successful, for in 1690-91 two more editions of this book appeared, under the conjoined names of Luchtmans and Du Vivié. Luchtmans would collaborate with Van der Aa on two more occasions, but other booksellers were involved in both of these projects. It may be the case that Luchtmans preferred to spread the risks of a partner such as Van der Aa among several parties. Usually Jordaan Luchtmans threw in his lot with Cornelis Boutesteyn, his partner in the stereotyping business, or with Johannes Du Vivié.

In the competition for scholarly copy, Luchtmans and Van der Aa were well matched. Personal contacts within the academic world were of vital importance in that endeavor, and so both booksellers took pains to court learned authors. Van der Aa was deft in winning over professors and regents, but Luchtmans profited from his Musschenbroek connection, and presumably also from his more solid reputation. In addition, due to the shortcomings of Abraham Elzevier, the scholarly fodder was rich enough to support two newcomers at the trough: the names of the academic stars of the day appear on the lists of both publishers, although Luchtmans scored better than Van der Aa in the field of theology.

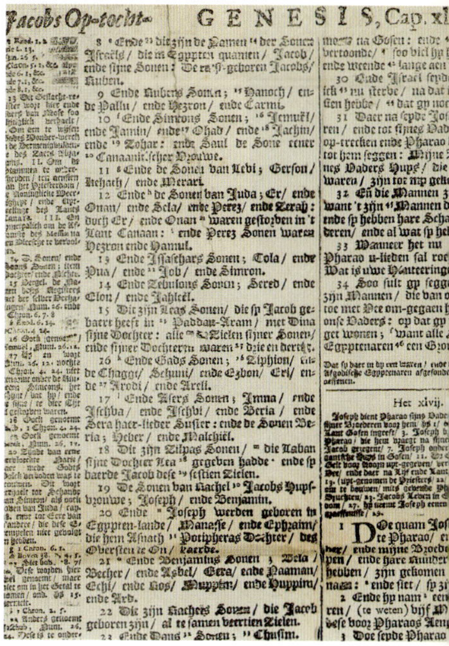

Jacobs Op-tocht. GENESIS, Cap. xl

In 1863 J. T. Bodel Nijenhuis made a print from an old stereotype printing plate that had not been melted down. It was one of the plates that had been used by Luchtmans in the eighteenth century for printing a folio Bible. It is no surprise that the last edition of 1791 proved to be unsalable: because of wear and tear on the plate, the printing is of inferior quality. LA/ULA

Graphic medical instruction in > head surgery. Engraving from J. B. van Lamsweerde, *Joannis Sculteti Armamentarium Chirurgicum*, published by Jordaan Luchtmans in 1693. ULA

Heidelberg Catechism and Syriac Grammar

In the twenty-five years between 1683 and 1708, Jordaan Luchtmans published 170 works, six or seven a year on average. Twenty of these referred to catalogs of the book auctions he organized, and another ten fall under the heading of occasional publications—eulogies, orations, and the like. The Dutch segment of his publishing list consisted of more than twenty titles, chiefly of a theological nature. The popularity of such edifying booklets should not be underestimated: the *Oefeningen over den Heidelbergschen catechismus* by Hendrik Groenewegen reached no fewer than seven editions, while David Knibbe's *Leere der gereformeerde kerk* was good for three editions. Apparently there was a good market in Holland for such religious self-help books. Luchtmans not only provided spiritual balm for the souls of his customers, he also looked out for their physical needs: the *Nieuw ligt der vroet-vrouwen* by Hendrik van Deventer (about midwifery), and the *Redenering en aanmerkingen omtrent de ziektens ter zee voorvallende* by William Cockburn (about diseases aboard ships) met the demand for medical information.

The larger part of Luchtmans's publishing list consisted of 120 scholarly works in Latin, the exception to this rule being a single medical handbook in French. With thirty-nine titles, the field of medical science dominated the list, reflecting the productivity of the corresponding faculty of the University during these years. Traditional humanist scholarship was almost equally well represented by thirty-fve titles devoted to philology or ancient history. At times philology merged into theology, as in Johannes Leusden's *Philologus Hebraeo-Graecus* of 1685. This volume inaugurated a tradition of publishing in Judaica that is still maintained by Brill. Brill's present-day offerings in the field of Syriac studies likewise have their antecedents in works published by Luchtmans in the late seventeenth century, including the *Schola Syriaca* (1685) by Johannes Leusden and the *Opus Aramaeum complectens grammaticam Chaldaico-Syriacam* by Carolus Schaaf (1686). Theology in the strict sense of the word ranked third, with about twenty titles. Other fields were meagerly represented in the publishing list: the natural sciences and jurisprudence contributed only a few titles each.

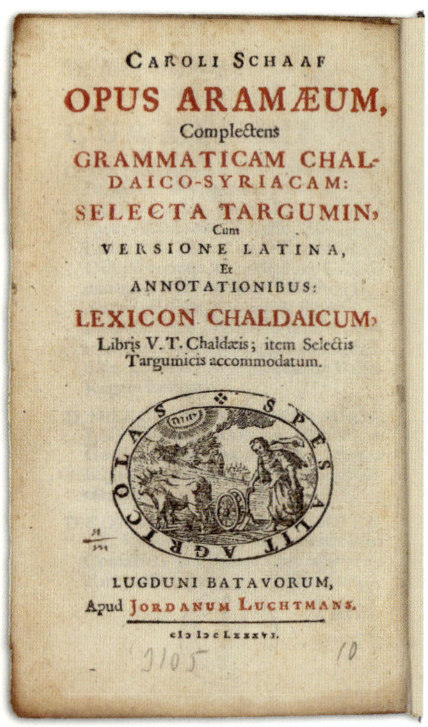

As the *Opus Aramaeum* of Carolus Schaaf (1686) shows, Jordaan Luchtmans was already publishing in Syriac and on the Syriac language at an early stage. In 1717 his son Samuel brought out a *Novum Testamentum Syriacum*, manufactured with the technique of stereotype printing. The Syriac tradition of Luchtmans is continued at Brill to the present day; for instance, in 1993 a stout six-volume *Concordance to the Syriac New Testament* was published. The most recent publication in this field is B. ter Haar Romeny, *The Peshitta: Its Use in Literature and Liturgy* (Leiden, 2007). In addition, Brill is the publisher of the journal *Aramaic Studies*, devoted to Aramaic and Syriac language and literature. ULA

TABVLA XXXII

SAMUELIS
BOCHARTI
OPERA
OMNIA.
Lugduni Batavorum,
Apud Cornelium Boutesteyn, et Jordanum Luchtmans,
Trajecti ad Rhenum,
Apud Guilielmum vande Water, M.DC.LXXXXII.

Jordaan Luchtmans died on June 18, 1708, at the age of fifty-six, a few weeks after his silver wedding anniversary. On that occasion his tenant Hendrik Snakenburg had written the poem "Silver Crown," of which the first page is shown here. Snakenburg (1674-1750) was deputy headmaster and later headmaster of the Latin School in Leiden. He also was a compulsory poetaster, seizing on every opportunity to craft a commemorative poem. He lived for more than half a century with the Luchtmans family in their house, first with Jordaan and later with Samuel. The heirloom poet shared life's joys and sorrows with three successive Luchtmans generations. After Snakenburg's death in 1750, Samuel published a large volume of his collected poems (*Poezy*, 1753). From the preface he wrote it is evident how fond he was of this friend of the family. ULA

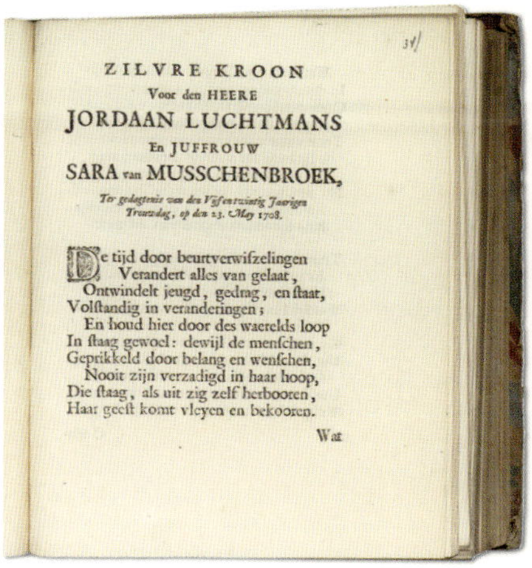
ZILVRE KROON
Voor den HEERE
JORDAAN LUCHTMANS
En JUFFROUW
SARA van MUSSCHENBROEK,
Ter gedagtenis van den Vyfentwintig Jaarigen Trouwdag, op den 23. May 1708.

De tijd door beurtverwisselingen
Verandert alles van gelaat,
Ontwindelt jeugd, gedrag, en staat,
Volstandig in veranderingen;
En houd hier door des waerelds loop
In staag gewoel: dewijl de menschen,
Geprikkeld door belang en wenschen,
Nooit zijn verzadigd in haar hoop,
Die staag, als uit zig zelf herbooren,
Haar geest komt vleyen en bekooren.

Wat

Samuel Luchtmans I: Consolidation and Expansion, 1708-1755

Jordaan Luchtmans died on June 18, 1708, shortly after a double jubilee. A month before he died, his firm marked its twenty-fifth year of operation, and barely three weeks earlier he had celebrated his silver wedding anniversary. He was buried in the family tomb of the Musschenbroeks in the Hooglandse Church in Leiden. Although his wife Sara bore him four sons, only one, Samuel (1685-1757), named after his grandfather Musschenbroek, survived. After the death of his father he took over the management of the firm, although his mother formally remained the owner until her death in 1710. Samuel had learned the book trade from his father, but thanks to a solid education he was also familiar with books in the context of scholarly activity: he attended the Latin school and studied law at Leiden University for a number of years. He would manage the firm until 1755, building on the foundations that had been laid down by his father. He also followed in his father's footsteps when choosing a spouse: in 1721 he married his cousin Cornelia van Musschenbroek (1699-1784), who was fourteen years his junior and with whom he would have nine children in all.

When Samuel took over the business, Luchtmans was already an established name in the Leiden book trade. Under the so-called *Familiegeld* tax for 1715, a total of thirty-five booksellers in the city were assessed, but only four of them had to pay the highest rate of twenty guilders: Samuel Luchtmans, Pieter van der Aa, Daniël van den Dalen, and Anthony de la Font, publisher of the *Gazette de Leyde*.[9] In 1714 Samuel balanced his accounts, adding up the value of all his books, copyrights, and other properties. His calculation resulted in the impressive sum of *f* 64,360 and 9 stivers. This amount corresponded to the market value he assigned to his earthly goods at that moment ("if it had to be sold right now, following my death"). The actual value of his estate in the longer run ("if the Almighty God should allow me to live for a few more years") would be about thirty thousand guilders higher, he thought.

< Engraved title page of the *Geographia Sacra* (1692) by Samuel Bochart, a joint publication of Jordaan Luchtmans, Cornelis Boutesteyn, and the Utrecht bookseller Willem van de Water. A costly publication, but the geography of the Holy Land was a religious accessory in great demand. ULA

Portrait of Hendrik Snakenburg by Hiëronymus van der Mij. The painting shows the interior of the Luchtmans mansion on the Rapenburg. SML

Samuel Luchtmans I as a solid citizen in 1748. Portrait by Hiëronymus van der Mij. SML

Cornelia van Musschenbroek, wife of Samuel Luchtmans. Portrait by Hiëronymus van der Mij, 1748. SML

At the time he drew up this balance sheet, Samuel Luchtmans was not yet thirty years old, and with God's help he was to reach the ripe old age of seventy-two. In 1747 he balanced his accounts once again, and now he calculated the value of his property at well over a hundred and twenty thousand guilders, nearly twice as much as in 1714. This total did not include any of his real estate, and so we may conclude that he had managed his affairs well in the intervening years.[10] This impression is confirmed by the Leiden register of tax assessments for 1742, from which it appears that only two of the thirty-two assessed booksellers had an annual income of more than two thousand guilders. Hendrik van Damme's income was estimated at between *f* 2,500 and *f* 3,000, but this turned out to be an overestimate: upon further consideration he was placed in the more modest income bracket of *f* 1,200 to *f* 1,500. Samuel Luchtmans figured as the only Leiden bookseller in tax group 12, which means that his annual income was estimated at between *f* 4,500 and *f* 5,000.[11] By that standard he was a solid member of the middle class, at a time when the annual income of the very rich reached *f* 12,000. With some right, Samuel was justified in striking the respectable, self-congratulatory pose recorded in 1748 by the painter Hiëronymus van der Mij.

Scholarship and a Cuckoo's Egg

Back in 1714, the second Luchtmans had published a catalog listing the titles of the 331 books he carried in stock at that time.[12] The majority (261 titles) consisted of scholarly works in Latin, but in addition Samuel had 70 Dutch books available. The offering of French books amounted to only 4 titles; later in the century, French was to claim more space in the shop and the catalogs, corresponding to the space it took up in public opinion. About 60 percent of the Latin works were published by Jordaan or Samuel Luchtmans, in some cases in combination with other booksellers. Among the Dutch titles—chiefly sermons and edifying works for a lay public—the proportion of their own publications was also around 60 percent.

The heart of the Latin division consisted of traditional humanist scholarship: well over 30 percent of the titles listed were devoted to philology or classical history, including some Hebraica and Syriaca. Theological works accounted for a good quarter of the supply of scholarly books; another 20 percent were medical works, and 10 percent addressed juridical topics. The remaining 15 percent of the catalog consisted of titles in the fields of philosophy and natural science, mainly seventeenth-century works by Descartes, Gassendi, Geulinx, Hobbes, Swammerdam, Leeuwenhoek, and Huygens. Only in the 1720s would Newton's physics and the paradigm of "empirical natural philosophy" catch on in Leiden.

Luchtmans was a bookseller of strict morals, but among his edifying Dutch titles he laid a less edifying cuckoo's egg. Between Soermans's *Kerkelijk Register der Predikanten van Zuydholland* and Steengragt's *Binnenste Heyligdom geopend om te sien de gantsche Godgeleertheyd* one comes across a book briefly described as *Spinoza regtsinnige Theologant*—that is, *Spinoza, Orthodox Theologian*. The title is all the more intriguing because, according to contemporary opinion, the philosopher Spinoza was not in the least orthodox. The complete title of the book is *De rechtsinnige theologant, of Godgeleerde Staatkunde,* and on closer examination it proves to be a translation of Spinoza's *Tractatus Theologico-politicus*. The *Tractatus* appeared in 1670 in Latin and, apart from his *Principles of the Philosophy of Descartes,* it was the only work of Spinoza to be published during his lifetime. A few years later, the book was banned by the Holland Court of Justice on account of its "blasphemous and pernicious" nature.

Around that time the *Tractatus* had already been translated into Dutch, but for the sake of his own peace of mind and safety, Spinoza blocked its publication. Several years after his death in 1677, this translation was finally brought out in two clandestine editions entitled *Rechtsinnige Theologant* (1693-94). The book made the rounds of the underground circuit and had to be sold under the counter. It is an outstanding example of the intellectual movement now refered to as the "Radical Enlightenment." The *Orthodox Theologian* is not a book one would expect to find in the inventory of an orthodox bookseller like Samuel Luchtmans. It is somewhat surprising that he listed the title in his catalog. He risked a heavy fine, like the one imposed on his Amsterdam colleague Gerrit Bom for selling a book by Spinoza as late as 1761. Judging by Samuel's note in the catalog, he had eleven copies in stock, perhaps a part of his inheritance from his father.[13]

Under the counter at Luchtmans: *Een rechtsinnige theologant, of godgeleerde staatkunde* (1694), with the fictitious imprint "Bremen, [published] by Hans Jurgen von der Weyl." An earlier edition (1693) had allegedly appeared in "Hamburg, [published] by Henricus Koenraad." The last imprint had in 1670 also been used for the prohibited *Tractatus theologico-politicus* by Spinoza, of which the *Rechtsinnige theologant* was the Dutch translation. The publishers behind the two clandestine publications are not known, but one of them might be the Amsterdam bookseller Aart Wolsgryn. For selling Spinozist books he was in 1698 sentenced to eight years in prison, twenty-five years of banishment from Holland, and a fine of *f* 4000. ULA

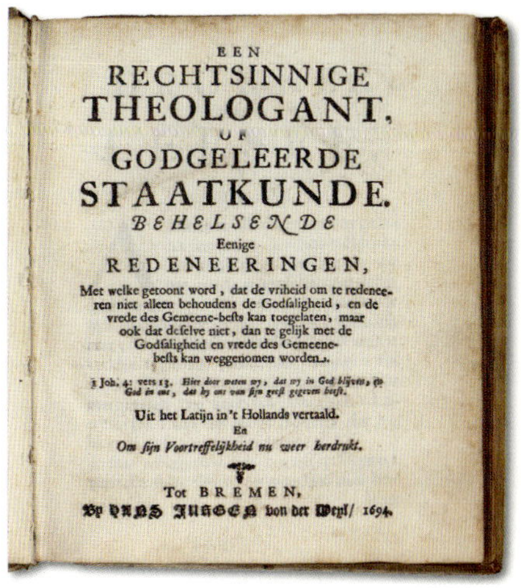
EEN
RECHTSINNIGE
THEOLOGANT,
OF
GODGELEERDE
STAATKUNDE.
BEHELSENDE
Eenige
REDENEERINGEN,
Met welke getoont word, dat de vriheid om te redeneeren niet alleen behoudens de Godsaligheid, en de vrede des Gemeene-besls kan toegelaten, maar ook dat deselve niet, dan te gelijk met de Godsaligheid en vrede des Gemeene-besls kan weggenomen worden.
1 Joh. 4: vers 13. *Hier door weten wy, dat wy in God blijven, en God in ons, dat hy ons van sijn geest gegeven heeft.*
Uit het Latijn in 't Hollands vertaald.
En
Om sijn Voortreffelijkheid nu weer herdrukt.
Tot BREMEN,
By HANS JURGEN von der Weyl/ 1694.

A printer's mark was the signboard of a publisher, but also a hallmark of authenticity and a protection (or so it was hoped) against pirated editions. From 1683 onwards Jordaan Luchtmans used a pastoral mark featuring a plowing farmer with the motto *Spes alit agricolas* (Hope nourishes the farmers). Pallas Athena, the goddess of learning and wisdom, was introduced into the firm by Samuel I in 1714. Optimistically she indicates that she is safe and sound behind her shield—*Tuta sub aegide Pallas*. The shift from the toiling farmer to the hopeful goddess reflects the difference between the first and second generations: Samuel no longer needed to build up the business from scratch. As a symbol of learning, Pallas also referred to the chief pillar of Luchtmans's publishing house. Perhaps her secure self-confidence had something to do with the Peace of Utrecht (1713-14), which had recently put an end to the long War of the Spanish Succession.

Pallas was a keeper, although other marks were used during the years 1745-1755. They were probably experiments of the third generation, for they appeared during the time when the firm presented itself as "Samuel Luchtmans and Sons." A woman bearing the flame of inspiration on her head and surrounded by allegorical props indicates that she lets herself be guided by God, ingenuity, art, vigilance, and effort. (She needed quite a mouthful of Latin: *Deo duce ingenio arte vigilantia labore*.) Another lady in an idyllic setting betokens the combination of business with pleasure (*Utile dulci*). These emblems were symbolical sins of youth committed by the brothers Samuel II and Johannes, who after 1755 returned to a stylized Pallas. In the nineteenth century printers' marks became obsolete, but at the beginning of the twentieth century the house of Brill reestablished the old motto, *Tuta sub aegide Pallas*.

The Knight of San Marco

Following the death of Abraham Elzevier in August 1712, the office of printer to the university and to the city stood vacant. One person's death is another person's chance to make a living; in all probability Samuel Luchtmans attempted to qualify for this vacancy, but he was unsuccessful. Was he considered too young, or did the curators of the university require candidates to own their own printing shop? Luchtmans was not the only applicant, for Pieter van der Aa also sought to obtain the lucrative and honorable office for himself. Anticipating the future, the ambitious publisher had been working for some years to secure the nomination, for instance by offering to publish at his own cost a new catalog of the university library. This generous offer was gladly accepted by the curators, but evidently it was not sufficient to win him an appointment as printer to the university. The bookseller and printer Jacob Poereep, who was also beadle of the university, was appointed as successor to Elzevier.

Van der Aa did not take this lying down, and he went out of his way to obtain the post of academic printer for himself after all. First he secured the support of the curator Jacob van Wassenaer Obdam, to whom he dedicated one of his publications. Then he bought the larger part of Abraham Elzevier's estate, including both the inventory

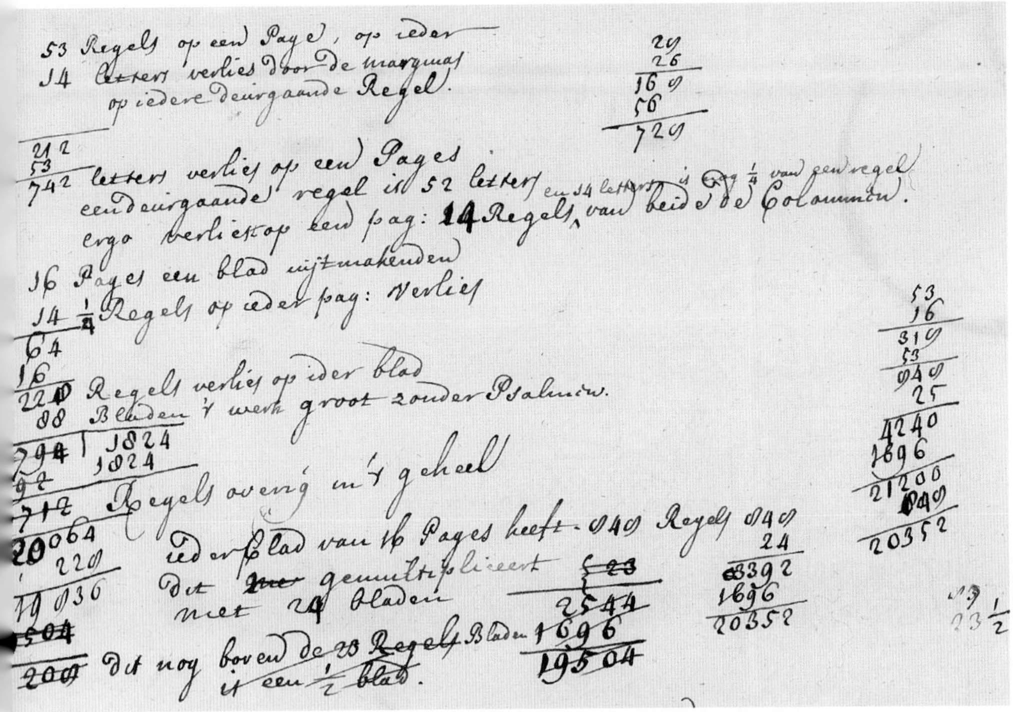

A publisher's worries. Rough draft from 1717, on which Samuel Luchtmans calculated the amount of type on a line and the number of lines on an octavo page. By extrapolation he estimated the number of sheets (each containing sixteen pages) that would be required. With a different typeface he would need less paper, but in that case he would have to have new type cast. The calculation concerns the Hungarian bible published by Luchtmans in 1718 (*Magyar Biblia Avagy az O és Uj Testamentom*). The circumstances that occasioned this Hungarian sidestep are not clear. Samuel corresponded about the book with a certain Desobrie, perhaps a representative of the Protestant community in Hungary. The vague half-circle in the right corner of the note is an imprint of Samuel's teacup. LA/ULA

of the latter's print works and his premises on the Rapenburg. The old houses were demolished and in their place Van der Aa had an impressive new complex erected, consisting of a private home with an adjoining shop and print works. Hitherto he had only been registered with the guild as a bookseller, but now he also had himself registered as a printer. His flanking maneuver had the intended result, all the more so because Poereep was not very successful in the post. Thus, in May 1715 Van der Aa was appointed printer to the university. He had already been appointed printer to the city a few weeks earlier.

From 1715 until 1730 Pieter van der Aa was the shining light at the center of the Leiden book trade. Samuel Luchtmans also built up a prosperous business in those years, but he could only thrive in the shadow of his neighbor. The publications of Van der Aa in his heyday were unsurpassed—the Doge of Venice was so impressed by one of his publications that he appointed the bookseller knight of the Order of San Marco. With such a fine-sounding title, the university printer could hold his head high on the Rapenburg. The culmination of his production was the sublime *Galérie Agréable du Monde* (1729), the finest book of plates ever to appear in the Netherlands. It was also the typographic swan song of Van der Aa, who in his advancing years increasingly struggled with health problems.

In August 1730 he had no choice but to resign as printer to the city and the university, and in the spring of 1731 he disposed of his print works. Samuel Luchtmans organized the auction in which the inventory of the print works was sold. Pieter van der Aa died in 1733, without a male heir; his widow continued to operate the bookshop on the Rapenburg for some time, but in 1735 the shop was also shut down.[14]

44
I
Vau He Daleth Gimel Beth Aleph
Lamed Caph Jod Teth Heth Sajin
Tzade Pe Hajin Samech Nun Mem
Thau Schin Resch Koph
Abrahams Alphabêt.
Jos. 24.3.
Enochs Alphabêt.
II
Gen. 5. 24.
III
Hebreeus Alphabêt van EZDRAS.
Esdre IV. Boek. Cap. 14. v. 24.

Samuel's Heyday

Once again, one man's death gave another man a better chance to make a living. Pieter van der Aa's disappearance from the scene was greatly profitable to Samuel Luchtmans. On August 8, 1730, he was appointed printer to the university when his neighbor resigned the office on the grounds of ill health. This time it was Luchtmans who had deliberately anticipated the future: already in 1728 he had published the *Wetten ende Statuten van de Universiteyt tot Leyden* [Laws and Statutes of the University of Leiden]. On February 7, 1730, eight months before his appointment as university printer, he had promised the curators that he would "at his expense... have a certain Arabic manuscript printed in folio."[15] It was the same strategy that Van der Aa had adopted in order to get into the good graces of the university governors.

This edition appeared at the publisher's expense in 1732 under the title *Vita et res gestae Sultani Almalichi Alnasiri Saladini*, with Arabic text and Latin translation juxtaposed in two columns. This account of the life and deeds of Sultan Saladin was the first Arabic publication issued by the house of Luchtmans, making it the overture to Brill's tradition in Oriental studies. The Latin translation was the work of the theologian Albert Schultens, founder of a dynasty of Leiden Arabic scholars that would last for three generations. A close cooperation developed between the Schultens family and the Luchtmans family.

< The development of the Hebrew alphabet through Abraham, Enoch, and Ezra. Engraving from Van der Aa's *Galérie Agréable du Monde* (1729), a highlight in Dutch printmaking. Private Coll.

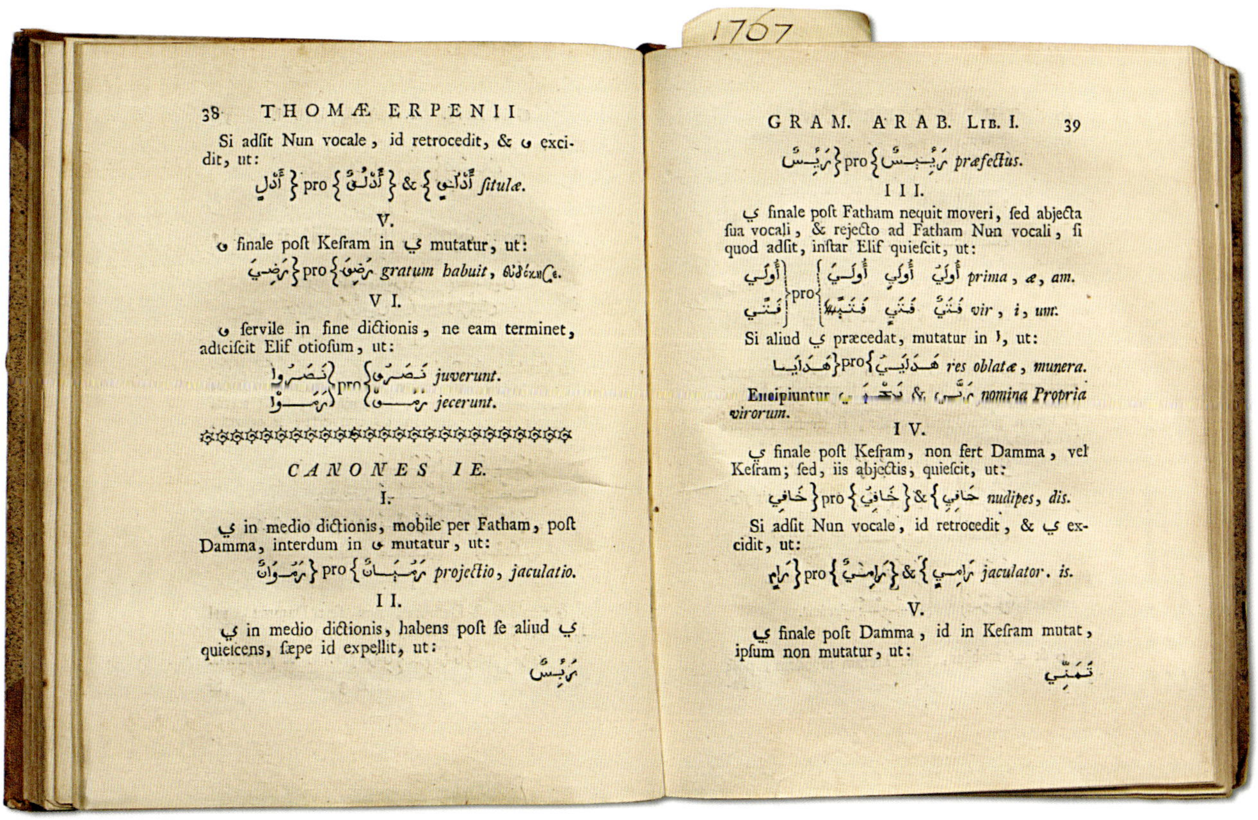

Interior of the *Grammatica Arabica*, first published by Samuel Luchtmans in 1747 and reedited by his sons in 1767. The Arabic scholar Albert Schultens adapted in his book the older grammar of Thomas Erpenius. Brill Coll.

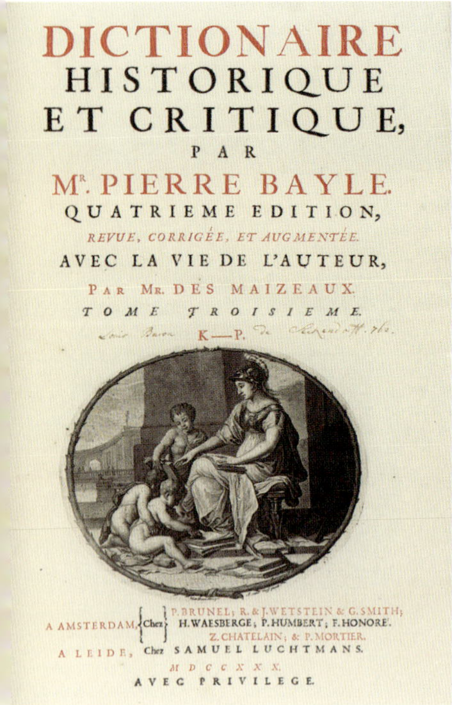

DICTIONAIRE
HISTORIQUE
ET CRITIQUE,
PAR
M^R. PIERRE BAYLE.
QUATRIEME EDITION,
REVUE, CORRIGÉE, ET AUGMENTÉE.
AVEC LA VIE DE L'AUTEUR,
PAR MR. DES MAIZEAUX.
TOME TROISIEME.
K—P.

A AMSTERDAM, Chez P. BRUNEL; R. & J. WETSTEIN & G. SMITH; H. WAESBERGE; P. HUMBERT; F. HONORE. Z. CHATELAIN; & P. MORTIER.
A LEIDE, Chez SAMUEL LUCHTMANS.
M D C C X X X.
AVEC PRIVILEGE.

The monumental fourth edition of Pierre Bayle's *Dictionaire Historique et Critique* (1730) was a mammoth production of Luchtmans and seven Amsterdam booksellers. As time went by, the book sold out and in 1740 a fifth edition was published. This time no fewer than fifteen booksellers took part in the enterprise. Samuel put up a twelfth share of the costs, in exchange for a twelfth part of the print run. The total costs for 3,288 copies amounted to *f* 46,000, a staggering sum in those days. Samuel had to invest well over *f* 3,800 and was entitled to 275 copies, at a cost of *f* 14 each. ULA

In 1730 the new university printer was also appointed official printer to the city, which did not mean that he actually ran a printing shop; town and gown had agreed that their printing was to be farmed out. The disappearance of Van der Aa created the opening in which Luchtmans could develop his business, an opening he exploited to the fullest. The years between 1730 and 1755 were the heyday of Samuel I, especially with regard to his publishing activities. The dissertations, disputations, and orations issuing from his appointment as university printer increased his turnover, even if not all of them were equally profitable. In his scholarly publications, Samuel stuck to the familiar pattern of theology and philology, but he also broke new ground. The spirit of Newton had come to preside over Leiden University, and his influence was also manifest in the publications of the university's *typographus academiae*.

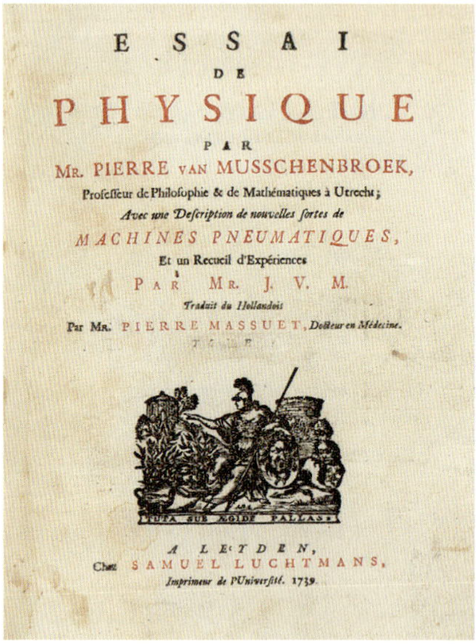

ESSAI
DE
PHYSIQUE
PAR
MR. PIERRE VAN MUSSCHENBROEK,
Professeur de Philosophie & de Mathématiques à Utrecht;
Avec une Description de nouvelles sortes de
MACHINES PNEUMATIQUES,
Et un Recueil d'Expériences
PAR MR. J. V. M.
Traduit du Hollandois
Par MR. PIERRE MASSUET, Docteur en Médecine.

TUTA SUB AEGIDE PALLAS

A LEYDEN,
Chez SAMUEL LUCHTMANS,
Imprimeur de l'Université. 1739.

Petrus van Musschenbroek was a brother-in-law and first cousin of Samuel Luchtmans. The famous physicist was also one of his best-selling authors. LA/ULA

Whereas books in the field of natural science were almost completely absent from the publishing list of Jordaan Luchtmans, they held an important place in his son's list. As early as 1727 Samuel published the *Matheseos universalis elementa*, the book with which W. J. 's Gravesande introduced Newton's concept of "universal mathematics" in the Netherlands. In developing this new domain Luchtmans once again profited from the connections with his inlaws: his cousin and brother-in-law Petrus van Musschenbroek (1692-1761) became one of the luminaries of the new physics. After his studies in Leiden, Musschenbroek served as a professor in Duisburg and then in Utrecht, returning to Leiden in 1740 as successor to 's Gravesande. He published most of his works with his cousin Samuel Luchtmans. Until the 1760s his *Elementa Physicae* (1734) was a bestseller, reprinted at regular intervals and also published in French and Dutch translations.

Publishing multilingual editions in order to reach a broader public was a strategy that Luchtmans adopted more and more frequently in those years. The Enlightenment not only took place in the lofty sphere of great minds and scientific discoveries; it was also equally manifest in coffee houses, salons, reading groups, and learned societies. It was in such circles that an inquiring clientele developed, thus boosting the sales of the publishing house. The book trade and the spirit of the age had a mutually profitable relationship.

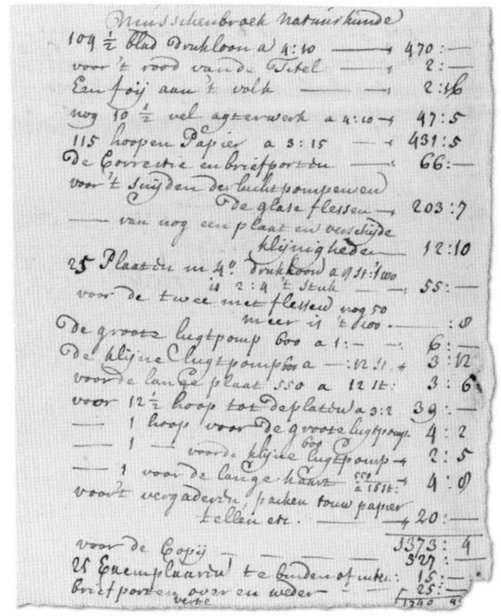

Even in the case of his cousin Petrus van Musschenbroek, the publisher reckoned his costs precisely. LA/ULA

From Father to Sons

Thus Samuel became a man of distinction and his bookshop became an important business, while in the meantime he and Cornelia produced nine children. They were prosperous times in all respects. As time went by the two oldest sons, Samuel II (1725-1780) and Johannes (1726-1809), were taken into the firm. They both attended the Latin school and then studied for some years at the university. Like all educated people of their day they were proficient in Latin and French, while at the same time they received a thorough training in German, English, and Italian. These languages fell outside the scope of the normal curriculum, but they came in useful in the book trade.

In 1741, at the tender age of sixteen, the younger Samuel was registered with the guild as a bookseller. This somewhat unusual procedure was facilitated by his father's leading position within the book guild. Apparently the elder Samuel wanted to ensure the continuity of his business, for in this same year young Samuel was also appointed his successor as printer to the city and to the university. The boy was still a student and did not actively join his father in the business until later in the 1740s. Johannes became part of the firm in 1749; he was to remain attached to it for sixty years, making him the Luchtmans family member with the longest record of service.

Henceforth the family business sailed under the flag of "Samuel Luchtmans and Sons," until the father retired in 1755. Having reached the age of seventy, he began to feel the burden of old age. Two years later, in the winter of 1757, Samuel Luchtmans passed away. He was buried in the family tomb that he had purchased in the Pieterskerk, a location befitting his rank in life. Cornelia survived him for many years and did not join him until 1784.

The Firm of S. & J. Luchtmans, 1755-1848

Samuel Luchtmans II at the age of thirty. Portrait (1755) by Nicolaas Reyers. SML

The firm would continue under the name of S. & J. Luchtmans for almost a century, although the brothers Samuel II and Johannes jointly managed the family business only until 1780. They were nearly the same age, and because they were inseparable they created the impression of being twins. Their brotherly unanimity extended into other spheres of life: each married a Reytsma girl. In 1763 Johannes was joined to Maria Johanna, and eighteen months later Samuel wedded her sister Constantia Elisabeth. As printers to the university and to the city they followed in their father's footsteps, and like him they held leading positions within the guild. Unlike their father, they did not need to work their way up to the position of solid citizens, since they had been provided with this status by birth. They were not counted among the ruling class of Leiden, but as businessmen of substance they came close to the city's upper crust. Whereas the Luchtmans family had previously been members of the Dutch Reformed Church, the brothers and their wives went over to the Walloon Church. The reason for their switch is not clear; perhaps they felt more at ease in the environment of the Église Wallonne, or they believed that this denomination was more congenial to their rank.[16]

Beyond the Borders

It was not only on the Rapenburg that the brothers conducted their business affairs, periodically they took various journeys abroad. Their fondness for travel was not inherited from their father, who was a cosmopolitan in spirit but quite the opposite in body. One gets the impression that Samuel I was more of a homebody; at any rate there is no sign that he ever attended the *Buchmessen*, or book fairs of Frankfurt and Leipzig. From a business point of view, it was not essential for him to put in an appearance there, because like most Dutch booksellers he could have himself represented by an agent. The wanderlust of the third generation reminds us instead of their grandfather Jordaan, who toward the end of the seventeenth century visited the German book fairs several times.[17] Judging by Samuel's balance sheet of 1714, for a while Jordaan even maintained branches in Duisburg and Lingen, which folded up due to the war in the first decade of the eighteenth century.

Johannes Luchtmans in 1755. Portrait by Nicolaas Reyers. SML

The Luchtmans archive preserves five travel diaries in which Samuel and Johannes recorded their experiences abroad.[18] The Leipzig book fair, which over the course of the century eclipsed that of Frankfurt, was their favorite foreign destination; furthermore, Samuel traveled to France in 1768, while Johannes spent some time in England during 1772.[19] The brother's constant companionship was interrupted only by such travels, as one of them always remained in Leiden in order to man the bookshop.

A journey from Leiden to Leipzig could easily take some ten days, and on account of the jolting of the stagecoaches on bad roads it was not an unqualified pleasure. The books going to the fair were transported separately, usually by water: from Amsterdam to Hamburg and then up the river Elbe to Leipzig. The books, mostly unbound, were packed in waterproof barrels. To recover all travel and accommodation expenses, as well as the costs of transport, it was of vital importance to do a brisk business in Leipzig. With all the hassle involved, it is hardly surprising that on average only two or three Dutch booksellers visited the book fair each year.[20]

The participants at the Book Fair in Leipzig socialized at the Richter coffeehouse. St. Mus. Leipzig

The advantage of such an international market was that it provided the opportunity for direct contact with colleagues. People could sell their own books and purchase foreign titles of interest to the domestic market. Moreover, the journey to Leipzig was not only undertaken for business, but also for pleasure: the fair was an exuberant gathering where there were lots of things to do and see. This latter aspect, however, cannot easily be deduced from Samuel's account of his visit in May 1764. By the look of it, this serious young man was busy networking and sought his pleasure chiefly in meetings with other booksellers:

> 26 May. For lunch at Mr. Reich's, where I met Mr. Kraus with his wife, from Vienna, Mr. Walther with his wife and son, from Dresden, and Mr. Nicolai with his wife, from Berlin, also the gentlemen Bohn and Brand from Hamburg, all booksellers, and who entertained us well. I have . . . been to see the burgomaster Mr. Bom on the New Market; Mr. Meisnar from Wolfenbüttel and Mr. Mumine from Copenhagen were also staying there.[21]

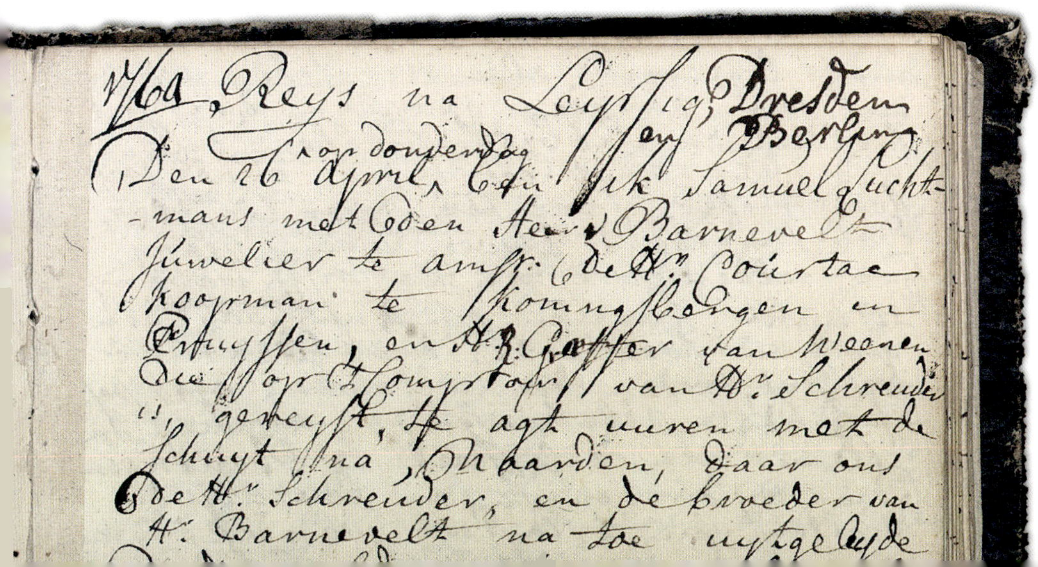
1764 Reys na Leipzig, Dresden en Berlin
Den 26 April op donderdag ik Samuel Luchtmans met den Heer Barnevelt Juwelier te Amst. de H.r Courtac Koopman te Koningsbergen in Pruyssen, en H.r Graffer van Weenen die voor t Comptoir van H.r Schreuder gereyst, te agt uuren met de schuyt na Naarden, daar ons de H.r Schreuder, en de broeder van H.r Barnevelt na toe uytgeleyde

Account by Samuel Luchtmans II of his journey in 1764 to Leipzig, Dresden, and Berlin. LA/ULA

Merchants with Style

Whereas their father had been more of a publisher than a bookseller, his sons were more booksellers than publishers. Under the brothers' management, the publishing house continued to produce a steady flow of unspectacular works, mainly in the field of classical languages. In addition to annotated text editions by classical scholars currently at the university, many older works from the firm's publishing list were reissued. The publishing house had lost its sparkle, a phenomenon not unrelated to the fact that both Leiden University and the city of Leiden were in decline during the second half of the eighteenth century. On the other hand, the brothers carried an assortment of books that was absolutely astonishing in comparison to that offered by their father.

Thousands and thousands of titles were listed in the bulky catalogs issued regularly by S. & J. Luchtmans.[22] They included many antiquarian works, even incunabula from the last quarter of the fifteenth century. Samuel and Johannes managed the shop with great care and energy. In order to acquire their enormous stock, they corresponded with innumerable booksellers at home and abroad. Their cosmopolitan correspondence covered Germany, France, Belgium, England, Switzerland, Italy, Spain, Portugal, Denmark, Sweden, Russia, and Hungary; even a bookseller in faraway Bombay occasionally received mail from Leiden. In part, these contacts were due to the brothers' diligent networking at the book fair. From behind their writing desks on the Rapenburg they did the same thing that Samuel did in person in Leipzig: they established profitable relations with fellow booksellers.

Family Chronicle

In 1780 the brothers' unity was broken by the death of Samuel II, whereupon Johannes continued the business on his own. The hereditary succession was secured in the person of Samuel son of Samuel, born in 1766; Johannes had two daughters, but his only son had died shortly after birth. When his father died, Samuel III was just fourteen years old, so that he first had to finish his education before going to work. He joined the firm after obtaining his law degree, but his heart was not in the book trade. He left the management of the family business in the hands of his uncle and preferred to devote himself to the administration of the city: during the years of the Batavian Republic and the period of French rule, he held various offices in Leiden. Johannes Luchtmans managed the bookshop until 1809, when he died in harness at the age of eighty-three. Samuel III then took charge of the business, but his management would last for only three years. The last scion of the Luchtmans dynasty died in 1812 without male offspring.

By tradition, the firm continued to do business under the name of S. & J. Luchtmans, but it vacated the time-honored address of Rapenburg 69: around this time the bookshop moved across the canal to Nos. 78-80. The business was passed down through the female line by way of Johannes's daughter Magdalena Henriëtta, who was married to the Amsterdam physician Evert Bodel Nijenhuis. This couple had two children, Johannes Tiberius and Catharina. When the mother died in 1799, the father was unable to raise the small children by himself. Johannes Tiberius and Catharina grew up in the home of their grandfather Johannes in Leiden and were mainly raised by their spinster aunt Cornelia. The grandson was the preordained successor to his grandfather, but at the time of the latter's death he was far too young to take over the business.

Illustrated religious history: > engravings from Ysbrandt van Hamelsveld, *De gewigstigste geschiedenissen des Bybels, afgebeeld in twee honderd en vijftig* printverbeeldingen. The book was published in 1791 by Johannes Luchtmans. ULA

Richt. XIII.

den Engel vaart op na den hemel in 't aangesigte van Manoah en zyn huisvrouw.

Apparition de l'Ange à Manoah & sa Femme.

J. Folkema fec.

Richt. XIV.

Simson verscheurt den Leeuw. || *Samson déchire un Lion.*

Johannes Luchtmans at the age of 65. Pastel by Johann Anspach, about 1791. SML

It is at this stage in the family chronicle that the name of Luchtmans becomes entwined with that of Brill. Because Samuel III had other things to attend to and Johannes was getting on in years, in 1802 they had taken on the Leiden printer Brill as their manager. Johannes Brill (1767-1859) descended from a race of Dutch ministers, but did not intend to become a minister himself. Nor had he in his early days been destined for the printing trade. Since 1786 he had been employed in the secretariat of Willem V of Orange, but in 1795 he was left behind without a job when the French invaded the country and the prince took refuge in England. Brill was naturally reputed to be an Orangeist, which in the days of the French-sponsored Batavian Republic was not exactly a recommendation. In order to support himself he established a printing shop in Leiden, and in this capacity he executed printing commissions for the Luchtmans firm. From 1802 he led a curious double life as both an independent printer and the manager of Luchtmans, a dual status that he would maintain until 1848. He became the house printer for Luchtmans, although he also did printing jobs for others.

When Samuel III died in 1812, Johannes Brill was fully initiated into the secrets of the book trade. The manager now acted as administrator of S. & J. Luchtmans, until the day when the young Bodel Nijenhuis would come of age. Bodel received the same kind of education as his eighteenth-century ancestors: he attended the Latin school and subsequently studied law at the university in Leiden. In his studies he combined the history of the family business with his own future as a publisher. In 1819 he obtained his doctorate with a historical-juridical thesis on the rights of printers and booksellers, which of course was published by S. & J. Luchtmans.[23]

Joint Leadership

Thus, from a theoretical point of view Bodel was fully prepared to enter the business in 1821. He was less well prepared for the practical end of the book trade, but it was his good fortune to have the experienced Brill at his side. Until 1848 they jointly managed the firm, Brill as business chief and Bodel as intellectual mentor. Bodel, more of a bookman than a bookseller, was the one who maintained relations with the scholarly world. The Luchtmans firm was still printer to the university, which guaranteed a steady turnover in dissertations and academical publications. As in the past, text editions of the classics remained a fixture in the publishing program.

Equally important in these years was the systematic publication of Arabic manuscripts from the famous Legatum Warnerianum of Leiden University. Successive Arabic scholars such as Hamaker, Juynboll, and Dozy published their editions of these manuscripts through Luchtmans. This tradition in Oriental studies built on previous Luchtmans publications and anticipated Brill's later list. With the arrival of professors such as Reuvens and Janssens, the archaeology department acquired institutional status within the university, which was reflected in various publications in this field. From 1839 onwards, Egyptology was embodied in the impressive series *Aegiptische Monumenten*, afterwards continued by Brill until 1904.

Political developments had their repercussions in the publications of S. & J. Luchtmans. For instance, the participation of Leiden students as volunteer-grenadiers in the Ten Days' Campaign against Belgium was acclaimed in *De terugkomst der vrijwillige jagers* (1831), a high-sounding and patriotical booklet by the theologian N. C. Kist.

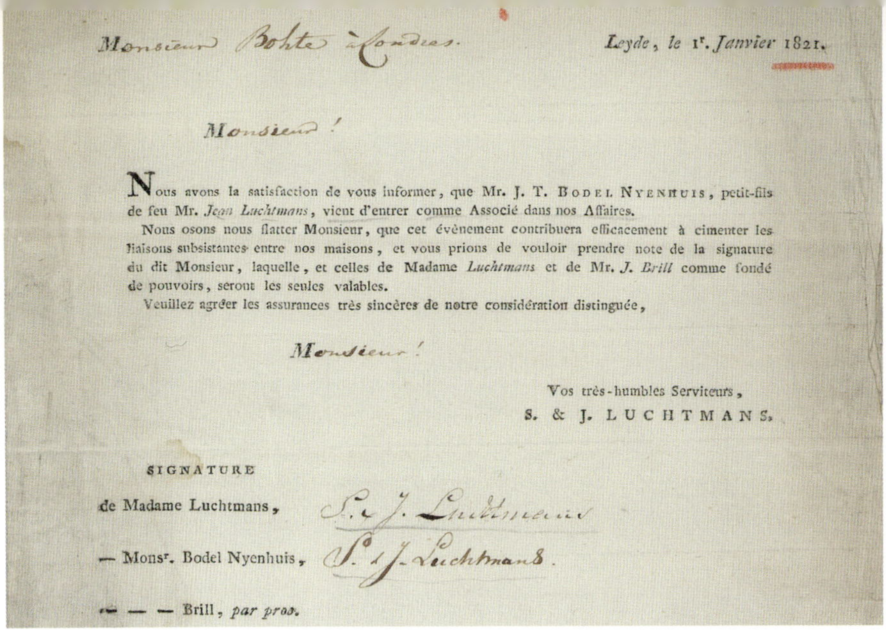

Monsieur Bohte à Londres. Leyde, le 1r. Janvier 1821.

Monsieur!

Nous avons la satisfaction de vous informer, que Mr. J. T. Bodel Nyenhuis, petit-fils de feu Mr. *Jean Luchtmans*, vient d'entrer comme Associé dans nos Affaires.

Nous osons nous flatter Monsieur, que cet évènement contribuera efficacement à cimenter les liaisons subsistantes entre nos maisons, et vous prions de vouloir prendre note de la signature du dit Monsieur, laquelle, et celles de Madame *Luchtmans* et de Mr. *J. Brill* comme fondé de pouvoirs, seront les seules valables.

Veuillez agréer les assurances très sincères de notre considération distinguée,

Monsieur!

Vos très-humbles Serviteurs,
S. & J. LUCHTMANS.

SIGNATURE

de Madame Luchtmans, S. & J. Luchtmans

— Monsr. Bodel Nyenhuis, S. & J. Luchtmans.

— — — Brill, *par proc.*

A circular letter in French from 1821, announcing that J. T. Bodel Nijenhuis has joined the firm of Luchtmans. LA/ULA

Another result of the Belgian revolt was the so-called "policy of perseverance" of King Willem I, who until 1839 vainly tried to win back his southern territory. The great increase in military expense in the mother country led in turn to a more intensive exploration and exploitation of the East Indian colonies. This in its turn, back in Leiden, stimulated the scientific and scholarly interest in the East and boosted the number of publications by Luchtmans in this field. The effects of the profitable *Cultuurstelsel*, the new program for cultivating the colonies by forced labour, could be felt on the Rapenburg: "By order of the King" (and thus with the government's support) Luchtmans published in 1839-44 a magnificent three-volume *Natuurlijke geschiedenis der Nederlandsche overzeesche bezittingen* [Natural History of the Dutch Overseas Possessions] by C. J. Temminck et al. This typographic *tour de force* formed the overture to the East Asian tradition that was afterwards cultivated by Brill.

Other publications reflected Bodel's interest in history, such as the monumental publication of sources by Guillaume Groen van Prinsterer, the *Archives de la Maison d'Orange-Nassau*. Bodel was on friendly terms with Groen, and he himself prepared the index for the innumerable volumes. Bodel's religious feelings were close to those of his friend and presumably he was also an adherent of the Réveil, the current revival movement. Groen's *Ongeloof en Revolutie* [Unbelief and Revolution], by and large a song of praise to "God, the Netherlands, and the House of Orange," was published with Luchtmans in 1847. The poet Isaäc da Costa, after his conversion from Judaism the personification *par excellence* of the Réveil, also published some works with Luchtmans.

Thus, a publishing house is clearly interwoven with its surrounding world in all sorts of ways. Even more so, it is a medium in which contemporary movements converge. Bodel was a man of his time, even if, like Da Costa, he harbored objections against "the spirit of the age" and, like Groen van Prinsterer, was a conservative who abhorred the heritage of the French Revolution. Grandfather Johannes, born in 1726, would have understood little of the nineteenth-century environment of his grandson. The world had changed, and with it the firm of Luchtmans. And yet through all these changes the firm of Luchtmans maintained its identity, steadfastly going its way while constantly remaining in tune with the changing times.

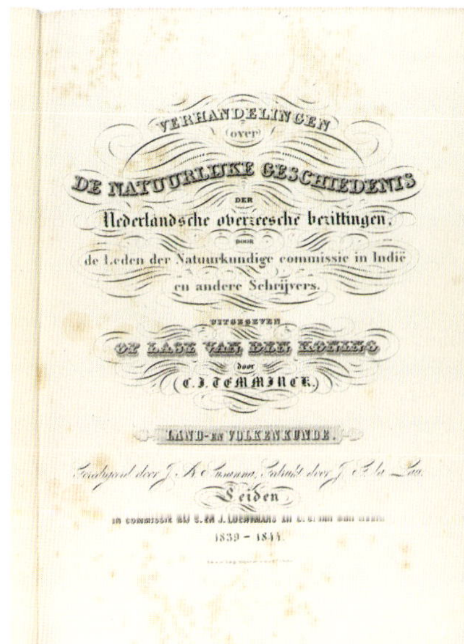

Verhandelingen over de Natuurlijke Geschiedenis der Nederlandsche overzeesche bezittingen, door de Leden der Natuurkundige commissie in Indië en andere Schrijvers. Uitgegeven op last van den Koning door C. J. Temminck. Land- en Volkenkunde. Leiden 1839 – 1844.

C. J. Temminck et al., *De Natuurlijke Geschiedenis der Nederlandsche overzeesche bezittingen* (3 vols., 1839–1844): a government sponsored showpiece on the natural history of the Dutch East Indies. ULA

SIMIA SATYRUS.

The New Man

More change was in the air. Since July 1, 1829, the seventeen-year-old Evert Jan Brill had been working with the firm, as a document from 1831 indicates.[24] Evidently the young man had made a favorable impression, for S. & J. Luchtmans wished to strengthen his ties to the business. They decided "to pay the said son of Mr. J. Brill in order to encourage him, for every two years he has been working, as of the 1st of July 1829, the sum of one hundred and fifty guilders, and to continue this payment for another two years in full confidence that the said son of J. Brill, under the training of his father, has met expectations and will continue to do so."

Quite a mouthful from Bodel, but it turned out that Brill Jr. was more than deserving of this trust and the biennial bonus of a hundred and fifty guilders. Under his father's guidance, he developed into an all-around professional—printer, publisher, and bookseller. In the course of the forties he even had a number of books published under his personal imprint "E. J. Brill." In 1846 he supervised the publication of a French book on the Dutch East Indies by C. J. Temminck, director of the National Museum of Natural History and the man responsible for the colonial showpiece that had been published by Luchtmans shortly before. Apparently Evert Jan had the ambition to become a publisher himself, but he was expected to succeed his father as manager of Luchtmans.

Things were coming to a head in 1848, the year of revolution, as described at the beginning of this chapter. Perhaps current events contributed to Bodel's decision to retire from the business. He wanted to devote himself exclusively to his intellectual pursuits, although some of his remarks also suggest that the firm's profitability had decreased. Brill Sr. had already indicated that he wished to start enjoying a quiet old age in the village of Scherpenzeel. It was not a foregone conclusion that Evert Jan, presumed successor to his father as manager, would take over the firm of Luchtmans under his own steam: Bodel initially intended to sell the business to the well-known bookseller Frederik Muller in Amsterdam.

The latter declined the offer, wondering twenty-five years later whether he had done so "in an ill-fated or felicitous hour."[25] When no other interested parties presented themselves, it was decided to transfer the business to Brill Jr. Although the financial details of the transfer are not known, one would expect, considering the record of service compiled by the two Brills, that S. & J. Luchtmans offered accommodating terms. Even so, Evert Jan Brill must have assumed considerable financial obligations. His self-confidence was apparent not only in his decision to take over the firm of Luchtmans, but also in his decision to operate it henceforth under his own name. Brill intended to prove himself without relying on the old Luchtmans glory.

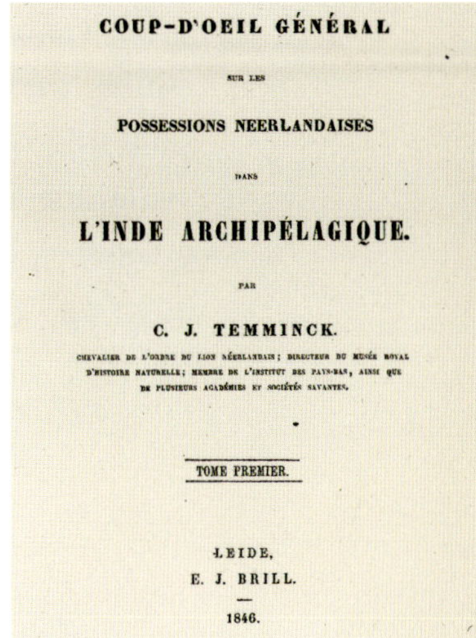
COUP-D'OEIL GÉNÉRAL

SUR LES

POSSESSIONS NEERLANDAISES

DANS

L'INDE ARCHIPÉLAGIQUE.

PAR

C. J. TEMMINCK.

CHEVALIER DE L'ORDRE DU LION NÉERLANDAIS; DIRECTEUR DU MUSÉE ROYAL D'HISTOIRE NATURELLE; MEMBRE DE L'INSTITUT DES PAYS-BAS, AINSI QUE DE PLUSIEURS ACADÉMIES ET SOCIÉTÉS SAVANTES.

TOME PREMIER.

LEIDE,
E. J. BRILL.
1846.

While still working as an employee at Luchtmans, E. J. Brill published in 1846 under his own name another work by Temminck about the East Indies. ULA

J. T. Bodel Nijenhuis around 1840. Portrait by J. L. Cornet. ULL Coll.

< The lithographies in C. J. Temminck's *Natuurlijke Geschiedenis der Nederlandsche overzeesche bezittingen* are of a stunning quality. The plates are partly hand-colored. ULA

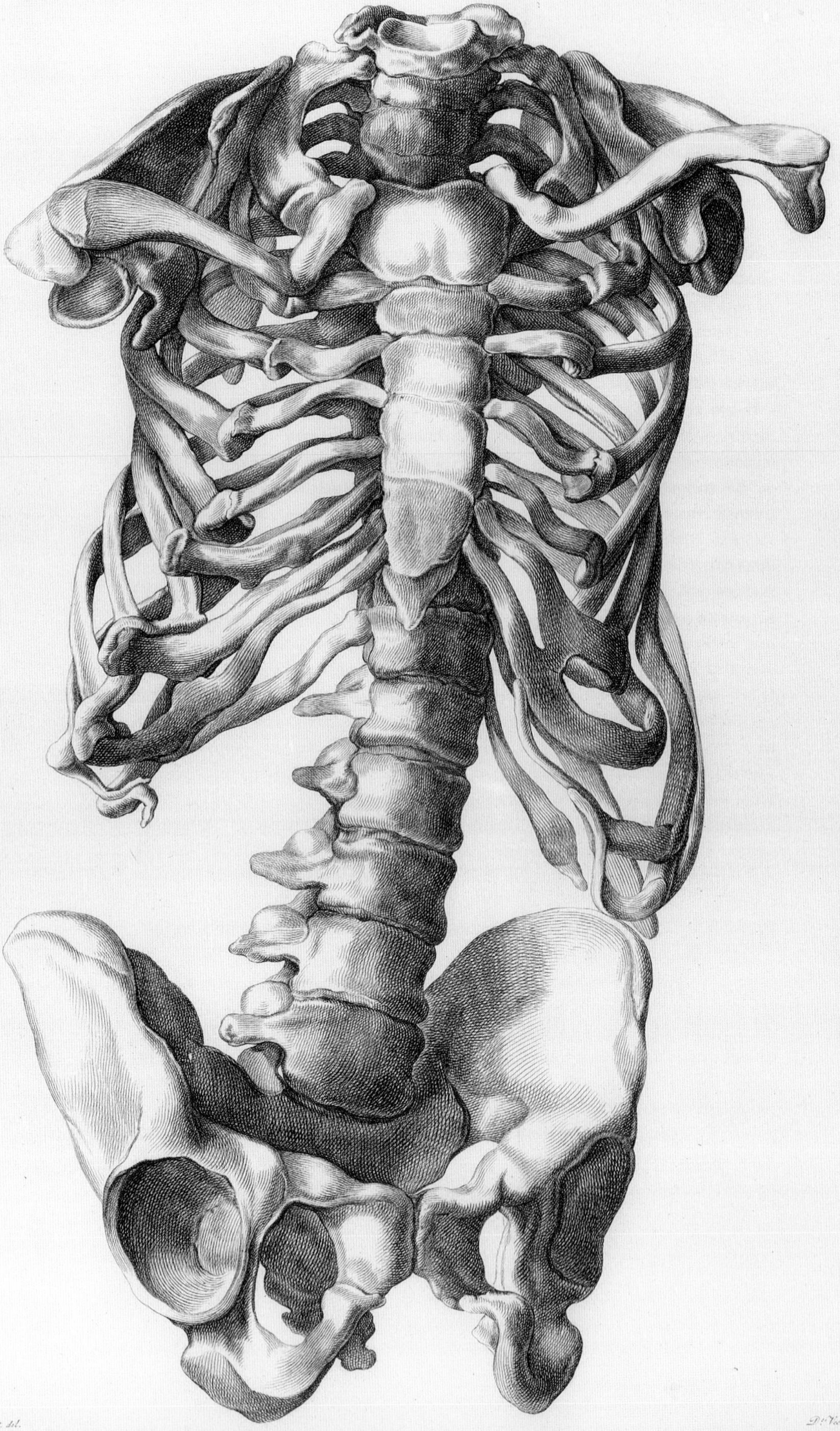

G. Sandifort del. D. Veelwaard sculp.

The Luchtmans Archive

The archive of the Luchtmans firm covers almost the entire period between 1683 and 1848 and forms a unique source for the history of the book trade in the Netherlands. No other Dutch archive covers such a long period of time and illuminates such a broad spectrum of the book trade. The eighteenth-century archive of the Enschedé firm in Haarlem has also been partially preserved, but it covers a shorter period of time and is less complete. Besides, in those days Enschedé was not an internationally renowned booksellers' establishment, but primarily the printer and publisher of a newspaper, the *Oprechte Haarlemsche Courant*. The Luchtmans archive is now housed among the Special Collections of the Amsterdam University Library and comprises about eleven linear meters of material. Here we may take stock of the most important elements.[26]

To start with, an impressive series of thirty-one folio volumes has been preserved, the so-called "Booksellers' Accounts" or "Booksellers' Debt-ledgers." With the exception of the first volume, which spans the years 1683-1697, they document a continuous period from 1697 to 1845. These ledgers record the transactions of the Luchtmans firm with booksellers both at home and abroad. The dealers bought books from one another, and they also engaged in commission selling on one another's behalf: the Leiden firm sold books published by other publishers, who in turn held Luchtmans's publications on consignment.

Practically all the well-known names of the eighteenth-century book trade can be found in these ledgers. In foreign countries, Luchtmans maintained relations with booksellers in Germany, England, France, Italy, the Southern Netherlands, and Switzerland. Each of these business partners had a charge account in the booksellers' ledgers, in which debits and credits were recorded. Relations between booksellers were often long-lasting and were based on mutual trust. On occasion settlement was effected over a period of years, and it did not necessarily involve cash. The bartering of books was a usual way of settling accounts (during the period 1741-1788 such transactions were also recorded in a series of "Exchange Ledgers").

Luchtmans's network of business relations can also be traced in a series of "Auction Ledgers" covering the years 1706-1806. The purchase of books usually took place at booksellers' auctions, mainly within the province of Holland. Booksellers purchased not only books themselves, but also the rights to books. The copyright was not just the right to print a certain book, in the hope that this would deter pirated editions; the right was transferable and could also legitimize the reprint of a certain number of copies. The Auction Ledgers did not only record purchases at auctions, but also Luchtmans's expenditures on the publication of new books, whether or not in cooperation with others. The purchase of paper, the costs of shipping, as well as payments to printers, translators, correctors, and engravers—all the expenses incurred by the publisher were meticulously recorded.

Transactions with individual customers can be found in the so-called "Private Accounts," also known as "Private Debt-ledgers" (nine volumes covering the period 1702-1842). These books record the purchases of individual customers, usually in the form of an outstanding account with a term of one year. On the basis of these ledgers

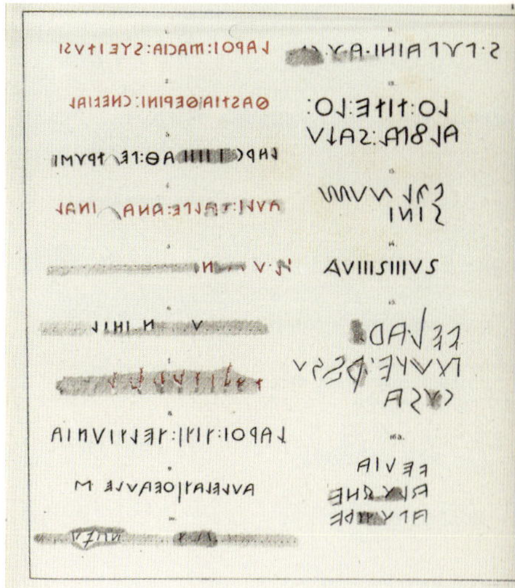

Etruscan inscriptions from L. J. F. Janssens, *Musei Lugduno-Batavi Inscriptiones Etruscae*, published in 1840 by S. & J. Luchtmans. In 1854 E. J. Brill published a Dutch edition of the work under the title *De Etrurische Grafreliëfs*. ULA

< Engraved plate from G. Sandifort, *Museum Anatomicum Academiae Lugduno-Bataviae*, volume IV. The imposing anatomical atlas produced by the father-and-son team of Sandifort was a long-term project of Luchtmans. The first volume appeared in 1793, the fourth in 1835. ULA

1773 Den Heer, M. M: Reÿ debet

Date	Qty	Description	f	st	Bladeren
29 Jan:	1	Harris de morbis Infantum in 8°	—	17	
12 Juny	2	Bielfeld Instit. Polit. Tome 3e			132
	1	Yden 4° T. 3e			69
14 July		Sperslot in boeken Schuldig			473
1774. 15 Aug	1	aan Hr. D. v. Damme bet.	149	5	
		te rug den 27 Aug: 1774			
	2	Campement de Maillebois 4°	10	—	
	2	Loisirs d'Eon d°	31	10	
	1	Campement des Russes d°	6	—	
	1	Oeuvres de Diderot d°	7	10	
	4	Conversion de Struensee d° 1e p.	3	4	
	5	2e p.	4	—	
	11	Caracter van Fagel d°	1	13	
	6	Loix de Minos d°	2	8	
		een assignatie op den Hr. Cuyk van Mierop	130	14	
		geliquideert den 30 Aug: 1774	355	1	674

1774

Date	Qty	Description	f	st
13 Jan:	1	Plutarchus Rualdi. fol. 2 voll.	42	—
	1	Aristides ed. Jebb. 4° 2 Voll.	15	15
	1	Manethonis Apotheles m.	1	10
	1	Frontinus Oudendorpii.	2	10
	1	Antiquae Musicae Scriptores.	7	10
28	te rug 1	Journal des Scav. 12° Jan. 1774		
3 Febr.	3	Bielfeld Institutions polit. T. 3e	9	—
27 Dec.	1	Michaelis in Hagiographos in 4° 3 Voll.	11	10
		Aan gelt 99:15 bet.	12	13
		Geliquideert den 6 Juny 1775	102	9

1775

Date	Qty	Description	f	st
10 Maart	2	Bielfeld Institut. polit. T. 3e	6	10
27 July	5 en ½	pond uyt Leipzig	1	2
31	1	Schultens Opera Minora.	4	15
	1	Schroeder Gramm. hebr. 4°	2	6
2 Aug	1	Agathon d. in 12° 4 Voll:	3	2
5	1	v. Swieten Commentarii 5 voll:	26	12
		een assignatie op Guerin 44:7	103	5
		geliquideert den 5 Aug: 1776	147	12

it is possible to identify the regular visitors of Luchtmans's shop and consequently to determine the makeup of the clientele.[27] Unfortunately, not all customers were solvent—certainly not in a university town such as Leiden. For instance, in 1714 Samuel I observed that his accounts due exceeded *f* 2,200, but that well over one third would have to be written off as "bad debts."[28]

Day-to-day expenses, along with other notes, were recorded in cashbooks, while three balance sheets (for the years 1714, 1747, and 1810) show an average of the permanent and floating assets of the business. Warehouse records registered the stocks of books. Outgoing correspondence was recorded in copy books. In addition, the archive contains a large quantity of unbound documents: contracts, internal correspondence, and notes. As can be expected in a publisher's archive, many book catalogs, either printed or in manuscript, have also been preserved. Finally, there are such curiosities as the above-mentioned travel diaries in which Samuel II and Johannes set down their experiences during their travels abroad.

< Booksellers' Accounts of Luchtmans, 1773: the debit record of the Amsterdam bookseller Marc Michel Rey, whose outstanding bills were crossed after payment. LA/ULA

From Leiden to Amsterdam

The year 1848 does not form a strict watershed between the old and the new management: the last of Luchtmans's booksellers' accounts contains notes by Evert Jan Brill, made after the liquidation of the old firm. The most recent portion of the Luchtmans archive, accumulated after the relocation in the early nineteenth century, was housed in the business premises at Rapenburg 78-80. Bodel Nijenhuis continued to live in the old family home at Rapenburg 69B, and in 1852 he annexed the neighboring premises at 69A for his expanding collection of prints, maps, and books.[29] The archive covering the period before 1800 must have remained in his home; he dabbled in history and regularly rummaged in the old papers, as is evidenced by various remarks he made.

Bodel Nijenhuis died on January 8, 1872. He had been married twice, but both marriages were childless. After the death of his second wife he had his last will drawn up on June 22, 1866, in which he bequeathed his unique collection of prints and maps to Leiden University.[30] His remaining possessions went to the children of his late sister Catherina Johanna, widow of Louis Pierre Bienfait. His nephew and executor Henri Bienfait inherited, in addition to a gold watch and diamond tiepin, a collection of family papers that probably consisted of the oldest portion of the Luchtmans archive up to 1800. In his obituary of Bodel, Frederik Muller mentioned that Bodel had left the old family papers to his relatives.[31]

Some time afterward, the archive covering the period between 1800 and 1848 also ended up in Bienfait's home on the Sarphatistraat in Amsterdam. The transfer of this portion can be dated to 1883, in connection with a relocation of the firm of Brill within Leiden. Evert Jan Brill had died at the end of 1871, six weeks before Bodel Nijenhuis, and after his death the business was taken over by Adriaan van Oordt and Frans de Stoppelaar, two gentlemen who will make their appearance in the next chapter. The Luchtmans archive was probably transferred to Henri Bienfait in 1883, when the business moved from the Rapenburg to its new premises on the Oude Rijn.

Picture of J.T. Bodel Nijenhuis around 1870. Brill Coll.

After the death of Bienfait in 1885, his son contacted the Association for the Promotion of the Interests of the Book Trade. It had come to the attention of Bienfait Jr. that the Association was collecting materials for the history of the Dutch book trade, and he wished to transfer the archive of "the famous firm of Luchtmans" to this institution.[32] His offer was gratefully accepted, although the Association proposed to have four portions of the materials "destroyed as [they are] worthless": a series of daybooks for the years 1782-1839, containing drafts of outgoing letters; forty-eight parcels of letters received from booksellers during the years 1801-1848; and finally a large quantity of receipts from the first half of the nineteenth century. Fortunately Bienfait objected to the destruction of the daybooks and the letters, so that only a boxful of receipts ended up in the trash.[33]

In 1958 the Association, now renamed the Royal Society of the Dutch Book Trade, gave its entire collection on loan to the library of the University of Amsterdam. Since 2005 these holdings, including the Luchtmans archive, have formed the Library of the Book Trade. It is housed in the Department of Special Collections of the University Library on the Oude Turfmarkt in Amsterdam.

Catalog from 1714, with annotations by Samuel Luchtmans I. LA/ULA

...TALOG...

LIBROR...

SAMUEL LUCHTMAN...

ALbini (*Bernardi*) Oratio de
Progressu Medicinæ. 4.
—— Oratio de Incremento
Artis Medicæ Seculi XVI
Anatomie & Ame des Plantes,
Srs. N. Grew, R. Boyle, &
du. 12. avec fig.

Arents Commentarius in Historiam Tentationis C
sti a Diabolo illatæ, in locum Matth. 4: 1-12.

Arriani Expeditio Alexandri Magni & Historia In
ca cum notis J. Gronovii, Græc. & Lat. in Fol

—— Ars Tactica, acies contra Alanos, Periplu
Ponti Euxini, Periplus Maris Erythræi, liber de
Venatione &c. Gr. & Lat. cum notis Blancardi. 8.

Ars magna & Admirabilis variis speciminibus confirma-
ta, qua Pandectarum tituli, eorumque præcipuæ
materiæ, Ope figurarum Emblematicarum brevissi-
me & Jucunde memoriæ imprimi & firmiter conti-
neri possunt. 8. cum V. Tabellis in plano.

Astori (*Joh. Ant.*) Commentariolum in Antiquum
Alcmanis Poëtæ Laconis Monumentum allatum è
Græcia, *Venet. cum fig.* in Fol.

—— Epistola de Deo Brotonte ad Illustriss. A-
postolum Zenum. *Venetiis*, in Fol.

Avancini Poësis Lyrica. 12.

A 2 Bach-

Fac-simile de l'écriture d'al-Makrizi

Al-Mokaffá, man. 1366, 3e volume.

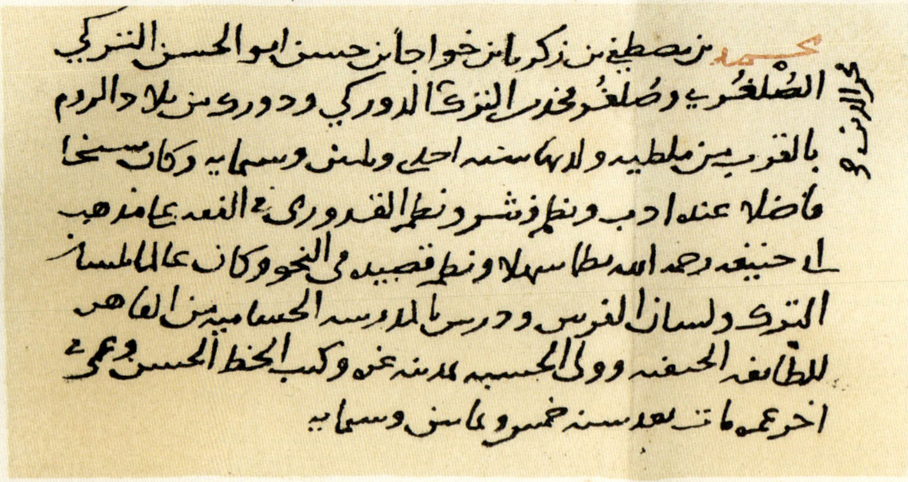

محمد بن مصطفى بن زكريا بن خواجا بن حسين ابو الحسن التركي
الصلغري وصلغر بطن من الترك الدوركي ودوركي من بلاد الروم
بالقرب من ملطية ولد بها سنة احدى وسبعين وستماية وكان شيخا
فاضلا عنده ادب ونظم ونثر ونظم القدوري في الفقه على مذهب
ابي حنيفة رحمه الله نظما سهلا ونظم قصيدة في النحو وكان عالما باللسان
التركي ولسان الفرس ودرس بالمدرسة الحسامية من القاهرة
للطايفة الحنفية وولي الحسبة بمدينة غزة وكتب الخط الحسن وعمر
اخر عمره ومات بعد سنة خمسين وسبعماية

Fac-simile de l'écriture du copiste d'al-Makrizi

Traité des monnaies musulmanes, man. 560 (2).

Notes marginales de l'auteur

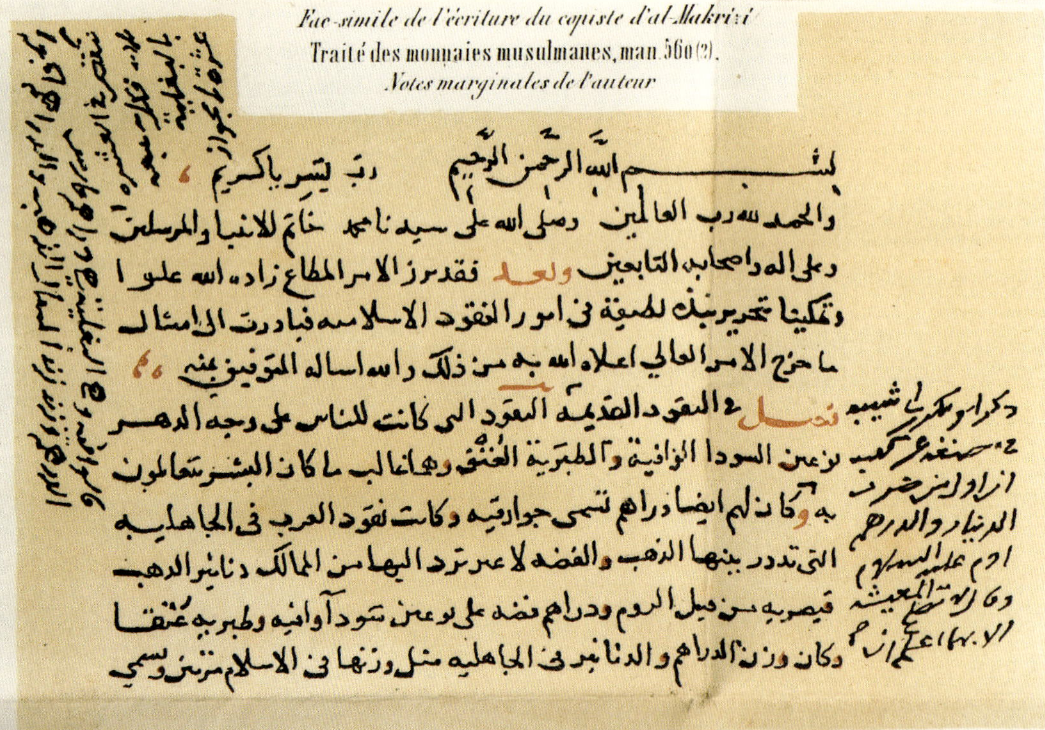

بسم الله الرحمن الرحيم رب يسر يا كريم
والحمد لله رب العالمين وصلى الله على سيدنا محمد خاتم الانبيا والمرسلين
وعلى اله واصحابه التابعين وبعد فقد برز الامر المطاع زاده الله علوا
وتمكينا بتحرير نبذة لطيفة في امور النقود الاسلامية فبادرت الى امتثال
ما خرج الامر العالي اعلاه الله به من ذلك والله اساله التوفيق بمنه
فصل في النقود القديمة النقود التي كانت للناس على وجه الدهر
نوعين السودا الوافية والطبرية العتق وهما غالب ما كان البشر يتعاملون
به وكان لهم ايضا دراهم تسمى جوارقية وكانت نقود العرب في الجاهلية
التي تدور بينها الذهب والفضة لا غير ترد اليها من الممالك دنانير الذهب
قيصرية من قبل الروم ودراهم فضة على نوعين سود وافية وطبرية عتق
وكان وزن الدراهم والدنانير في الجاهلية مثل وزنها في الاسلام مرتين ويسمي

Lith. de Hooiberg à Leide.

THE FIRM OF E. J. BRILL, 1848-1896

Between the Old Days and the New: Evert Jan Brill, 1848-1871

The house of S. & J. Luchtmans bid farewell to the world with a spectacular book sale.[1] The former firm disposed of all the stock that had been piling up over the course of one and a half centuries in the shop and the warehouses—an unparalleled outpouring of books. The Luchtmans auctions were in 1848-49 the outstanding event in the Dutch book world. Evert Jan Brill took responsibility for their organization, and as a novice entrepreneur thus had the additional task of disposing of the legacy of his predecessors. No doubt, when drawing up the inventory for the auctions, he set apart the books he wanted to keep for himself; he acted on insider information, so to speak. Taking over the entire Luchtmans stock of books could hardly have been an option for Brill. It would have saddled him with enormous financial obligations, not to mention an enormous stock of unsalable books.

Between October 1848 and April 1850, the Luchtmans stock of bound books was sold at four consecutive auctions. The proceeds of the first auctions were mainly used to settle debts and to cover the operating expenses of the firm in its last days. The stock of unbound books came under the hammer beginning on August 20, 1849, in the Odeon building on the Singel in Amsterdam. This large-scale literary ball was organized by the Amsterdam merchants Radink and Van Kesteren, in cooperation with Brill. There was a large crowd in attendance, and among the interested parties were well-known booksellers such as Frederik Muller, Martinus Nijhoff, and the Van Cleef brothers. Even German and French booksellers made a special journey to Amsterdam for the auction.

In addition to more recent Luchtmans publications, the catalog listed many eighteenth-century works that had long been thought to be out of print. Indeed, the auctions brought to light some copies of the fourth edition of Bayle's *Dictionaire* from 1730, the above-mentioned mammoth project of Samuel I and a couple of Amsterdam booksellers. The catalog included more than three thousand items: 540 copyrighted Luchtmans titles and an assortment of 2,634 titles without copyright. In the bound state, this massive pile of printed paper would correspond to around fifty thousand books.

Disappointing Sale

The quantity of unbound books offered at the auction was overwhelming, but sales were disappointing. Many titles yielded less than expected, and some seven hundred and fifty items had to be withdrawn due to lack of interest. Luchtmans was saddled with a host of unsalable merchandise that could hardly be given away. In 1849, monuments of eighteenth-century scholarship had not yet attained the status of valuable

R. P. A. Dozy, *Notices sur quelques manuscrits Arabes* (1847-1851, with the imprint "E. J. Brill"). Reinhart Pieter Anne Dozy (1820-1883) was one of the most prominent Arabic scholars of his day. Some of his works are still authoritative until this day, one hundred and fifty years after their publication. The book contains a facsimile of the manuscripts of the scholar al-Makrizi and his copyist. The facsimile is a multicolor lithograph, made by the Leiden lithographer T. Hooiberg. Dozy expressed his hope that autograph specimens would be published more often, as they "would considerably simplify research of this kind." ULA

From the beginning of the nineteenth century until 1883 the firm of E. J. Brill was established on the Rapenburg at Nos. 78-80. Brill Coll.

antiques, and they changed hands for a few pennies or quarters. After the deduction of the auctioneers' commission, the net proceeds of the sale amounted to *f* 25,464.44—a lot of money in those days, but less than the Luchtmans heirs had hoped for. Half of this sum went to Bodel Nijenhuis, the other half to his cousins. It was not until August 1850 that Brill was able to inform Bodel that all business had been wound up and that all debts had been paid. Unfortunately, there also proved to be "a mass of bad debts," since many of them were unrecoverable and had to be written off.

Brill himself was among the bidders at the Amsterdam auction. It was the first time he competed with the big names of the trade, although as a minor player: he bought 97 titles in all. He probably could not afford more, although the question remains whether he had wanted to acquire more. He intended to build up a publishing list of his own and had no interest in Luchtmans's dead weight. He acquired 48 copyrighted titles, but one third of these consisted of eighteenth-century scholarship of little commercial value. The medical work of Albinus, published in 1747 by Samuel I, was a curiosity at best; the rights were even older and dated from the days of Jordaan Luchtmans. Well over thirty of the copyrighted titles he purchased were publications from Luchtmans's more recent past, mainly in the field of classical philology and theology. Publications in Arabic were to become a cornerstone of his own publishing list, but such books were not included in the Luchtmans legacy: in recent years, Brill had already begun to publish Arabic texts under his own name. He did buy a work by the Arabist R. P. A. Dozy, an author who would contribute substantially to his publishing list in the years to come. Brill's desire to court particular authors also seems to have inspired other purchases of recent work.[2]

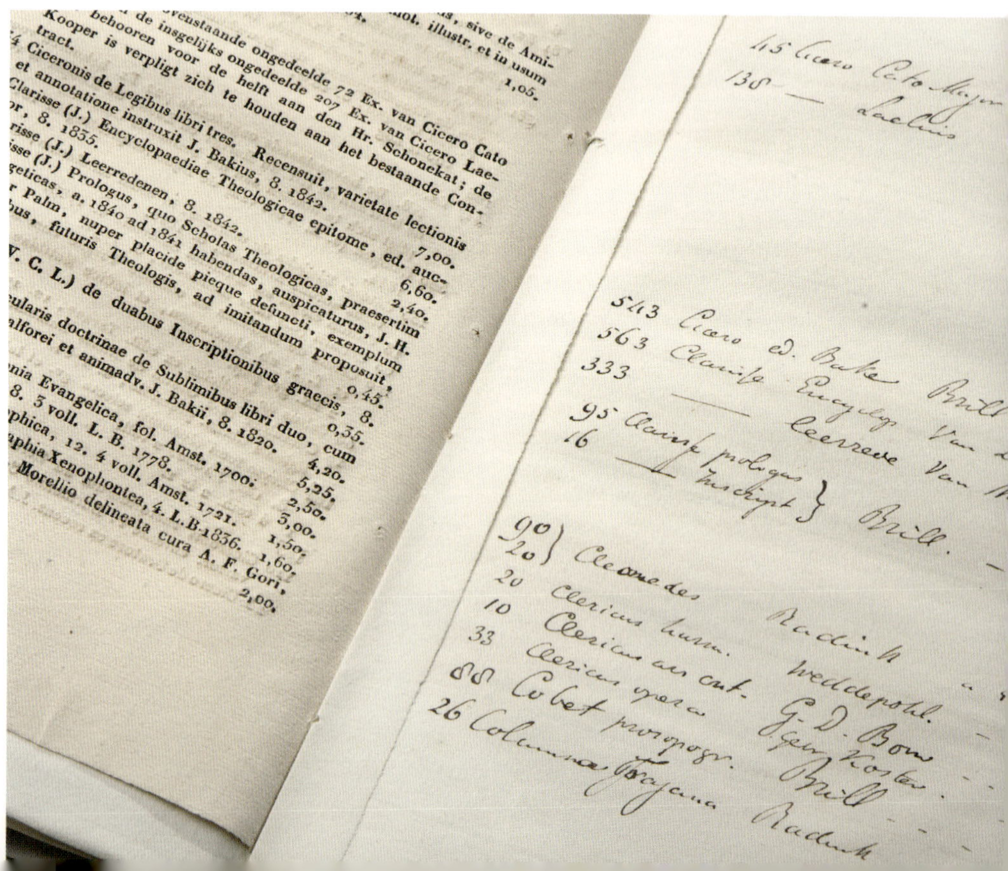

In his copy of the catalog, E. J. Brill recorded which books he bought at the Luchtmans auction in 1849. LA/ULA

The amateur theologian Jacob Brill (1639-1700) was probably an ancestor of Evert Jan Brill. The Leiden weaver and catechist was a follower of the Zeeland minister Pontiaan van Hattem (ca. 1641-1706). In orthodox circles this preacher had a bad reputation on account of his mystical pietism, which was somewhat related to the ideas of Spinoza. Van Hattem and his followers emphasized personal communion with the divine and rejected original sin. Such attitudes were regarded as anathema in the Reformed Church of those days. Jacob Brill was also an adept of this pietistic and nonconformist way of thinking. He unfolded his religious ideas in a book that appeared in 1705, five years after his death: *De werken, klaar en grondig aanwijsende het pit en merg van de ware, wesentlijke en dadelijke God-geleerdheid*. One of the most vehement opponents of the Hattemists was another Zeelander, the minister and poet Carolus Tuinman (1659-1728). He did not have a good word for Jacob Brill:

> . . . There is a freethinker in his skin
> Who deceitfully seeks to hide himself in gibberish.
> His book, however foggy, can supply spectacles (*bril*)
> That give a clear view of the secrets of hell.

Brill's book appeared in 1710 in a German translation as *Der Weg des Friedens* [The Way of Peace]. The German edition contained the engraved frontispiece with laudatory poem, shown in the illustration. The author is praised by a sympathizer as a man of God who offers a way out of the Babel-like confusion of conflicting beliefs:

What kind of man of God Brill is
His writing will show to you, reader:
Here he leaves all sects behind,
And shows the way out of Babel.

Dedicated to the Business

Brill was a printer and a publisher, and in addition he operated his combined bookselling firm and antiquarian bookshop. After the takeover the printing shop had been incorporated into the firm, but Brill's manner of conducting business did not differ substantially from that of S. & J. Luchtmans. An abrupt change was hardly to be expected, since Brill had learned his trade there and even managed the firm in its latter days. Even so, he did not simply continue to do business on the same footing; he had one foot in the past and the other one in the future, so to speak. By comparison with Bodel Nijenhuis, he was a paragon of new professionalism, although he was only fifteen years younger than his former employer. Brill would not live to see the introduction of the steam engine into the world of printing, but he was much more of a nineteenth-century entrepreneur than his predecessor had been.

Illustration from C. G. C. Reinwardt, *Plantae Indiae Batavae Orientalis*; ed. W. H. de Vriese (1856). >
Caspar Georg Carl Reinwardt (1773-1854) was a Dutch botanist of German origin. He was the founder and first director of the botanical garden in Bogor on the isle of Java and became later (1823-1845) professor in Leiden. This botanical travel account is typical of the early nineteenth century, when scientific research and economic benefit went hand in hand for the first time. The descriptions of medicinal plants and hardwoods have been supplemented with information on their occurrence. The two-color lithographs were printed in Ghent. ULA

Picture of Evert Jan Brill in 1866, at the age of 55. Brill Coll.

The man Evert Jan Brill seems to have wholly identified himself with the firm of E. J. Brill. He was a bachelor, and for more than twenty years he lived exclusively for his business. He put all his energy and all his time into his work, which in the long run took its toll on his health. He was used to doing everything himself and was familiar with all three departments of the business. Given the small scale of the enterprise, it was physically possible for one person to direct the various activities. In the print works approximately ten men were employed: an overseer, two or three typesetters, just as many printers, and a few apprentices. A list of office furniture and equipment from 1871 suggests that about five people were employed in the shop and the publishing house. In the 1850s and 1860s, the total workforce of the firm of E. J. Brill would have included about fifteen persons.

Changing Times

Brill worked steadily to build up his business, and time was on his side. The Netherlands gradually woke from a long slumber and hesitantly began a period of revival. The core of this development took place after 1870, but its onset was noticeable in previous decades. The spirit of modern times also made itself felt in lethargic Leiden,

Changing times in Leiden: the new railroad station around 1850. The first Dutch railroad line was constructed in 1839 and ran from Amsterdam to Haarlem. It was extended to Leiden in 1842. Lithography from A. Montagne, *De Stad Leiden* (2 vols., 1850-51). ULA

V.

Q.M.R. Ver Huell ad nat. Sicc. del. 1856

I. Strobant Sc. & Lith. a Gand.

Eucalyptus Leucadendron. Rwdt.

where the stagecoach and the horse-drawn towing barge had to give way to the steam train. The innumerable reprints of Nicolaas Beets's *Camera Obscura* (1839) reflected the radical change in society: within a short while, the pleasant little world Beets described had become part of a past era that was nostalgically cherished. One might consider Beets as the Dutch counterpart of Charles Dickens, who owed his literary success partly to the same reasons. The rapid modernization of society was also accompanied by a strong increase in the demand for books, and the number of printing shops in the Netherlands more than doubled between 1850 and 1880. Science too was imbued with the spirit of the age, and with the approach of its third centenary, Leiden University developed new zeal. Discoveries were made in rapid succession, new disciplines were called into being, and international scholarly exchange was increasing.

At this critical juncture, Evert Jan Brill stands out as a transitional figure between bygone days and days to come—the last representative of the Luchtmans age, and at the same time the pioneer of a new era. Since 1853 he had been printer to the city and to the university, as the Luchtmanses had been ever since 1730. This office still conferred a certain standing and guaranteed a regular business in dissertations, orations, necrologies and the like. Auctioning private libraries continued to be an important sideline, with an average of two auctions a year. Brill regularly sent shipments of books to the book fair in Leipzig, although there is nothing to suggest that he himself ever attended. For that matter, the train made the journey a lot more comfortable than the jolting stagecoach Samuel Luchtmans had to rely on in his day.

Willem Gerard Brill (1811-1896), professor of Dutch language and literature in Utrecht. He was Evert Jan's twin brother, but not his spitting image. Brill Coll.

Brill's Publishing List

Brill continued the classical-philological tradition of Luchtmans with publications by Leiden classicists such as C. G. Cobet and J. Bake. Nevertheless, classical languages were less emphatically represented in his list than in that of his predecessors, in part because after 1850 the use of Latin as a scholarly language became increasingly obsolete. This development was in part counterbalanced by a series of classical texts for the gymnasiums, as a consequence of the Secondary Education Act. A new phenomenon in the field of classical studies was the journal *Mnemosyne*, founded in 1852 by Cobet and published by Brill. Over 150 years later, it is still being published by Brill.

At the time, journals were strongly in the ascendant and they constituted an attractive growth market for the publishing house. Brill began to publish more journals, such as the *Annales Academici* of the university, the journal of the Dutch Literary Society, and that of the Museum of Natural History. From his relations with the museum flowed other important publications, such as *Bouwstoffen voor een fauna van Nederland* [Materials for a Dutch Fauna; 3 vols., 1853-66] by J. A. Herklots, and *Plantae Indiae Batavae Orientalis* (1856-57) by C. G. C. Reinwardt. A similar association with the State Herbarium resulted in the illustrated *Museum Botanicum Lugduno-Batavum* of E. L. Blume (2 vols., 1849-56).

Thanks to the historian R. J. Fruin, the historical discipline acquired a new academic status, which was reflected in a strong historiographical component in Brill's publishing list. The same can be observed for Dutch language and literature. Willem Gerard Brill, the brother of Evert Jan, was a professor in this field of study in Utrecht and developed into a highly prolific scholar. Many of his works were published by his brother.

Up until the arrival of the twentieth century, the *Hollandsche Spraakleer* [Dutch Grammar] of W. G. Brill was the bible of students of Dutch language and literature. The first edition had been published by Luchtmans in 1847, and Brill was apparently determined to acquire it at any cost: his brother's grammar was the most expensive purchase he allowed himself at the auction of 1849.

Strange Characters

Brill's publications covered a wide range in the humanities, but personally he had a particular orientation in mind. What he intended to do found expression in *Het Gebed des Heeren in veertien talen,* which he brought out in 1855. Brill printed the Lord's Prayer in fourteen languages, using all of the exotic fonts he had at his disposal—Hebrew, Aramaic, Samaritan, Sanskrit, Coptic, Syriac, Arabic, Persian, Tartar, Turkish, Javanese, Malay, and Greek, some of them in several variants. More than a type specimen of the strange characters the printer had on hand, the booklet was a declaration of intent, perhaps even a kind of personal prayer offered by the publisher. Brill made it known that he wanted to specialize in languages beyond the range of other publishers. He thus laid a foundation that his successors are building on to this very day.

The famous series *Aegyptische Monumenten van het Nederlandsch Museum van Oudheden te Leiden* was published between 1839 and 1904 in twelve volumes, in both a Dutch and a French edition. It was the magnum opus of Conrad Leemans, director of the Museum of Antiquities in Leiden, and was continued after his death by his successor Willem Pleyte. The fine plates were made by the Leiden lithographer T. Hooiberg. The first volumes were published by Luchtmans and the continuation encompassed the entire working life of E. J. Brill. The reproduced plate is from the third volume of 1846. ULA

In 1855 E. J. Brill published a book in which he printed the Lord's Prayer in fourteen exotic languages (*Het gebed des Heeren in veertien talen*). The illustration shows the Coptic version. ULA

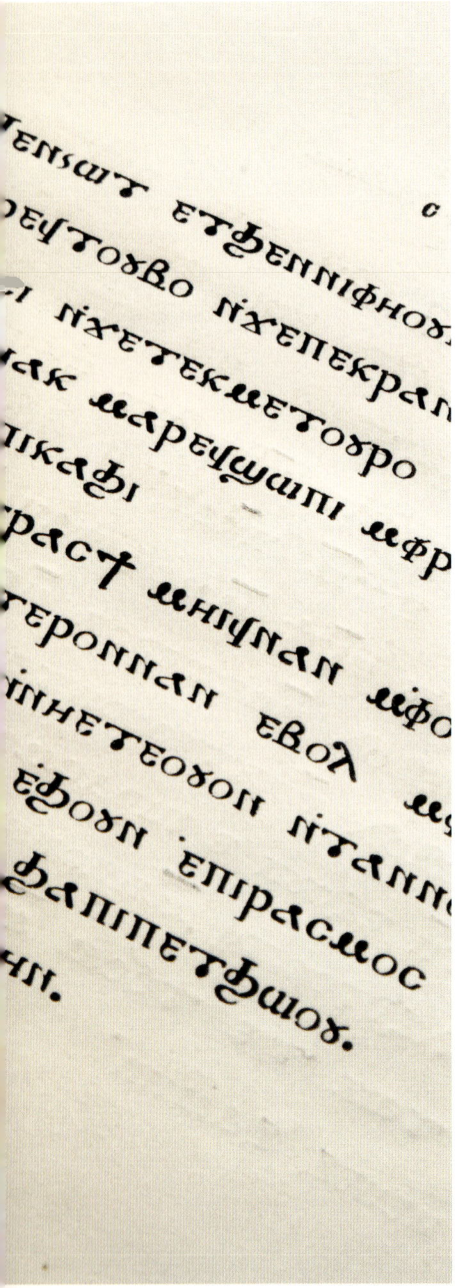

To be sure, the Luchtmanses had also brought out books in Arabic or on the Arabic language, but these were occasional publications. As mentioned above, during the second quarter of the nineteenth century the firm began the systematic publication of Arabic manuscripts from the Legatum Warnerianum. The books were printed by Johannes Brill and published by Luchtmans, and thus Evert Jan was exposed to Arabic at an early age. It was the passion of his youth and he cherished it when he was older. In 1854 his enthusiasm led him to participate in a remarkable educational experiment, namely the publication of an Arabic grammar for the gymnasiums. Its author, J. J. de Gelder, hoped to promote the Arabic language as a regular element of the school curriculum, but his project did not succeed.

Brill's love for Arabic was encouraged by the eminent Arabic scholars who were working at Leiden University at the time. By cooperating with scholars such as R. P. A. Dozy and M. J. de Goeje, he acquired a reputation for his "Oriental" publications. Dozy in particular, who specialized in the history of Moorish Spain, was an extremely prolific author. Arabic scholars from different countries collaborated on some text editions, contributing to Brill's reputation abroad as a publisher of Arabica. Such international collaboration on long-term projects would also characterize Arabic studies later on.

While Arabic publications were already a regular feature in the publishing list during Brill's lifetime, in other languages represented in his edition of the Lord's Prayer he was a pioneer. For instance, it was not until the 1870s that Indology became an established discipline in Leiden, whereas Brill already published a book about Sanskrit in 1851. In 1856 he published a Malay epic poem, but it was not until after his death that the study of Indonesian languages would flourish. He would have printed the Lord's Prayer in Chinese or Japanese, were it not that he lacked these fonts at the time. In 1858, however, the university acquired a collection of printing types for the two languages, and in 1864 Brill published the *Ta Hio* or *Dai Gaku* in Chinese and Japanese. The texts were edited by J. J. Hoffmann, who in 1855 had been appointed the first professor of the languages of the Far East. Three years later, in a joint production with the Leiden firm of A. W. Sijthoff, there appeared the same author's *Japansche Spraakleer, gedrukt met 's Rijks Chineesche en Japansche drukletters* [Japanese Grammar, printed

A manual for Sanskrit typesetters: A. Rutgers, *De Sanskrit-drukletters typografisch gerangschikt en met eene proeve van sanskrit-tekst voorzien* (1851). Antonie Rutgers (1805-1884) was the preceptor of Hendrik Kern, who later became professor of Indology at Leiden University. The book was intended as a correction of a comparable publication by P. P. Roorda van Eysinga, who "was lacking in the required knowledge of the Sanskrit characters," according to Rutgers. At the request of Professor H. A. Hamakers, the printing types were purchased by the university, and after his death they were put at the disposal of Brill "on some conditions in the interest of Leiden University." The arrangement of the type in its cases was wrong, but with the help of this manual the type could be used for setting the complex Sanskrit language. The book was Brill's first publication in Sanskrit. ULA >

One of the few children's books published by E. J. Brill: H. Tollens, *Die Holländer auf Nova Zembla* [The Dutch on Nova Zembla, 1850]. In 1596 Willem Barentz.and Jacob van Heemskerck tried to sail to the East Indies via the Northeast Passage, but their ships became trapped in the ice near the Russian island of Nova Zembla. The seamen built a lodge out of the wreckage and kept themselves alive by shooting arctic foxes and polar bears. The poet Hendrik Tollens devoted a warm and sentimental epos to the ice-cold wintering, which was translated into German "for the education of the young." The brave Dutchmen tried to make it through the long polar night by singing hymns and patriotic songs about the fight against the Spaniards. In the spring of 1597 the survivors built boats and set out for civilization. Unfortunately the courageous Barentz. died a week after departing from Nova Zembla. ULA

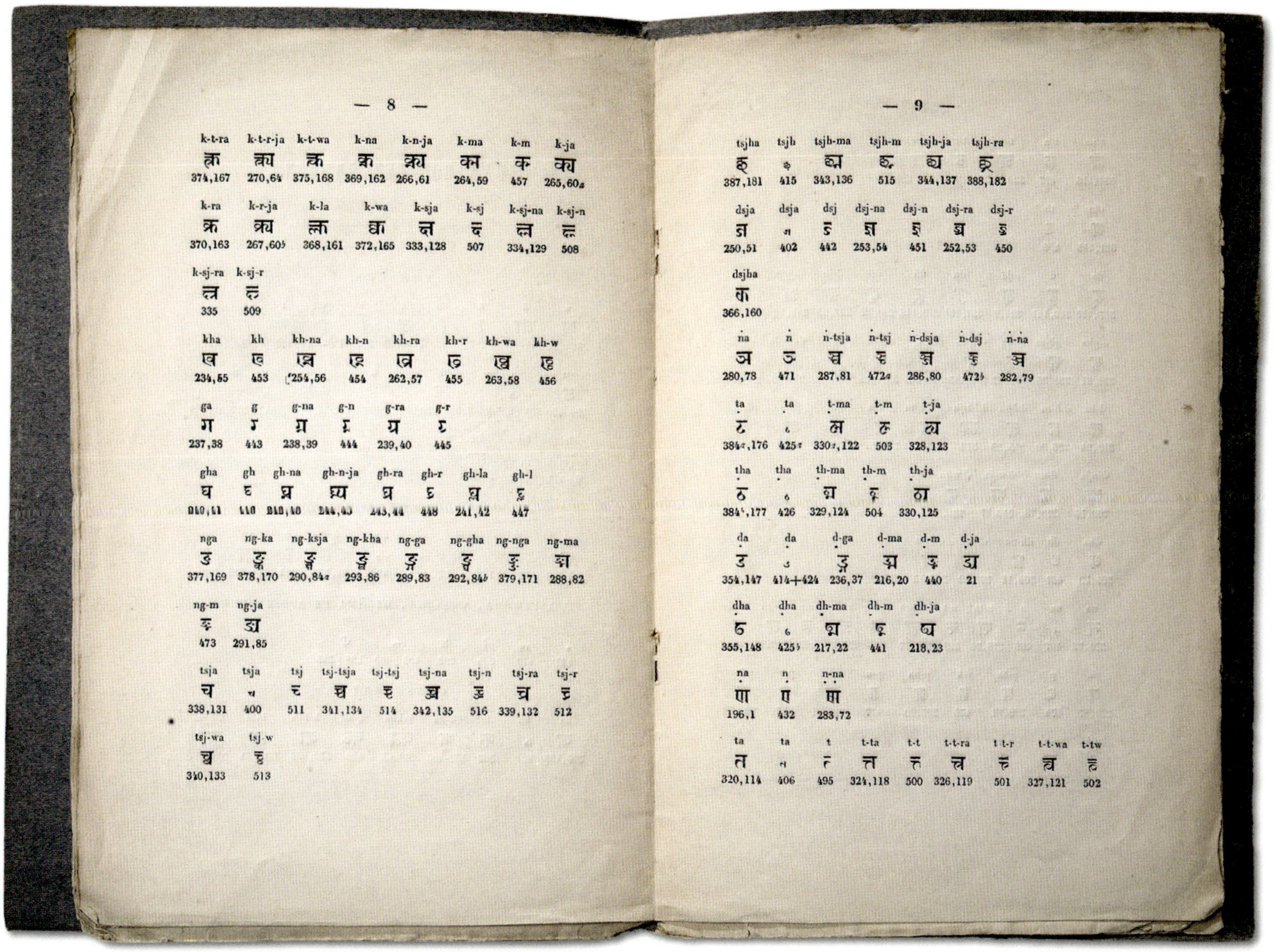

day.

otation of hours.

dial shows the two methods of marking the hours in u

in the Government's Chinese and Japanese type-fonts]. An English edition of the book was published by Brill alone in 1868. These, too, were precursors, anticipating the development of Chinese and Japanese publications under his successors.

Egyptology was an older tradition in Leiden, as evidenced by the before-mentioned series *Aegyptische Monumenten*, which started in 1839 under Luchtmans and continued until the beginning of the twentieth century at Brill. What was new, however, was the printing of hieratic and hieroglyphic script, first practiced by Brill in the three-volume *Études égyptologiques* (1866-1869) of W. Pleyte. The author himself had designed his ancient Egyptian printing types and subsequently had them cut and cast at the Tetterode type foundry in Amsterdam.[3]

"While I Am Still Alive"

After more than twenty years of unremitting labor, Brill decided to go easier on himself. His circumstances enabled him to relax, since his business was doing well and required less involvement. Perhaps he was also forced to step down by his declining health. Early in 1871 he organized a sale of unbound books, titles he had either bought at auctions or published himself. As usual, the catalog was sent out to the fraternity of booksellers, and in its preface Brill explained the motive for the sale: in the absence of a successor, he wanted to put his affairs in order "while I am still alive." The undertone of worry in his words was unmistakable. Furthermore, he announced that "my publications in Oriental languages" had been withheld from the auction. Brill was keeping his crown jewels for himself.

The auction was held on March 14, 1871, at the sales-room "Eensgezindheid" on the Spui in Amsterdam. Brill offered 157 titles, about one third of which he himself had bought at the Luchtmans auction of 1849. Eighteen copies of F. Pomey's *Pantheum Mysticum* (Amsterdam, 1777), acquired at the time for three guilders apiece, were now allowed to sell for *f* 1.25. It is to be feared that some of Luchtmans's slow movers had also lingered too long at Brill's shop. The purchase price of J. Bake's *Over de vertegenwoordiging der wetenschap* [On the Public Role of the Scholar, published in 1846] had been *f* 0.60, while the recommended price in 1871 was *f* 0.55; of the 280 copies Brill had purchased in 1849, 96 were left. There was even less of a demand for the *Oratio de re herbaria* by the botanist W. H. de Vriese (1845): in 1849 Brill had bought eighteen copies at *f* 0.30 apiece, and now he wanted to sell the remaining fifteen at the same price.[4]

The net income from the auction is unknown, but its purpose is plain: Brill was holding a clearance sale in order to reduce his baggage. Shortly after putting his business affairs in order, he did the same in his private life: on May 4, 1871, he married Cornelia Hermina Dibbets. The marriage would last only a short time. On November 29 of that year, Evert Jan Brill died suddenly at the age of sixty.

< Illustration from J. J. Hoffmann, *Japanese Grammar* (1868). At the insistence of Hoffmann, the first Leiden professor of the languages of the Far East, the Ministry of Colonial Affairs purchased a collection of Chinese and Japanese printing types in 1858. The *Japanese Grammar* (1868) by Hoffmann was one of the first Japanese books printed by E. J. Brill. The dial shown here explains how the Japanese clock works. Brill Coll.

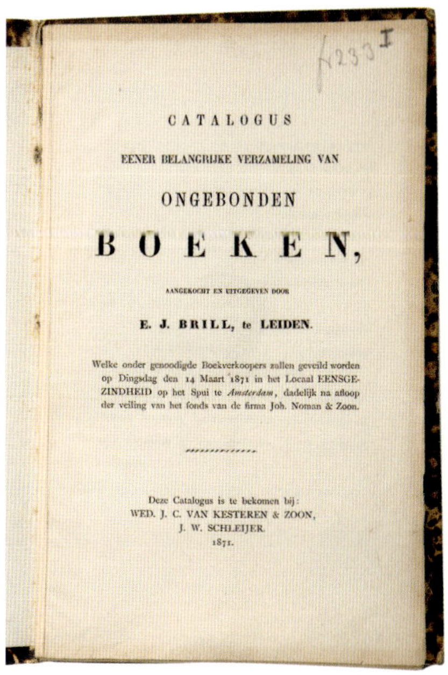

N233 I

CATALOGUS

EENER BELANGRIJKE VERZAMELING VAN

ONGEBONDEN

BOEKEN,

AANGEKOCHT EN UITGEGEVEN DOOR

E. J. BRILL, te LEIDEN.

Welke onder genoodigde Boekverkoopers zullen geveild worden op Dingsdag den 14 Maart 1871 in het Locaal EENSGEZINDHEID op het Spui te *Amsterdam*, dadelijk na afloop der veiling van het fonds van de firma Joh. Noman & Zoon.

Deze Catalogus is te bekomen bij:
WED. J. C. VAN KESTEREN & ZOON,
J. W. SCHLEIJER.
1871.

Catalog of the auction of 1871. Brill recorded in this copy his instructions for the auctioneer. For some titles the minimum price has been indicated; most carry the notation "sell," indicating that the item should be sold at any price. BA/ULA

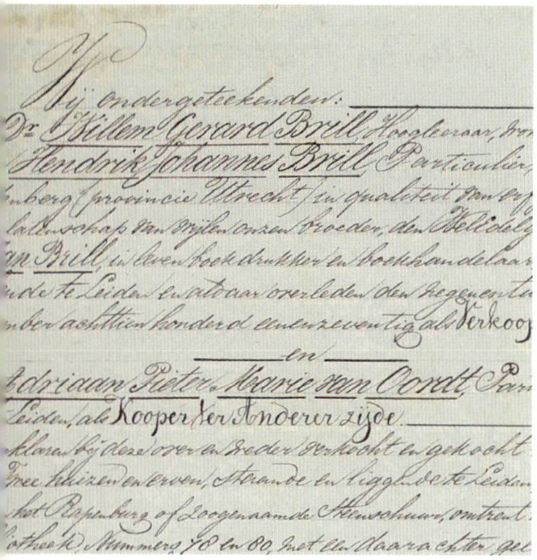
Wij ondergeteekenden:
Dr. Willem Gerard Brill, Hoogleeraar, ...
Hendrik Johannes Brill, Particulier,
...berg (provincie Utrecht) in qualiteit van erf-
...latenschap van wijlen onzen broeder, den WelEdele...
...an Brill, in leven boekdrukker en boekhandelaar
...de te Leiden en aldaar overleden den negenentw...
...mber achttien honderd een en zeventig als Verkoop...
en
Adriaan Pieter Marie van Oordt, Par...
Leiden, als Kooper ter Anderer zijde
...klaren bij deze over en weder verkocht en gekocht
...twee huizen en erven, staande en liggende te Leiden
...het Rapenburg of zoogenaamde Steenschuur, omtrent
...otheek Nummers 78 en 80, met een daarachter gel...

Deed from the sale of the business of E. J. Brill to A. P. M. van Oordt, January 21, 1872. BA/ULA

Adriaan Pieter Marie van Oordt (1840-1903). KVB/ULA

Men of the New Era: Adriaan van Oordt and Frans de Stoppelaar, 1872-1896

On December 5, 1871, the *Nieuwsblad voor den Boekhandel*, a trade paper, carried a statement by Brill's executors, Mart. Nijhoff and N. H. de Graaf. They announced that the bookselling firm and printing office of the late E. J. Brill would continue to operate on the same footing for the time being. But how was the firm of Brill to continue without Brill? The deceased had named his two brothers as heirs to the business: Willem Gerard, the previously mentioned professor of Dutch language and literature in Utrecht, and Hendrik Johannes, a draughtsman and author of children's books by profession, who lived in the village of Woudrichem. In consultation with Brill's widow, the executors and heirs came to the conclusion that selling was the best option.

Almost immediately, a buyer appeared in the person of Adriaan Pieter Marie van Oordt (1840-1903), originally a theologian. After completing his studies he had made a journey through America, which in the 1860s still was an adventurous undertaking. When he returned to his native country, he worked on a dissertation, but unfortunately it turned out that a German theologian had just obtained his doctorate with a thesis on the same subject. Van Oordt abandoned his dissertation and did not become a minister either; his poor health and possibly a weak vocation forced him to explore other options. In 1871, just after his marriage, he settled down in Leiden with the purpose to study law. At the end of his first term as a law student, however, the Brill establishment was put up for sale. Van Oordt subsequently decided to change his tack and try his luck in the book trade.[5]

The Estate of Brill

As of February 15, 1872, Van Oordt was entitled to call himself proprietor of the business. According to the deed of sale, Evert Jan Brill had owned the premises at Rapenburg 68-70 (the bookshop, along with the residence and publishing house), and to the rear of these, No. 74 (the printing shop, with a separate entrance on the former Begijnhof). Together the three properties fetched *f* 8,000. All fonts, type cases, presses, paper stocks, and other appurtenances of the printing shop were included in the purchase, as were the titles on the publishing list, along with the associated rights.

Page from W. Pleyte. *Catalogue raisonné de types Égyptiens hiératiques de la fonderie de N. Tetterode* (1865). The Egyptologist Willem Pleyte (1836-1903) was curator and later director of the Museum of Antiquities in Leiden. He designed a typeface for the hieratic script, which was used in ancient Egypt alongside the more familiar hieroglyphs for writing on papyrus. The printing types were numbered, which made it possible to typeset texts without knowledge of the script. The typesetter received a series of numbers indicating which characters to choose. The printing types were used for the first time for Pleyte's *Études égyptologiques* (1866-69), printed and published by E. J. Brill. Afterward, in 1883, Pleyte sold his Egyptian types to the firm of Brill. ULA >

...rresp.
, ch. 9,
...ce corresp.
3.
1. 7.

Nombre du type.	Type.		Repr...
60.		Visage.	
61.		Tête.	
62.		Chévelure.	
63.		Oeil.	
64.		Oeil ouvert.	
65.		Oeil versant des larmes.	
66.		Sourcil.	
67.		Bouche.	
68.	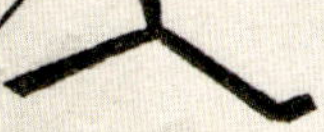	Langue.	
69.		Épine du dos.	
70.		Mammelle.	
71.		Poitrine entre deux bras.	
		Deux bras levés.	
		Deux bras	

Accounts payable and receivable, reckoned by the state of affairs on November 29, 1871—the day of Brill's death—, were transferred to the new owner. The cash balance of the bookshop was also transferred to Van Oordt, amounting to a grand total of *f* 27.75.

The price of all moveable property was fixed at *f* 32,000, which, combined with *f* 8,000 for the real estate, resulted in a total purchase price of *f* 40,000. The office furniture—bookcases, a desk, three tables, two lecterns, some chairs, two stoves with accessories, and a few ladders—was valued at *f* 150 and had to be paid for separately, for reasons that can no longer be determined. Van Oordt agreed to make an initial payment of *f* 25,000 (plus *f* 150 for the office furniture) on February 15, 1872. He would pay off the remaining *f* 15,000 in five annual installments of *f* 3,000, with the first payment due on February 15, 1873.[6]

According to article 7 of the deed of purchase, Van Oordt was at liberty to continue the business under the name of Brill, with the option of combining it with his own name. The new owner did not think it necessary to name the business after himself and preferred to retain the established name of "E. J. Brill." On the other hand, the same article stipulated that Van Oordt was not allowed to transfer the right to the name of Brill, nor to bequeath it to his heirs. Evidently, later generations were no longer aware of this clause, which, strictly speaking, would have made it impossible for the name "Brill" to be transferred to the present company.

Frans de Stoppelaar (1841-1906).

BA/ULA

The Spirit of Brill

Because Van Oordt was entering the book trade unprepared, he asked his friend Frans de Stoppelaar (1841-1906) to assist him as codirector. For that matter, De Stoppelaar could not claim much experience either: he was a teacher of Dutch at the recently established State High School in Deventer and the author of a widely used schoolbook.[7] Nevertheless, he plunged himself into his friend's Leiden adventure and burned his bridges in the eastern province of Overijssel. According to a deed of partnership dated October 17, 1872, the cooperation began with a trial period that would end on December 31, 1873. If either of the two gentlemen wanted to dissolve the partnership, he would have to give his partner six months' notice in writing. Otherwise the agreement would be tacitly renewed, always for one year at a time. It would turn out to be a lifelong agreement.[8]

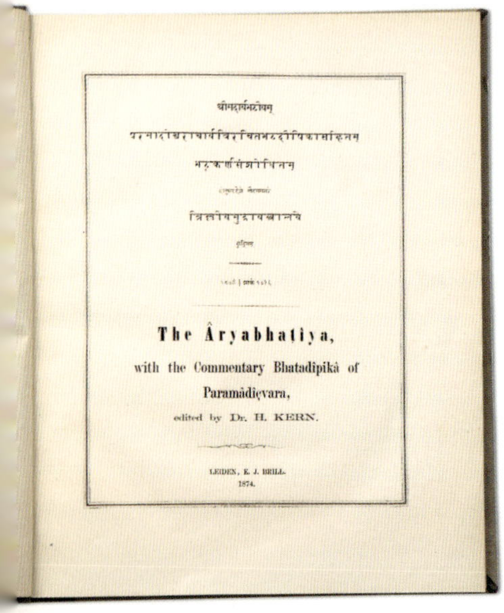

< H. Kern, *The Āryabhaṭīya. A manual of astronomy with the commentary Bhatadīpikā of Paramādīcvara* (1874). The Indian mathematician Āryabhata, born in 476, wrote a treatise in verse on the mathematics and astronomy of his day. Already at that time mathematical and astronomical knowledge had reached a surprisingly high standard in India: Āryabhata arrived at a very accurate calculation of the number π and was aware of the fact that the apparent orbit of the heaven was caused by the rotation of the earth on its axis. The text was edited by Hendrik Kern, professor of Sanskrit in Leiden since 1865. Kern's book is a classic of Indology and was translated into Hindi in 1906. ULA

The Amsterdam bookseller Frederik Muller, who had been associated with the firm for many years through his friendship with Bodel Nijenhuis and Brill, worried at first about the new owners' lack of experience. He feared that they would not meet the high standards that people were accustomed to expect from Brill and from Luchtmans. Muller even felt compelled to admonish the two gentlemen in the *Adresboek van den Nederlandschen Boekhandel* (1875), a trade publication, that the takeover of a renowned company also involved obligations: "Noblesse Oblige."

The old gentleman's fears were unwarranted. It is remarkable how Van Oordt and De Stoppelaar managed to carry on the business in the spirit of Brill, in spite of the fact that they had never known their predecessor. What they lacked in experience during those first years, they made up for by their commitment and intelligence. Moreover, they took over a successful business that had been molded by Brill and was imbued with his spirit. They reaped what he had sown and continued to advance along the lines he had set out. The takeover by Van Oordt and De Stoppelaar was marked by continuity, as had been the case in 1848 when Brill took over the firm.

The new owners also continued Brill's auction activities. Bodel Nijenhuis died on January 8, 1872, less than six weeks after Brill. In 1873-74, Van Oordt and De Stoppelaar, in cooperation with Fred. Muller, organized a series of seven auctions at which Bodel's large estate was put up for sale. Not only his library, but also the prints that were not included in his bequest to Leiden University went under the hammer. The book auctions took place in Bodel's residence at No. 69 on the Rapenburg, which had been owned by the Luchtmans family since 1697. On this occasion the auctioneers

Arabesque decoration on the untitled cover of *Beoefenaren der Oostersche talen in Nederland en zijne Overzeesche Bezittingen* [List of the Orientalists in the Netherlands and the Dutch Overseas possessions]. The book was a sumptuous commemorative volume published by the firm of Brill on the occasion of the third centenary of Leiden University in 1875. ULA

○錦雞ハ山どりに
似て小く羽色ハ又
文なり孔雀のごとく
鵔乃ごとし鷩雉
糸鶏並同
○白鷴ハ山雞に似
てもろし色白く黒き文
あり尾の長さ三四
尺ばかりあり食を
きがゆ仏補ひ毒
と解を

themselves bought, among other things, an old Dutch Bible that had belonged to the Luchtmans family. According to custom, successive generations had recorded the genealogy of the family on the flyleaf. The new owners of the firm of Brill thus showed their reverence for tradition and the Luchtmans legacy.[9]

Arabic Studies

The continuity of Brill without Brill was promoted by the fact that several authors remained faithful to the publishing house. This was true of the Arabic scholars in particular, who knew enough to appreciate the expertise of Brill's typesetters and printers. R. P. A. Dozy, who was nearing the end of his life, published in 1877-81 an impressive two-volume dictionary (*Supplément aux dictionnaires arabes*). His pupil M. J. de Goeje and the latter's pupil C. Snouck Hurgronje maintained the tradition of Arabic studies, along with the tradition of publishing their work through Brill. Relations between the Leiden Arabic scholars and the publishing house were very close in those years; De Goeje himself was a personal friend of De Stoppelaar and later worked for the firm. The first volume of his series of editions of Arabic geographical texts (*Bibliotheca Geographorum Arabicorum*) appeared in 1870, while E. J. Brill was still alive; the eighth and last volume was published in 1894.

A similar long-term project was the edition of the *Annals of* al-Tabarî, which had been initiated by De Goeje and was published in sixteen volumes between 1879 and 1901.[10] This complex publication required the efforts of fourteen Arabists from six countries, as well as the enduring commitment of the firm of Brill. Such monumental series testified to the courage of the publishers, who had to assume considerable risk. Around the turn of the century, this pattern of international cooperation in a long-term project coordinated by Brill would also be the foundation of the famous *Encyclopaedia of Islam*.

Indology and East India

In 1865, J. H. Kern had been appointed as the first professor of Sanskrit at Leiden University. E. J. Brill himself had already acquired a set of Sanskrit printing types for a project in 1851, but it was not until after his death that Indology would flourish. The publications of Kern and his Utrecht colleague W. Caland led foreign authors as well to submit their Indological works to the publishing house. Van Oordt and De Stoppelaar recognized their opportunity to develop this field of study, too, into a specialty of Brill.

< Illustration from L. Serrurier, *Encyclopédie Japonaise. Le chapitre des quadrupèdes* (1875). Serrurier dedicated this work to his preceptor, J. J. Hoffmann. The small encyclopedia was a popular reader for children in Japan and a textbook for students in Leiden. It contained a facsimile of the Japanese edition, phonetic transcriptions of the Japanese text, a literal word-by-word translation, and a running translation. In addition to real animals the book also features mythical animals such as the unicorn. Whereas in European mythology the unicorn is a gentle and shy creature that allows itself to be petted only by virgins, in Japanese mythology it is a carnivorous monster that attacks the bad guys and spares the good guys. ULA

Histoire des Musulmans d'Espagne. This history of the Arabs in Spain is the chief work of the historian and Arabic scholar Reinhart Pieter Anne Dozy (1820-1883). At the age of twenty-four, Dozy obtained his doctorate in the Faculty of Arts, in 1850 he became extraordinary professor, and in 1857 full professor in Leiden. Dozy was one of those universal scholars who engaged in the study of history as well as in the study of language and literature. He published innumerable scholarly treatises and also brought out text editions of Arab historiographers. The four-volume *Histoire des Musulmans* reads like a novel and still ranks as a standard work. ULA

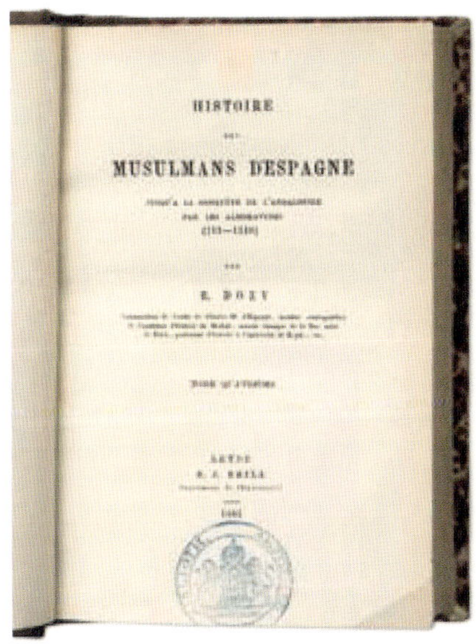

Schlegel et Pollen R. s. l. Faune d. Madagascar.

ARTAMIA BICOLOR.

< Illustration from F. P. L. Pollen and D. C. van Dam, *Faune de Madagascar et de ses dépendances* (1867-77). This five-volume work (of which only four volumes were published because the third was never completed) is a typically nineteenth-century publication. Faraway regions were being thoroughly explored, which meant that scientific curiosity went hand in hand with the investigation of economic opportunities. This publication appeared in loose-leaf form, so that buyers themselves had to have the showpiece bound. It consists of travel accounts, scientific descriptions, and a collection of lithographs. These are remarkable: it is only too obvious that some of them have been made on the basis of photographs and thus lack the unconscious pathos of an artist. One portion of the illustrations was hand-colored; another portion was printed in color and then touched up by hand. ULA

In his day, E. J. Brill had published a few books in Malay, but his successors produced a wide range of publications on the Dutch East Indies. Once again the spirit of the age bore fruit at the publishing house: the opening up of the Dutch colonies to private capital was accompanied by a growing scientific and scholarly interest in the Indonesian archipelago. A new philological tradition in Leiden focused on the publishing of Indonesian manuscripts, literary texts, and oral traditions.

As a result of the growing Dutch presence in the colonies, the demand for books in a variety of native languages increased greatly during the last quarter of the nineteenth century. Brill published dictionaries of Malay and Javanese, but also of the lesser-known languages of the archipelago—Madurese, Rotinese, Tontemboan, Bare'e, Toba-Batak, and so on. The geography and ethnography of the Dutch empire were amply represented in the publishing list. Scientific interest in the East was stimulated by the Royal Institute for Linguistics, Geography, and Ethnography, founded in 1851 and located first in Delft, afterwards in The Hague, and finally, since 1966, in Leiden (now as the Royal Netherlands Institute of Southeast Asian and Caribbean Studies). The authorities organized several scientific expeditions to the coastal regions and the interior of Indonesia, the results of which were published by Brill in substantial series. The Arabic scholar Snouck Hurgronje remained in the East for a long time and made an important contribution to its ethnography with his *Atjehers* (2 vols., 1893-94).

One of Brill's star authors in these years was the Arabic scholar and Islam expert Christiaan Snouck Hurgronje (1857-1936). When his dissertation *Het Mekkaansche feest* was published by Brill in 1880, the author had not yet visited the Holy City of Islam. In 1884, however, Snouck traveled to the Arabian Peninsula and lived for a while in Mecca. As the first Westerner he photographed the sanctuaries, inhabitants, and utensils of the Holy City. For the sake of his field research he called himself Abd al-Ghaffar and dressed in the local attire, as can be seen in this photograph. He stretched his assimilation to the point of converting to Islam. The photographs were used for his books *Mekka* and *Bilder aus Mekka*, published by Brill in 1888-89. Afterwards Snouck worked in the Dutch East Indies, and in 1906 he was appointed professor of Arabic in Leiden. Snouck's *Mekka* was republished in 2007. ULL Coll.

DRIEHOOFDIG. DRIEMAANDELIJKSCH. 1009

Driehoofdig 三頭 *sam t'ǒ*; 有三頭 *iú sam-t'ǒ*; 有三首 *iú sam-siú.*

Driejarig 三歲 *sam soè*; eene —e koe 犙 *sǫ*; 犙 *tsam*; 牛三歲 *giû sam soè*; een — paard 駣 *tiaō*; 騑 *hui*; 馬三歲 *mǎ sam soè*; —e onthouding van het uitoefenen van een ambt gedurende den rouw voor zijne ouders 予寧 *i lîng*; 博士弟子父母喪、予寧三年 *p'ok-sū tē-tsú hū-bǒ song, î-lîng sam liên*; — (eens in de drie jaren) 三年一次 *sam liên it ts'ù*; het — examen 三年一度開科舉 *sam liên it tǫ k'ai k'o-kí*; het groote examen 大比 *taī pī* of 大科 *taī k'o* genaamd; — (om de drie jaren) 每三年 *moé sam liên*; 三年一次 *sam liên it ts'ù.*

Driekant / **Driekantig** 三邊 *sam pien*; 三面 *sam biēn*; 以三面 *í sam biēn*; 有三口 *iú sam k'ǒ*; *een —e hood 三稜冠 *sam-lîng koan.*

***Drieklank** 諧三音 *haî sam-im*; 三字之音 *sam-dzū tsi im.*

Driekleur 三色 *sam sik*; de — (vlag) 三色旗 *sam-sik kî.*

Driekleurig 三色的 *sam-sik tsik.*

***Driekoningen** 主顯之節 *Tsú hiên tsi tsiet.*

***Drielettergrepig** 三音之言 *sam-im tsi gân*; 三字之言 *sam-dzū tsi gân*; v. Tweelettergrepig.

Drieling, een' — baren, 一胎産三子 *it t'ai sán sam tsú*; 生三子 *sing sam tsú*;

2) — (wijnkelk) 觚 *kǫ*; 鄉飲爵之稜 *hiang ím tsiak tsi lîng.*

Driemaal 三次 *sam ts'ù*; 三回 *sam hoê*; 三遍 *sam piên*; 三遭 *sam tso*; 再三 *tsaì sam*; zich — bedenken 三思 *sàm su*; denk gij er — over! 足下三思 *tsiok-hē sàm su*; ik bedenk mij altijd eerst — 我亦時常想再三 *ngǒ ik sî-siâng siáng tsaì-sam*; — 's jaars 歲凡三次 *soè hoān sam ts'ù*; gij hebt mij — geslagen 爾乃策我者三 *dzí naī ts'ik ngǒ tsiá sam*; hij boog zich — ter aarde 伏地三拜 *hók tē sam paì*; dit geschiedde tot —len 如是者三 *dzî-sī-tsiá sam*; ik ben — gegeeseld 余三次受杖 *î sam-ts'ù siū-tiāng*; nadat zij — het (letterkundig) strijdperk betreden hadden 二人共入三場滿 *dzī-dzîn kiōng dzip sam ts'iâng boán*; — drie is negen 三三如九 *sam-sam dzî kiú*; — acht is vierentwintig 三八二十四 *sam pat dzī-síp-sù*; v. Keer; Maal; — meer 加三倍 *kǫ sam-poē*; — grooter dan 三倍大於○○○ *sam-poē taī i.*

Driemaandelijks / **Driemaandelijksch** 三個月的 *sam-kò goát tik*; — (per kwartaal) 季 *kuì*; 每三月 *moé sam goát*; — de huur betalen 按季出租 *àn kuì ts'ut tsǫ*; de huur zal —, zonder uitstel of vertraging, moeten betaald worden 其租分四季交清、毋得拖欠 *kî tsǫ hun sù-kuì kao-ts'ing, bû-tik t'o-k'iêm*; v. Vierendeel.

Sinological monument: a page from the *Nederlandsch-Chineesch Woordenboek* by Professor Gustav Schlegel, which was published by Brill in four substantial volumes between 1886 and 1891. ULA

The Far East

In Sinology and Japanese studies as well, Van Oordt and De Stoppelaar followed in the footsteps of their predecessor. In 1877 G. Schlegel was appointed professor of Far Eastern languages, as successor to J. J. Hoffmann. Two years earlier, in 1875, Van Oordt and De Stoppelaar purchased the Chinese and Japanese printing types that Brill had used in the 1860s for his first publications in these languages. They acquired this collection from the Ministry of Colonial Affairs for the substantial amount of *f* 3,514.45.[11] It was a considerable investment for the new entrepreneurs, but possession of these printing types put the publishing house in a unique position. From the midseventies onwards, Schlegel published a large number of books on the Far East with Brill, culminating in a monumental four-volume Chinese dictionary (1886-90). Foreign authors, too, increasingly brought their work to Brill, one of the few publishing houses in Europe featuring this expertise. From 1890 onwards Brill published the journal *T'oung Pao*, which was devoted to the study of the languages and cultures of the Far East. The journal, subtitled *Revue internationale de sinologie*, is still the leading serial in this field of study and is still being published by Brill.

The typesetting of Chinese and Japanese required some familiarity with the script. During a six-week training period, Schlegel introduced Brill's first typesetters in these languages to the basic features of the characters. In 1927, master typesetter J. P. van Duuren, dubbed "the Mikado" on account of his specialization in the Far East, told the Rotterdam journalist M. J. Brusse how he had been initiated into the secrets of the Chinese language by the professor fifty years earlier. In turn, Van Duuren had trained new generations of typesetters in Chinese. The Sinologist E. Zürcher recalled in 1983 how as a student he had become acquainted with the master typesetter P. W. Martijn at Brill, not long after the Second World War. Around 1912 Martijn had started to work with Brill as an apprentice, and he had learned the art of Chinese typesetting from Van Duuren over the years. Zürcher still held a vivid memory of the typesetter at work: "moving between his type cases like a Taoist priest performing a dancing ritual, and producing with incredible speed and accuracy any character from a collection containing nearly 8000 signs."[12]

The Spirit of the New Era

During the last quarter of the nineteenth century, the firm of E. J. Brill underwent a tumultuous period of growth. Under the management of Van Oordt and De Stoppelaar, the publishing house acquired an international reputation continued by today's Brill. The tone had been set in the fifties and sixties by Evert Jan Brill, with his penchant for strange characters; his successors had the good sense to build on this predilection and orient the business more and more emphatically toward the field of Oriental studies. By 1900, Brill had distinguished itself as an international scholarly publishing house with a specialization in exotic languages. The number of learned journals published by Brill had also increased noticeably. In addition, the company published a broad range of titles for the domestic market, especially in the fields of Dutch language and literature, history, and theology.

The international scale on which Van Oordt and De Stoppelaar operated would have been inconceivable for Evert Jan Brill. After 1870, the world underwent a process of

From 1883 until 1985 Brill was located at Oude Rijn 33a, as the facade clearly indicates. The immense building with its monumental entrance was originally part of the Almshouse for Orphans and Poor Children. By the sixties of the previous century, the premises on the Oude Rijn had become too small for the print works. In 1965 it was moved to a new building on the Plantijnstraat, on the outskirts of Leiden. The publishing house remained in the old business quarters for more than twenty years, until it followed the print works to the Plantijnstraat in 1985.

The photograph with the towing barge must have been taken in or shortly after 1883, when Brill moved to the Oude Rijn. Well over twenty-five years later, the artist L. W. R. Wenckebach (1860-1937) made a drawing after this photograph for the newspaper *Het Nieuws van den Dag*. By that time, the towing barge had already become a picturesque curiosity of the past. Wenckebach, a well-known illustrator in his day, included a small drawbridge that is not shown in the photograph. In reality it is a little farther away, but for the sake of the composition the artist brought it forward. Brill Coll.

Ground plan of the orphanage > complex on the Oude Rijn, showing the location of the steam engine ("Plaats van de gas-motor"). The city council of Leiden granted permission ("Voorloopige Vergunning") for the installation of the engine. BA/ULA

globalization unparalleled in history. European imperialism penetrated into the farthest corners of the earth, *laissez-faire* capitalism thrived, and the Industrial Revolution transformed manufacture and trade. Traveling abroad became increasingly easier, and international scholarly contacts were also multiplying. For instance, every three years an International Congress of Orientalists was held in an European city, where Arabists, Sinologists, Sanskritists, and practitioners of other exotic disciplines met each other. Frans de Stoppelaar was a regular visitor at these meetings, where he made many profitable contacts.

The spirit of the new era provided opportunities that Van Oordt and De Stoppelaar knew how to exploit fully. The international reputation they built for themselves was reflected in the foreign honors bestowed upon the company. At the 1873 World Exhibition in Vienna, the firm of E. J. Brill won a gold medal for its "Oriental printed editions." The award can be interpreted as a posthumous recognition of the man who gave the firm its name. At the Paris World Exhibition of 1878, the company won a gold medal once more. In 1883 Van Oordt was appointed knight of the Order of the Crown by the king of Italy, on account of his merits as a publisher. In 1889 the sultan of the Ottoman Empire awarded him the knight commander's cross in the Order of Mejidie, and in the same year he was knighted in the Order of Vasa by the Swedish king. De Stoppelaar left the foreign accolades to his friend, but he himself was appointed a knight in the Order of the Dutch Lion. Thus, the successors of Luchtmans ultimately outstripped old Pieter van der Aa, who at the beginning of the eighteenth century had advanced no further than the rank of "knight of San Marco."

New Quarters

Around 1880 the company outgrew its old premises on the Rapenburg, which no longer afforded enough space for the expanding business. New quarters were found in the former Holy Spirit or Almshouse for Orphans and Poor Children at No. 33a on the Oude Rijn, which after major renovations was occupied in the spring of 1883. All segments of the company—composing room, printing shop, bookshop, antiquarian bookshop, and publishing house—were housed in the old but spacious orphanage. On the first floor, facing the street, was the shipping department, where materials and other purchases arrived and the firm's books were dispatched to customers at home and abroad. The back of the first floor served as a warehouse and also contained the steam engine that made the presses work. The relocation had given Brill the opportunity to modernize its printing machinery.

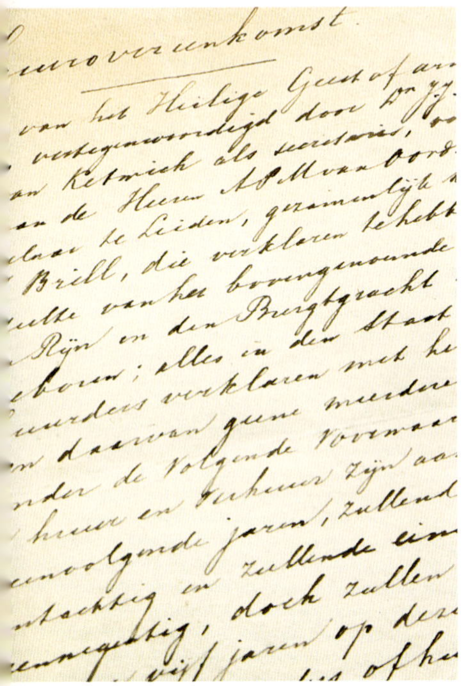

Van Oordt and De Stoppelaar rented the premises on the Oude Rijn from the governors of the Holy Ghost or Almshouse for Orphans and Poor Children. The illustration shows the rental contract between the two parties. BA/ULA

Extremely modern by the standards of the day were the two elevators that were driven by the steam engine and carried heavy goods, such as webs of paper, to the upper floors. On the second floor was located the office of the directors, as well as the composing room and the printing shop. The typesetting and printing of Arabic, Chinese, Japanese, and other exotic scripts took place in a separate room on the third floor; the printing of "Oriental" works continued to be done by hand long into the twentieth century.

The third floor also housed the bookshop and an exhibition space for new publications, as well as the stock of books for sale. Customers who wanted to visit the antiquarian bookshop had to ascend to the fourth floor, where Brill books that were in less

< Technical publications such as this *Leerboek der Stoomwerktuigkunde* [Manual of Steam Engines; 2 vols., 1882] by L. A. Dittlof Tjassens were an exception at Brill. The typographic skills that were employed to illustrate the mechanics of steam power leave nothing to be desired.

Brill Coll.

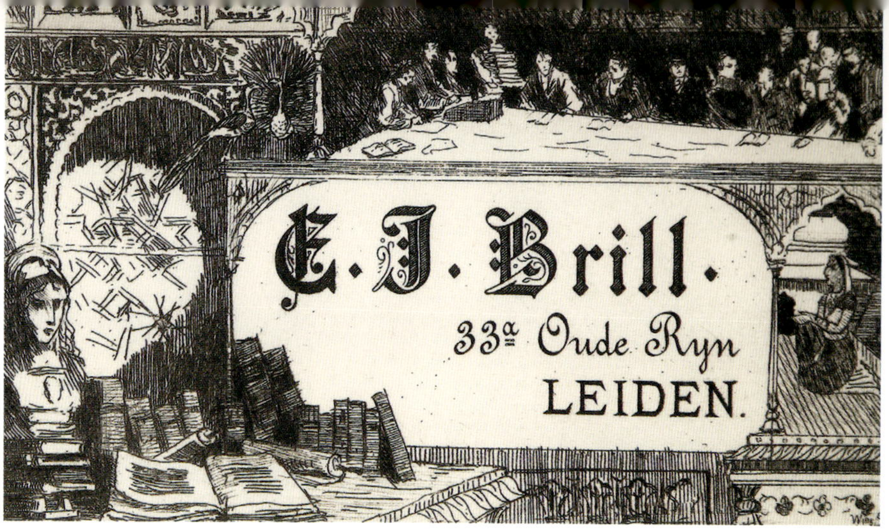

The firm of Brill chose this artistic business card to represent itself at the end of the nineteenth century. The somber book club in the background lends a Rembrandtesque touch, while arabesque motifs frame the company's name and address. The female bust in the foreground resembles more the French Marianne than the Greek Pallas Athena. The design is the work of a certain W. S. and dates from 1885. BA/ULA

demand were also stored.[13] Gas lighting was installed in the building, but the typesetters and printers were unhappy with the newfangled fixtures. The gas lamps gave off an unpleasant light and produced too much heat. At the instigation of the employees, paraffin lamps were reinstalled.[14]

New Statutes

The relocation required considerable investment, and as a result the statutes of the company were modified. Up to this time De Stoppelaar had been codirector while Van Oordt was the full owner of the business. According to a deed of January 23, 1881, Van Oordt relinquished his exclusive ownership and De Stoppelaar became joint owner of the firm.[15] All expenditures and dealings were now under joint account, and all assets of the company were considered to be joint property. The new status of De Stoppelaar was probably due to the fact that his in-laws provided the capital necessary for the relocation. He was married to Clara Lulofs, and his brother-in-law Jan Doekes Lulofs, banker and stockbroker in Amsterdam, acted as financier.

The new statutes also stipulated a division of tasks between the two directors. Owing to his poor health, Van Oordt would restrict himself to administrative work, including the supervision of the printing and paper budget. It was, however, emphatically stated that he retained the right to deal with any aspect of the business. De Stoppelaar was responsible for day-to-day management, with the exception of administrative work.

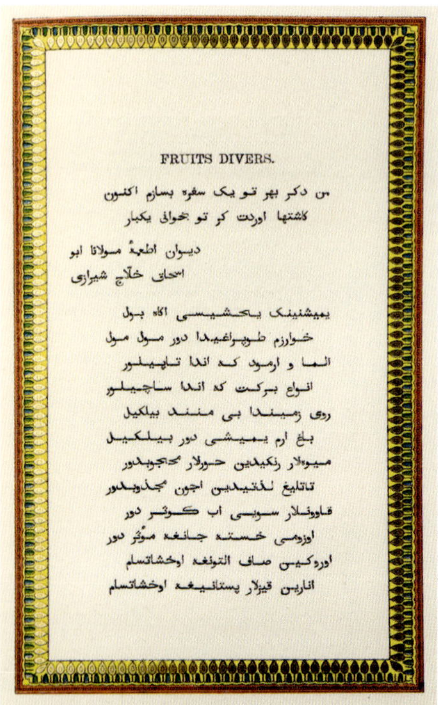
FRUITS DIVERS.

من دکر بهر تو یک سفره بسازم اکنون
کاشتها اوردت کو تو بخوانی یکبار

دیوان اطعمهٔ مولانا ابو
اسحاق خلاج شیرازی

یمیشنینک یخشیسی اکاه بول
خوارزم طوپراغیدا دور مول مول
الما و ارمود که اندا تاپیلور
انواع برکت که اندا ساچیلور
روی زمیندا بی منند بیلکیل
باغ ارم یمیشی دور بیلکیل
میوه‌لار رنکیدین حورلار بحجوبدور
تاتلیغ لذتیدین اجون مجذوبدور
قاوونلار سویی اب کوثر دور
اوزومی خسته جانغه موثر دور
اوروکیس صاف التونغه اوخشاتسلم
اناریں قیزلار پستانیغه اوخشاتسلم

Menu du diner offert au VIIe Congrès International des Orientalistes. Stockholm, le 7 sept. 1889. Another typographic *tour de force* from Brill: the menu of a dinner party held in 1889 to honor participants in the Seventh International Congress of Orientalists in Stockholm. Each course was supplied with a comment by a scholar, in the form of a pastiche of the writings in which he was a specialist: Arabic historiography, Chinese poetry, Javanese primitive art, Babylonian legal texts, and so on. Each contribution was printed in the appropriate script—vulgar Egyptian Arabic, Chinese, Ethiopic, Sanskrit, Malay, Hebrew, Manchurian, Javanese, Akkadian, Turkish, Coptic, hieroglyphic Egyptian, Bucharian, Japanese, Djagatai, and classical Arabic. The latter language was used by an abstemious theologian for a learned discourse on champagne. ULA

MENU
DU DINER OFFERT
AU VIIIme CONGRÈS INTERNATIONAL DES ORIENTALISTES
STOCKHOLM LE 7 SEPT.

The annual balance sheet had to be approved by both partners. De Stoppelaar was entitled to a preference dividend of two thousand guilders; the remainder of the profits was equally divided between the partners.

The Scholar of the Purified Garden of Delight

While books on the Arabic world featured prominently in Brill's publishing list, not many people from the Arabic world were to be seen in Leiden in those days. Around the turn of the century a Syrian typesetter was employed by the company for a year, working on a specialist Arabic publication, but he was a rare bird on the Oude Rijn. Some years earlier, in 1883, a certain Amien ibn Hassan Holwani al-Madani had paid a call on Brill. He originated from the holy city of Medina and called himself "the scholar of the Purified Garden of Delight," a high-sounding title derived from the madrassa where he used to teach. Afterward he traveled extensively throughout the Islamic world, with the purpose of collecting manuscripts. He had been living in Cairo for some time when the news reached him that in 1883 a World Exhibition would be held in Amsterdam.

Such a global bazaar seemed to Amien ibn Hassan an excellent opportunity to sell his manuscripts, on the assumption that they would be worth more in Europe than in Egypt. In high spirits he traveled to Amsterdam and sat down behind a table at the World Exhibition, but unfortunately not a single visitor was interested in his literary merchandise. His luck changed when Count Carlo de Landberg, a Swedish traveler and Oriental scholar, happened to visit the Exhibition. Landberg drew the attention of the salesman to the firm of Brill in Leiden, which might have an interest in the manuscripts. Thus the learned trader called at the Oude Rijn, where he was respectfully received by Van Oordt and De Stoppelaar. From a commercial point of view, his visit was a success, because the publishers bought his complete collection of 665 manuscripts. They in turn sold them to Leiden University, where they were added to the Legatum Warnerianum.[16]

The building of the World Exhibition in 1883 in Amsterdam. ULA

The Arabic scholar found his bread buttered on both sides in Leiden, since the Sixth International Congress of Orientalists was held in the city that year. As an unexpected representative of the Arabic world, Amien ibn Hassan was invited to take part in the event. He described his impressions of the congress in the *Al-Burhan*, a Cairo newspaper. His articles were translated into Dutch by Snouck Hurgronje and published in a booklet that was issued by Brill.[17]

The scholar of the Purified Garden of Delight was pampered by his hosts, and he visibly enjoyed the attentions bestowed on him. He was highly surprised by the scholarly curiosity about the East displayed in the West; he had not expected to find so much intellectual enthusiasm in a Europe corrupted by materialism. No fewer than three hundred scholars of all sorts—Indologists, Sinologists, Assyriologists, Egyptologists, and Arabists—had gathered in Leiden. Amien chiefly attended the meetings of the Arabists, with whom he could easily exchange ideas. He was the only Arab in a company of sixty European Arabists.

He was deeply impressed by their knowledge of the Arabic language and its literature, indeed to such a degree that he even found it somewhat alarming. In view of

Amien ibn Hassan Holwani al-Madani, the scholar of the Purified Garden of Delight. Lithograph from C. Snouck Hurgronje, *Het Leidsche Oriëntalisten-congres* (Leiden, 1883). ULA

their scientific zeal, he feared that the scholars of the West would take possession of the learning of the East: "for when the Franks [Europeans] once apply themselves to a science, they never give it up, but plunge into its seas and dive for the pearls at its bottom."[18] The notion that Arabic studies implied a form of intellectual imperialism was advanced about a century later by Edward Said in his well-known book *Orientalism* (1978).

Lead Colic and Child Labor

In 1890 a nationwide inquiry was held into working conditions in factories and workshops. Social issues were high on the agenda at the time, thanks to the fact that workers had begun to organize themselves in trade unions and socialism was gaining ground as a political movement. On August 5, 1890, the committee of inquiry investigated the state of affairs at Brill. The report provides a look at the daily routine of the business.[19] From a present-day point of view there is ample reason to criticize the working conditions at Brill, but in comparison with other print works they were quite decent.

Pieter de Groot de Bruin, thirty-six years old and a typesetter in Arabic, was questioned about his working hours by the commission. In the summer he worked 10.5 hours a day, from 6 a.m. until 7 p.m., with a rest break of 2.5 hours. In the winter he put in 10 hours a day, from 8 a.m. until 8 p.m., with a rest break of 2 hours. In a working week of 6 days, this amounted to 65 hours in the summer and 60 hours in the winter.

A harsh intervention by Van Oordt and De Stoppelaar in October 1894. A "seditious bulletin" issued by the General Dutch Typographers' Union had not gone down very well with them. They acknowledged their employees' right to associate, yet as employers they did not want to let themselves be bullied. The directors demanded that their printers and typesetters sign a statement that they were not members of this trade union. If the workmen failed to give this statement, they would be fired. All of them signed. BA/ULA

This compared favorably with the printing shop of P. W. M. Trap in Leiden, where the length of the working week was 70.5 hours in the summer and 63.5 hours in the winter.[20] The wages at Brill were just as high as those at other graphic arts firms in Leiden, perhaps a fraction higher. Typesetters who specialized in Oriental languages, such as De Groot, earned *f* 11 a week, while ordinary typesetters received between *f* 8 and *f* 9, depending on their skills. The printers earned just as much, and as with the typesetters, the specialists in foreign languages were better paid. Apprentices earned between *f* 1.50 and *f* 2.00 a week.

The commission questioned De Groot about hygienic conditions in the establishment. He reported that the composing room was regularly swept and scrubbed, but that the type cases were not kept clean. Given the "immensely large stocks of printing types" at Brill, it was in his opinion impossible to clean the dust from the type cases. Consequently, as was the case in all composing rooms, there was a lot of lead dust in the air, and lead poisoning, the dreaded occupational disease of typographers, also occurred at Brill:

> I was bothered by a constant stomachache, for which I eventually sought medical aid. Up to then I had treated myself with household remedies, since I understood the origin of the disease. It was lead colic, which makes one feel sluggish and causes the stomach a certain feeling of nausea when it receives food.

De Groot reported another case of lead poisoning, and he said that consumption (tuberculosis) also regularly occurred, although he did not know whether this illness was work-related. The level of absenteeism was high: "It has happened that out of forty people [in the print works and composing room] we had nine sick persons." The firm of Brill offered a sick pay of 60 percent of the weekly wage, which was not a statutory obligation in those days. Senior employees kept their jobs for many years while retaining their former pay. In the absence of a pension scheme, this too was a humane practice of the employers. De Groot cited the example of a printer who had been working for the company for sixty-seven years, which means that he had been apprenticed by Johannes Brill in 1823. The aged employee was free to come and go as he pleased and performed light work exclusively.

The commission was specifically interested in child labor. The Children and Young Persons Act of M.P. Samuel van Houten, which prohibited the labor of children below the age of twelve, dated back to 1874. Lately, there had been a growing body of public opinion in favor of raising the minimum age, in connection with the introduction of compulsory education. In December 1889, the Lower House of the Dutch Parliament passed a law prohibiting boys below the age of sixteen from working later than 7 p.m.

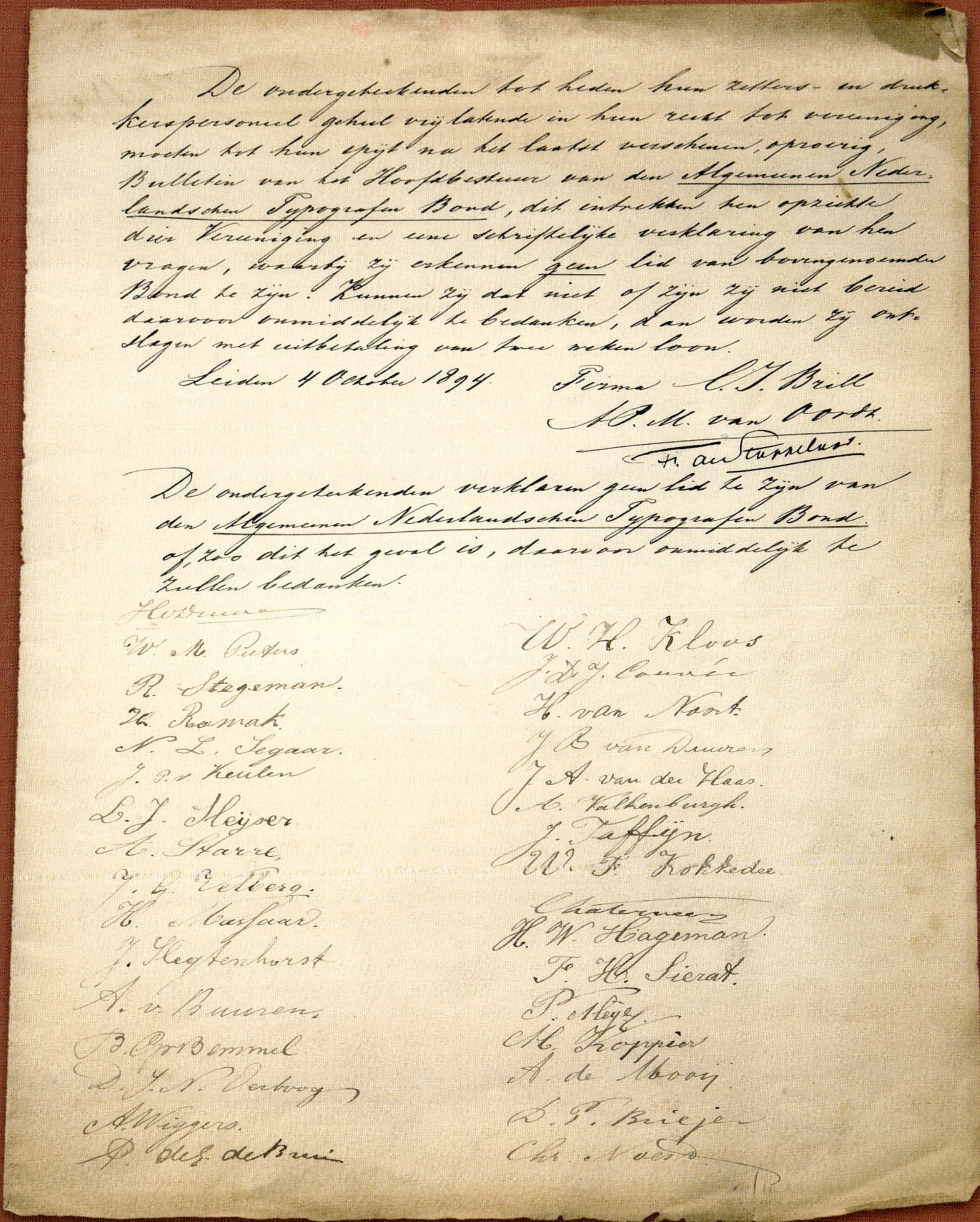

De ondergeteekenden tot heden hun zetters- en drukkerspersoneel geheel vrijlatende in hun recht tot vereeniging, moeten tot hun spijt na het laatst verschenen, oproerig, Bulletin van het Hoofdbestuur van den Algemeenen Nederlandschen Typografen Bond, dit intrekken ten opzichte dier Vereeniging en eene schriftelijke verklaring van hen vragen, waarbij zij erkennen geen lid van bovengenoemden Bond te zijn. Kunnen zij dat niet of zijn zij niet bereid daarvoor onmiddelijk te bedanken, dan worden zij ontslagen met uitbetaling van twee weken loon.

Leiden 4 October 1894. Firma E.J. Brill

A.P.M. van Oordt.

F. de Stoppelaar.

De ondergeteekenden verklaren geen lid te zijn van den Algemeenen Nederlandschen Typografen Bond of, zoo dit het geval is, daarvoor onmiddelijk te zullen bedanken.

[illegible]

W. M. Peeters
R. Stegeman.
H. Ramak.
N. L. Segaar.
J. P. v. Keulen
L. J. Meijser.
A. Starre,
J. G. Velberg.
H. Marsaar.
J. Slegtenhorst
A. v. Buuren.
B. Op Bemmel
L. J. N. Verboog
A. Wiggers.
P. Alex. de Bruin

W. H. Kloos
J. D. J. Couvée
H. van Noort.
J. B. van Deuren
J. A. van der Haas.
C. Valkenburgh.
J. Taffijn.
W. F. Kokkedee.

[illegible]

H. W. Hageman.
F. H. Sierat.
P. Meije.
M. Koppier
A. de Mooij
L. P. Brieje
Chr. Noord.

At the Paris World Exhibition of 1878, the firm of E. J. Brill was awarded a gold medal for its "Oriental printed editions." Brill Coll.

In his responses to the commission, De Groot did not show himself to be a supporter of such measures. The wages the boys brought in were a welcome supplement to the family income, and in his opinion typesetting was not a heavy burden for a boy of twelve or thirteen. Director Van Oordt was also questioned by the commission about the apprentices, and it turned out that he fully agreed with his employee:

> Question: Would the raising of the minimum age be regretted by you?
> Answer: For our trade, yes; a twelve-year-old boy has been sufficiently educated; in our trade his skills are continually being developed. The typesetter's skill is best acquired if the boy makes an early start in the trade.

Van Oordt may have regarded the measures against child labor with disfavor, yet in the context of his day he distinguished himself as an employer who cared for his people:

> Question: Would you welcome or regret the statutory obligation to take out accident and pension insurance for the employees, largely at the expense of the employer?
> Answer: The former.

The Twentieth Century in Sight

By working together harmoniously, the ex-theologian and the former teacher had built a flourishing business in twenty-five years. They had seized the opportunities that presented themselves, and because of their open-mindedness they were all the better equipped to do so. They had started in 1872 with fifteen employees and now employed about sixty people.[21] However, in the nineties they confronted the same problem as that faced by Evert Jan Brill in his day: they had no successor. Initially Van Oordt's son was to take over his father's position, but he died of tuberculosis at an early age. The two sons of De Stoppelaar pursued their own careers, and neither of them wanted to enter the business. The question of the future of the company became all the more urgent because Van Oordt wanted to be less involved in the daily routine on account of his poor health. The two directors decided to ensure the continuity of the business by turning the firm of E. J. Brill into a public limited company, in Dutch a "naamloze vennootschap." In the future the firm was to be called "N.V. Bookselling and Printing Firm, formerly E. J. Brill." Under this designation, the company entered into the new century and into a new phase of its existence.

EXPOSITION UNIVERSELLE INTERNATIONALE DE 1878
E.J.BRILL
PARIS
CHAPLAIN

KÅLÅ PRATJEKÅ. SÅRÅWITÅ. TÅGÅG KÅLÅ SRÅNÅ. KÅLÅ PRALĔMBÅ. MET EEN BRIEF IN DE HAND.

Rijks Ethnographisch Mus

THE N.V. BOOKSELLING AND PRINTING FIRM, FORMERLY E. J. BRILL, 1896-1945

The Turn of the Century, 1896-1906

A closer look reveals that the anonymous partners of the new public limited company had familiar names. Van Oordt and De Stoppelaar stayed on as directors in the new business entity and took on a third man as a reinforcement: Cornelis Marinus Pleyte, recruited with the intention of succeeding them in the long run. The supervisory board consisted of five members, all of them old acquaintances of the business or relatives of the directors: Michaël Jan de Goeje, professor of Arabic, a prominent author of the house of Brill and a friend of the family for many years; Albert Cornelis Vreede, professor of Indonesian languages and also a Brill author; the Egyptologist Willem Pleyte, director of the National Museum of Antiquities, a Brill author for thirty years and father of the newly-appointed co-director; and finally two brothers of the managing directors, namely Willem Hendrik van Oordt, mayor of the town of Valkenburg near Leiden; and Jan de Stoppelaar, a gentleman of independent means in The Hague.

The purpose of the partnership was described as "the continuation and further exploitation of the fully operative print works, bindery, and publishing establishment, as well as the trade in Oriental and antiquarian books and ethnographic literature, as these had been carried out so far under the firm of E. J. Brill." The share capital amounted to *ƒ* 100,000, divided into twenty nominative shares. All shares were in the hands of the directors and the supervisory directors: the two old directors had six shares each, the new director had three, and the five supervisory directors had one each. Van Oordt and De Stoppelaar did not contribute any capital in the literal sense of the word, but they did supply "the fully operative print works and bindery with all accompanying equipment, [and] the interior of the business with the accompanying furniture."[1]

The value of the business brought in by the directors was estimated to be *ƒ* 60,000, which meant that the actual amount of new capital in the form of shares amounted to *ƒ* 40,000. The N.V. Brill was listed on the Amsterdam Stock Exchange, not among the common stock funds but in the section of the so-called "Unlisted Companies": the shares were registered and were not freely negotiable on the exchange. The Amsterdam quotation was especially important because the founders intended to issue a bond loan through the stock market. The rapid growth of the business had been another reason for the transition to a public limited company, because in this form it would be easier for the business to attract investment capital. The limited number of registered shares guaranteed that power remained in the hands of the small Leiden inner circle, since bondholders had no managerial influence within the company.

L. Serrurier, *De wajang poerwa: eene ethnologische studie* (1896). This standard work on wajang puppets by Lindor Serrurier (1846-1901), director of the Leiden Museum of Ethnology, is as monumental as it is rare. The beautiful lithographs were outsourced by Brill to the printer P. J. Mulder in Leiden. The Dutch government had two hundred copies printed, which were presented to museums abroad and to foreign dignitaries on a state visit. ULA

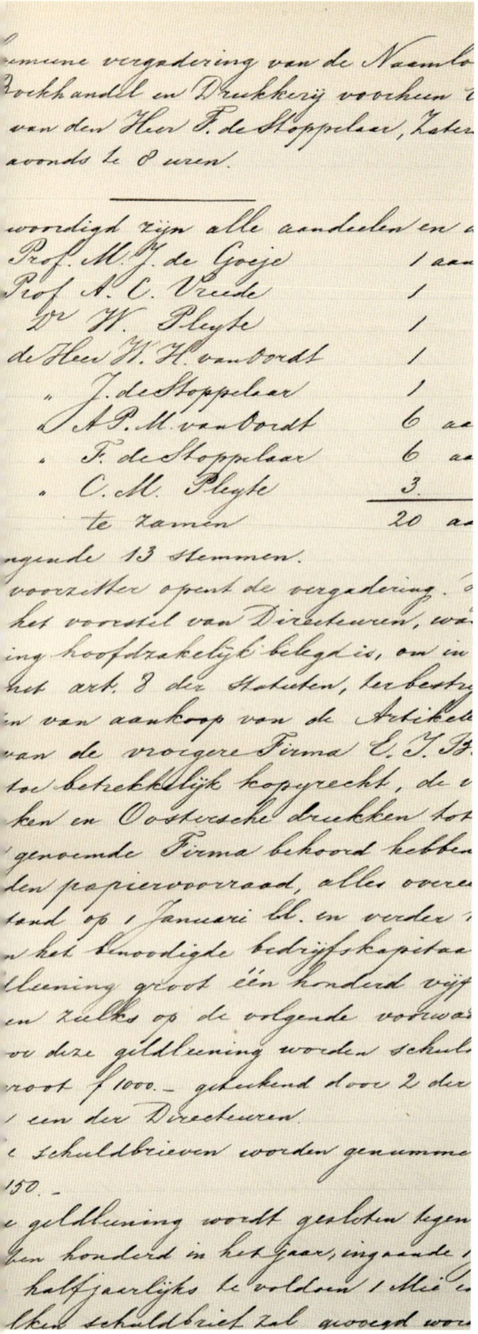
...meene vergadering van de Naamlo...
...Boekhandel en Drukkerij voorheen E...
van den Heer F. de Stoppelaar, ...
avonds te 8 uren.
...woordigd zijn alle aandeelen en ...
Prof. M. J. de Goeje 1 aan...
Prof. A. C. Vreede 1
Dr. W. Pleyte 1
de Heer W. H. van Oordt 1
" J. de Stoppelaar 1
" A. P. M. van Oordt 6 a...
" F. de Stoppelaar 6 a...
" C. M. Pleyte 3
te zamen 20 a...
...ngende 13 stemmen.
...voorzitter opent de vergadering.
...het voorstel van Directeuren, wa...
...ing hoofdzakelijk belegd is, om in...
...het art. 8 der Statuten, ter bestr...
...in van aankoop van de Artikel...
van de vroegere Firma E. J. B...
toe betrekkelijk kopyrecht, de ...
...ken en Oostersche drukken tot...
genoemde Firma behoord hebben...
den papiervoorraad, alles overe...
...stand op 1 Januari ll. en verder...
...het benoodigde bedrijfskapitaa...
...leening groot één honderd vijf...
en zulks op de volgende voorwa...
...ie deze geldleening worden schul...
...groot f 1000.- geteekend door 2 der...
een der Directeuren.
...e schuldbrieven worden genumme...
150.-
...e geldleening wordt gesloten tegen...
...een honderd in het jaar, ingaande...
halfjaarlijks te voldoen 1 Mei ...
...elken schuldbrief zal ... wor...

The minutes of the first general meeting of shareholders, held on March 28, 1896, at the home of De Stoppelaar. BA/ULA

Bonds

Van Oordt and De Stoppelaar had not transferred the publishing list and corresponding rights, the stock of books, or the paper stocks to the new business entity. Consequently, the public limited company was obliged to take over these assets from the former firm. The value of the publishing list was estimated at *f* 108,239.03, the stock of books at *f* 12,738.60, and the paper stocks at *f* 4,126.95. At the first general meeting of March 28, 1896, it was decided that the N.V. would issue a bond loan of *f* 150,000 for the purpose of this threefold acquisition. The one hundred and fifty bonds of a thousand guilders each at 4.5% had a term of twenty years, as of May 1, 1896, and would be paid off on the basis of redemption.

The established name of E. J. Brill inspired confidence among the investors, and the bond issue was easily subscribed. More than 80 percent of the proceeds were used to buy out the owners of the former firm, and the surplus—totaling *f* 24,895.41 and half a cent—served as reinforcement for the working capital. Together with the financial contribution of the shareholders—eight shares with a joint value of *f* 40,000—the company had an ample capital reserve of *f* 65,000 at its disposal. Part of this was used to acquire a new press and new printing types.

In 1872 Van Oordt had taken over the entire business of E. J. Brill for *f* 40,150, while in 1896 the publishing list alone was valued at *f* 108,239.03. Augmented by the inventory and the stock-in-trade, the total value of the firm at the time of its transformation into a public limited company amounted to well over *f* 185,000. In just under twenty-five years, the value of the company increased more than four and a half times, while the workforce experienced a comparable growth during the same period. Van Oordt and De Stoppelaar had managed their affairs well.

Attendance Fee

The directors were responsible for the day-to-day management of the firm, arranging their duties in mutual consent. The supervisory directors, three to five in number, had to be shareholders. They saw to it that the statutes were observed and supervised the other directors, and they were also authorized, should the occasion arise, to suspend a director. Appointment and dismissal of the directors, however, rested with the general shareholders' meeting—and because Van Oordt and De Stoppelaar held 60 percent of the shares between them, they did not need to worry much about this stipulation. The supervisory directors did not receive any salary, just a fee of ten guilders for each meeting they attended.

To cover these attendance fees an annual budget of *f* 250 was set aside, so that the five supervisory directors were able to hold five paid meetings a year at most. The statutes obliged them to meet at least twice a year. Each year, one of the supervisory directors had to resign, although he was immediately eligible for reelection. In meetings of the supervisory board, the directors had merely an advisory function, but in the shareholders' meeting they had the last word on the matter at hand. According to the statutes, a general shareholders' meeting had to be held once a year in Leiden, on the first, second, or third Thursday of June. (This stipulation was to cause some inconvenience during a managerial crisis at the end of the 1980s: the legitimacy of one such meeting was contested because it had taken place in Leiderdorp, just outside the city limits of Leiden.)

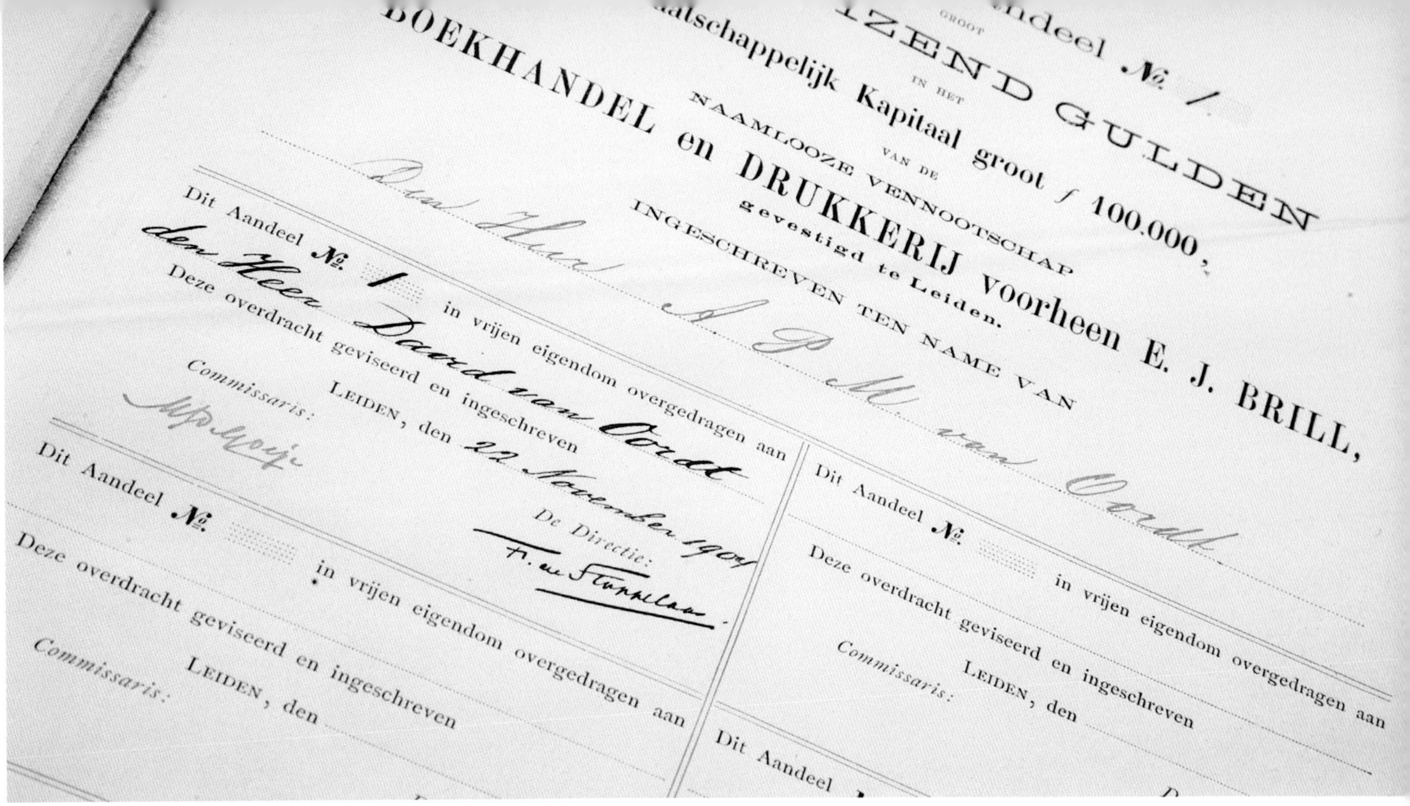

Shareholders' register of E. J. Brill N.V.

BA/ULA

Biblical Ups and Downs

At the meetings of the supervisory board and the shareholders' meetings, practically every aspect of the company was discussed. The minutes of those meetings reflect the state of affairs in the various segments of the business and form a rich source for the history of the N.V. Brill.[2] From these records it is also possible to glean some information about erroneous judgments and failed projects. For instance, at the first meeting of the supervisory board in 1896, De Stoppelaar proposed an ambitious project for an illustrated Bible, to be organized by Brill in cooperation with other publishers. A select group of painters from the Netherlands and beyond was enlisted to prepare around one hundred plates to illustrate the Bible. The publication was to be a matchless work of art that would also appear in English, French, and German editions. Perhaps it was meant as a successor and surpasser of the famous illustrated Bible of Gustave Doré, which had been published in 1865.

The costs of the projected Bible had been estimated at *f* 135,000, and Brill contributed *f* 10,000 to the partnership that had been established for the purpose of this publication. The project was very dear to De Stoppelaar in particular, and thus he recommended it wholeheartedly: "A favorable outcome is beyond doubt, and the profits show considerable promise even in the case of moderate success." The supervisory directors consequently decided that the N.V. would take over the firm's interest in this enterprise. In 1897 prospects were still favorable; in the following years, however, the tone gradually became more and more pessimistic. In 1902 the N.V. was forced to write off *f* 1,000 of its investment, and a year later wrote off another *f* 1,500, "without yet entirely despairing of success." From 1904 onwards *f* 1,000 was written off annually, "in the hope that eventually the day will come that will bring about a favorable turn in the affairs of the Illustrated Bible Partnership." This happy day never came,

Another fine illustration of wajang puppets from L. Serrurier, *De wajang poerwa: eene ethnologische studie* (1896). ULA >

SANGKOENI. DOERNA.

SOEJOEDÂNÂ. LESMÂNÂ.

Rijks Ethnographisch Museum.

F. E. Blaauw, *A Monograph of the Cranes* (1897). One of Brill's most beautiful publications is this book on cranes, of which only 170 copies were printed. The illustrations are based on watercolors that were painted from living specimens in the Artis Zoo in Amsterdam. Zoo director Westerman had wanted to write the book himself, but he assigned the work to Frans Ernest Blaauw (1860-1935), an amateur biologist who kept exotic animals threatened with extinction on his country estate, Gooilust. The binding is a fine example of the *Jugendstil* art that Brill sometimes applied in scholarly publications. ULA

and after a long period of muddling along the illustrated Bible became positively defunct in 1911. Brill's total loss in the failed enterprise amounted to well over *f* 16,000. As a balm for its wounded feelings, the firm received from the liquidation proceedings the painting *David Playing the Harp before Saul*, created by the well-known painter Jozef Israëls for the illustrated Bible. It was sold for *f* 2,000 so as to reduce the loss.[3]

Another Bible project had a more favorable outcome. Back in the 1880s, Van Oordt and De Stoppelaar had conceived a plan to bring out a new translation of the Bible. By the middle of the following decade, a group of translators under the direction of Professor H. Oort was actively engaged in a new translation of the entire Bible from the original sources. This so-called "Leiden Version" was intended as an alternative to the Dutch Authorized Version, in use since 1637. The Old Testament was published by Brill in 1906 and the New Testament in 1913, both volumes including introductions and annotations. It was a long-term project with an impressive result, although the new translation did not really succeed in supplanting the old one. In orthodox circles, the contemporary language of the Leiden Version was considered too liberal.[4] Brill was far ahead of its time: only in the 1950s would a new Bible translation find acceptance among the Dutch protestant churches, in its turn being replaced by a yet newer translation in 2007.

Miss Headstrong

Projects of this kind reflected the interests of Van Oordt, originally a theologian, and of De Stoppelaar, an active member of the Mennonite Congregation. The religious persuasion of the latter even generated a small wave of Mennonitica in the publishing house, and also the *Mennonite Contributions* were published by Brill for many years. For that matter, books in the fields of theology and church history were occasional phenomena rather than a staple feature of the publishing house at the time. It was only after the Second World War that the monograph series in the fields of Old and New Testament studies originated, continuing themselves into the present publishing list.

Whereas the former firm of E. J. Brill still presented itself as printer to the university, the public limited company dropped this time-honored epithet. The title had passed into disuse, after the theoretical monopoly on academic printing had been abolished in practice for a long time. In these years dissertations, orations, and publications by Leiden scholars were issued by various Leiden publishers, Brill on account of its tradition being no more than *primus inter pares*. The revival of the natural sciences at Leiden University was also reflected in Brill's publishing list, thanks to publications by the Nobel Prize winners H. A. Lorentz and H. Kamerlingh Onnes.

The "Oriental printed editions" formed the real pillars of the company, which stood firmly on the foundations that had been laid in the last quarter of the nineteenth century. The sixteen-volume series of De Goeje's *Annals of Al-Tabbari*, begun in 1879, was completed in 1901. In the course of the 1890s, a momentous new project began to take shape: the *Encyclopaedia of Islam*. Together with a number of foreign Arabists, De Goeje and De Stoppelaar had set up an international committee to get the publication underway, but between the initial dream and its realization there were many practical obstacles. When the Utrecht professor M. Th. Houtsma had assumed responsibility for coordinating the international collaboration in 1899, things began to move ahead at last.[5] Even so, it was not until 1908 that the first installment of articles beginning with the letter *A* was published. The first bound volume of the encyclopedia appeared in 1913, and the four-volume first edition would not be completed until 1936.

Around 1900 Brill had acquired a solid international reputation through its scholarly publications in Arabic Studies, Assyriology, Indology, Sinology, and related fields of study. More and more foreign authors and institutions entrusted their work to the publishing house. By tradition ethnography and biology had been important components of the publishing list, and these fields became increasingly important at the turn of the century. The results of a series of scientific expeditions to New Guinea (1903-1920) were published by Brill in sixteen volumes. In 1899-1900, the famous Siboga Expedition directed by Max Weber explored the farthest corners of the Indonesian archipelago, making innumerable discoveries and generating a series of more than one hundred and forty installments published by Brill. The company also issued the results of expeditions conducted by other nations. For instance, in 1903 the firm contracted with the Museum of Natural History in New York to publish the findings of the Jessup Expedition to Alaska and the northeast of Siberia.[6]

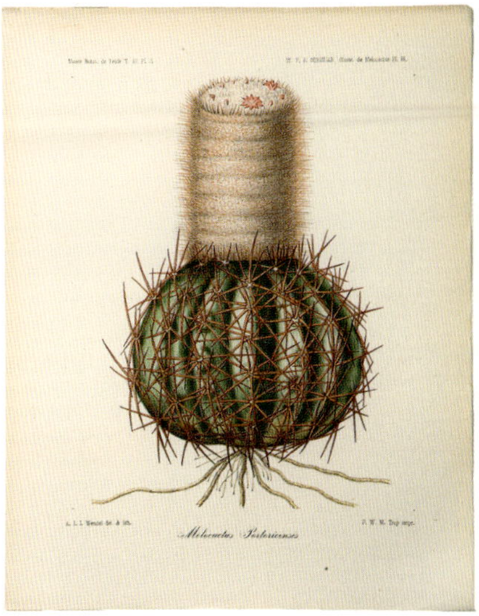

Illustration from W. F. R. Suringar, *Musée botanique de Leide* (E. J. Brill, 1897). Willem Frederik Reinier Suringar (1832-1898) was an important botanist, the director of the Botanical Gardens and the National Herbarium in Leiden. During the years 1884-85 he journeyed to the West Indies with his son Jan. He was especially interested in plants of the genus *Melocactus*, to which the *Musée Botanique* devoted a volume. In the Botanical Gardens he had a special greenhouse built for these cactuses, which were regularly sent to him from overseas. Later it turned out that the species so carefully distinguished by him unfortunately belonged to the same variety. The loose-leaf work contains drawings and photographs of cactuses. Photographs provided the best representation of reality, but some details could be rendered best in a drawing.

ULA

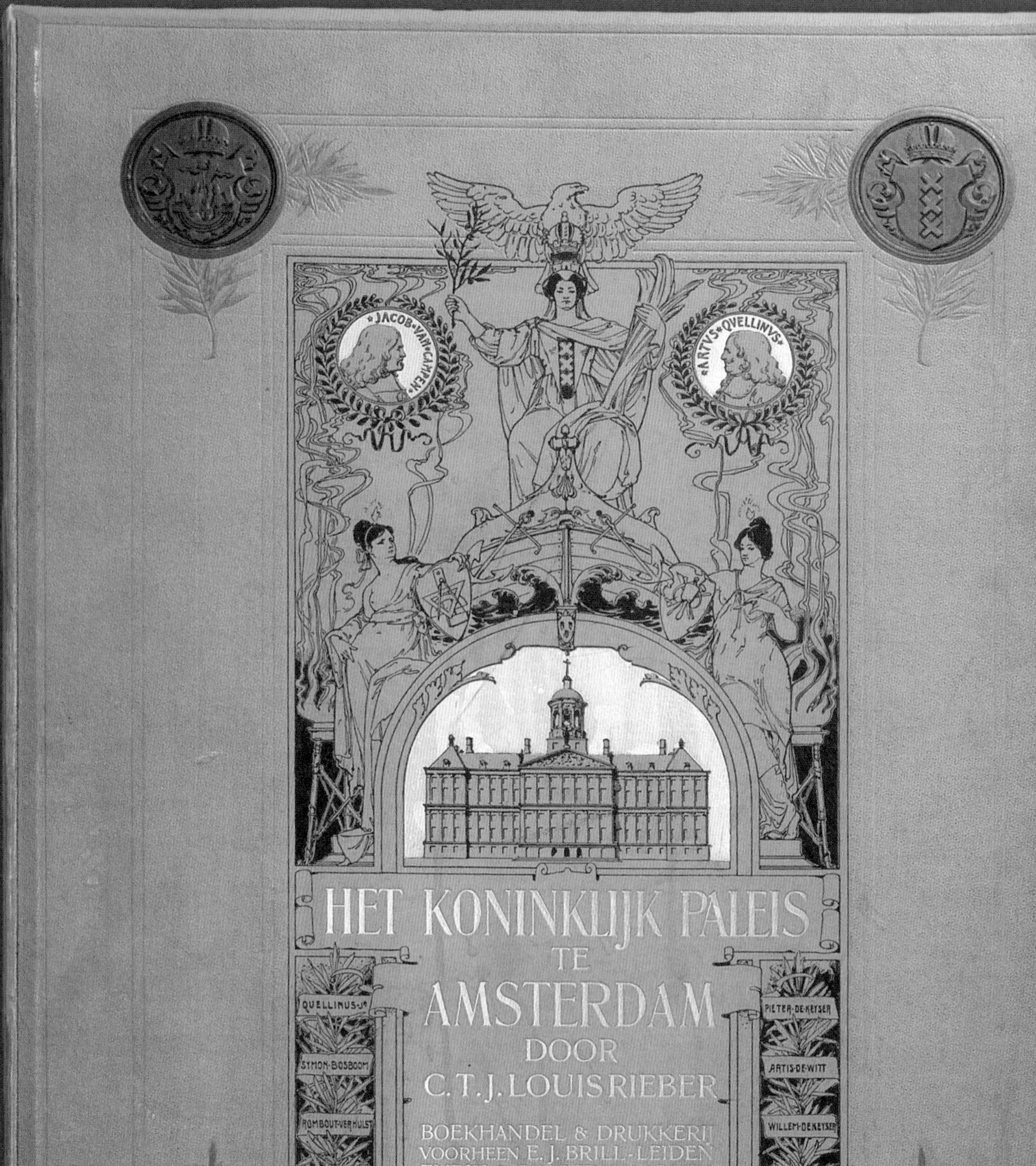
JACOB VAN CAMPEN
ARTVS QVELLINVS
HET KONINKLIJK PALEIS
TE
AMSTERDAM
DOOR
C. T. J. LOUIS RIEBER
BOEKHANDEL & DRUKKERIJ
VOORHEEN E. J. BRILL - LEIDEN
EMRIK & BINGER - HAARLEM
QUELLINUS-Jr
SYMON-BOSBOOM
ROMBOUT-VERHULST
ALBERT-VINCKENBRINCK
PIETER-DE-KEYSER
ARTIS-DE-WITT
WILLEM-DE-KEYSER
J-C-BRONCKHORST

Siboga-Expeditie

POLYCHAETA ERRANTIA OF THE SIBOGA EXPEDITION

BY

Dr. R. HORST

PART I

AMPHINOMIDAE

Monographie XXIV¹a of:

UITKOMSTEN OP ZOOLOGISCH, BOTANISCH, OCEANOGRAPHISCH EN GEOLOGISCH GEBIED

verzameld in Nederlandsch Oost-Indië 1899—1900

aan boord H. M. Siboga onder commando van Luitenant ter zee 1e kl. G. F. TYDEMAN

Dr. MAX WEBER

While this publishing program continued along lines set out in the past, around the turn of the century Brill also experimented in unexpected fields. For instance, in the course of the nineties the renowned scholarly publishing house brought out the *Miss Headstrong* trilogy by the German author Emmy von Rhoden—a milestone in the development of the pedagogically sound and politically correct girl's book. Another classic was the first Dutch edition of Lewis Carroll's *Alice in Wonderland* (1901), with illustrations from the English original. Children's books, however, would never develop into a full-grown corpus of publications within the publishing list; they remained in their infancy, so to speak.

The same applied to the novels Brill occasionally ventured to publish, without making any claim to be a literary publisher outright. Around the turn of the century, the firm also experimented with a series of publications in the field of technology, including such surprising items as a treatise on shipbuilding and a manual of masonry.

The members of the Siboga Expedition on the deck of the gunboat of the same name. Seated in the middle are the biologist Max Wilhelm Carl Weber (1852-1937), the leader of the expedition, and his wife Annie van den Bossche. The expedition of 1899-1900 explored the farthest corners of the Indonesian archipelago and acquired a wealth of knowledge: for instance, no fewer than 131 new species of fish were catalogued. It was not until the 1970s that Brill completed the series of research results, consisting of 142 volumes. ULA/Artis Zoo

< C. T. J. Louis Rieber, *Het Koninklijk Paleis te Amsterdam* (1900, reprint 1940). A showpiece in large folio format (46 x 66 cm) devoted to the old Amsterdam city hall, later the Royal Palace. To quote from Brill's prospectus: "The large book of plates by Rieber presents in an excellent fashion, fully worthy of the building, an impressive picture of all the splendors to be found there." Brill Coll.

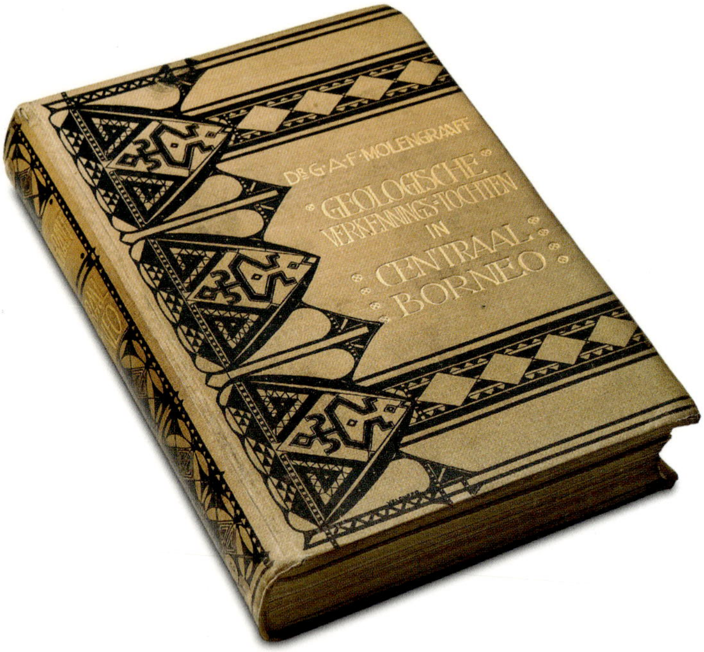

G. A. F. Molengraaff, *Geologische verkenningstochten in Centraal-Borneo* (1900). The Borneo expedition of the geologist Molengraaf (1860-1942) to the interior of this island lasted almost a year. This voluminous travel account did not only deal with rocks, but also with the customs and traditions of the inhabitants. Observations on siliceous wood are alternated with remarks on the building style of the Dayak people. The descriptions of bivouacking in torrential rains are beautiful. The fighting dogs of the Dayak disturbed the nocturnal rest of the explorer, woken by an "infernal yelling and screaming, which I was unable to compare with anything I had ever heard." The binding is a fine *Jugendstil* design by J. G. Veldheer. ULA

Unwittingly, such excursions into other areas highlighted the true character of Brill: a scholarly and internationally oriented publishing house with a specialization on "strange" languages.

Good Times

Brill Ltd. flourished during the first ten years of its existence and entered the twentieth century in good spirits. Turnover increased steadily and the company made a handsome profit year after year. A loss of *f* 16,000, such as that incurred by the illustrated Bible project, could easily be offset. The old steam engine of 1883 was due for replacement after twenty years of service; the purchase of a new engine capable of delivering a full six horsepower presented no problem at all, nor did the purchase of a new printing press costing *f* 6,000. With a view to future capital expenditure and the approaching redemption of the bond loan, the company built up a considerable capital reserve, which was invested as prudently as possible. During the first ten years, after deducting reserves and depreciation, the net profit was always fixed at an amount of *f* 8,000 to *f* 9,000, corresponding to a dividend of 6-6.5% per share. Time and again the supervisory directors were able to approve the balance sheet with confidence, for the business ran smoothly. In accordance with the statutes, they validated the figures not once but twice: first in their capacity of supervisory directors, and once again at the general meeting in their capacity of shareholders. For the sake of convenience, the general meeting of shareholders was often combined with a meeting of the supervisory board, which was held earlier on the same day.

The print works and composing room were running almost entirely on work supplied by the publishing house—an ideal combination. This triad of synergetic departments formed the heart of the company. The auction service and the larger part

On occasion the respectable publishing house of Brill indulged in frivolous book covers. Around 1900 many Dutch decorative artists worked in the style of the *Nieuwe Kunst*, the Dutch variant of *art nouveau* or *Jugendstil*. Well-known artists such as R. W. P. de Vries (1874-1952) and L. W. R. Wenckebach (1860-1937) designed book covers for Brill. The binding reproduced here was designed by the unknown H. H., who erroneously spelled "Brill" as "Bril." The stylistic idiom owes more to French *art nouveau* than to the *Nieuwe Kunst*. The series *Romans in proza*, the first volume of which appeared in 1897, was edited by the Leiden professor Jan ten Brink. Brill Coll.

Natalie Bruck-Auffenberg, *De vrouw "comme il faut"* (1897)
At times Brill published works of popular scholarship, such as this adaptation of an Austrian book on the Well-behaved Woman. It is remarkable how restrictive female etiquette merges here into emancipatory feminist ideology. The author makes a plea for the liberation of women, who by all means should go to university. In her opinion women are better suited to do so than men—a prophetic statement, judging by present student demographics. A broad range of female activities is discussed, from controlling the libido to offering tea, "for which at least the right glove is pulled off." ULA

of the antiquarian bookshop were split off when the firm became a public limited company. Two former employees of Brill, Burgersdijk and Niermans, continued the auctions under their own name and established an antiquarian bookshop with the stock of 250,000 books they took over from Brill. In the long run, the firm of Burgersdijk and Niermans became the preeminent antiquarian bookshop and auction house in Leiden.[7] Brill's Orientalia did not form part of this transaction, but continued to be sold through its own "Oriental" bookshop. This least successful side of the business seems to have been a perpetual problem child. Discussions of the antiquarian bookshop during meetings of the supervisory board generally boiled down to laments over the ailing institution and exhortations to bring it back to life. In 1910 there was even talk of closing this branch of the business for good, but the idea was dismissed as being too extreme.

The Son of the Egyptologist

The new director, Cornelis Marinus Pleyte (1863-1917), was expected to learn all aspects of the business, while at the same time strengthening the ethnographic component of the publishing list. Pleyte had worked for some time as a volunteer at the Ethnographic Museum in Leiden, which opened in 1883, and in 1887 got a job in Amsterdam as curator of the ethnographic collection at the Artis Zoo. He owed his position at Brill to the influence and financial contribution of his father Willem Pleyte—Egyptologist, director of the Leiden Museum of Antiquities, and supervisory director of the company.

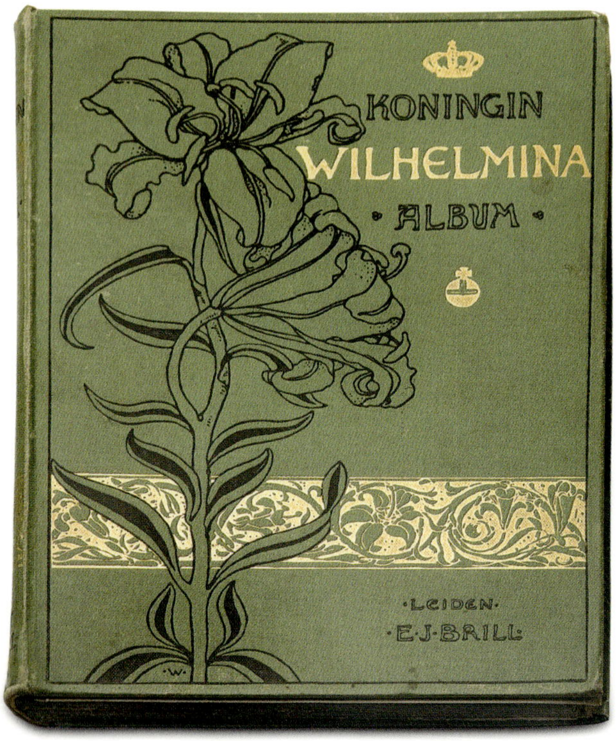

The beautifully designed *Koningin Wilhelmina Album* (1898) was edited by the Leiden poet Fiore della Neve (pseudonym of M. G. L. van Lochem). This literary coronation-gift to young queen Wilhelmina contained poems and short stories by famous contemporary authors, most of them forgotten by now. Cyriel Buysse wrote for eighteen-year-old Wilhelmina a charming story about the desperate love of a ship's doctor for a shallow American beauty. The decorative binding of the book was designed by L. W. R. Wenckebach. Van Lochem compared the coronation of the young queen with the arrival of spring, but most authors kept their adoration of royalty within bounds. ULA

Copies of outgoing mail were recorded in copy books. The reproduction shows a letter from 1900 by Peltenburg, then deputy director, to the Arabic scholar Snouck Hurgronje, who was staying in Batavia at the time. Brill Coll.

One is inclined to think that the younger Pleyte was a little too restless for the solid corporate culture at Brill's. To the annoyance of Van Oordt and De Stoppelaar, it turned out that their apparent successor was not in the least interested in the print works and the publishing business. Ethnography alone was dear to his heart, to the exclusion of other pursuits. Pleyte seized on every opportunity to travel abroad, using the company's interest as an excuse to take off to France, Germany or England. In 1898 he was invited by the Ministry of Colonial Affairs to travel to Indonesia and assemble a collection of objects of ethnographic interest, intended for the Dutch pavilion at the Paris World Exhibition of 1900. Under protest Van Oordt and De Stoppelaar reconciled themselves to his departure for the East, where, according to the optimistic assessment of the supervisory directors, he would be able to establish productive relationships on behalf of the company. The expedition was to last six months, but Pleyte enjoyed himself in the colonies and stayed away much longer. In the words of the author of his obituary: "This journey offered him much to enjoy and much to learn. Such a wandering life, moving on from one place to another, was highly attractive to him."[8]

When he finally turned up again in Leiden at the end of 1899, Pleyte felt out of place at Brill. The estrangement was mutual, although the process of severing ties was a rather sordid affair: after Pleyte submitted his resignation on the grounds of ill health, he tried to sell his shares to a third party, thus bypassing directors and supervisory directors. Thereupon angry words were traded at the meeting of supervisory directors, from which the elder Pleyte absented himself this time for tactical reasons. Van Oordt and De Stoppelaar were shocked by the disloyalty of the younger Pleyte. They availed themselves of the opportunity to recite his shortcomings and to calculate how much loss he had caused the company. After this discomfiture Pleyte abandoned his career as a publisher. He returned to the East, leaving behind his wife and children, and devoted the rest of his life to his ethnographic pursuits.[9]

M. F. Onnen, *De draadloze telegrafie en hare toepassing* (1906). In this brochure published by Brill, the government is called on to install a wireless telegraph system in the Dutch East Indies. Such a facility was naturally of major importance in the vast Indonesian archipelago. In this book Onnen briefly explains how wireless telegraphy works and why such a system should be in the hands of the government; finally he provides a detailed survey of the costs. In 1911 the Dutch East Indian Post Office began the installation, a process that was accelerated by the First World War. A wireless connection with the Netherlands was also established. ULA

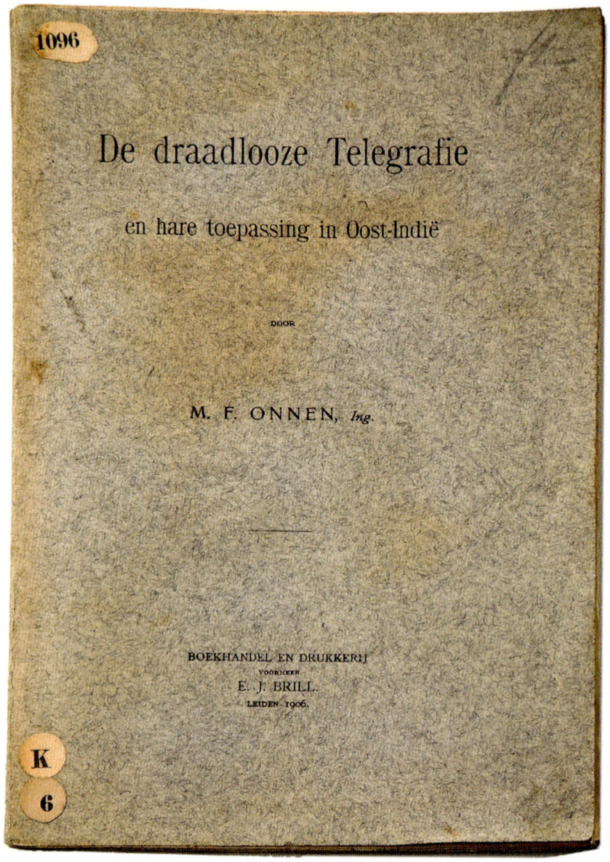

Apparently Van Oordt and De Stoppelaar had already doubted the suitability of their intended successor at an earlier stage, because in the spring of 1898 they recommended Cornelis Peltenburg as deputy director. Peltenburg, who had been employed at Brill since 1880, had recently been offered an interesting job elsewhere. Van Oordt and De Stoppelaar wanted to bind him to the company and so proposed that the supervisory directors appoint him deputy director. In time Peltenburg would be appointed full director, "if circumstances should require—which according to the course of events *must* happen sooner or later—that one of the present directors be replaced." [10] Peltenburg for his part had to confirm this agreement for the future with an oath of allegiance to Brill. The opportunity to replace one of the directors came sooner than expected: after Pleyte's departure in 1900, Peltenburg was appointed in his stead.[11]

Van Oordt and De Stoppelaar had done well to arrange for their succession, because other circumstances necessitated their own replacement. Adriaan van Oordt died on the last day of 1903, and Frans de Stoppelaar on June 8, 1906. They were both buried in the cemetery on the Groenesteeg in Leiden. They had spent all their lives together and continued their companionship after death.

The Firm Hand of Cornelis Peltenburg, 1906-1934

The General of Brill

Cornelis or Corneille Peltenburg was born in 1853 in the village of Oegstgeest, just outside Leiden (as a Francophile and a member of the Walloon Congregation, he had a predilection for the French form of his name). In his youth he had cherished the dream of becoming a professional soldier, but his father was opposed to a career in the army.[12] Instead, Cornelis received a thorough practical training in the book trade: at an early age he took service with the Hazenberg bookshop in Leiden, subsequently worked in bookshops in The Hague and Amsterdam, and then returned to Hazenberg. In 1880 De Stoppelaar brought him to Brill, where he worked his way up from sales representative to office manager and co-director. After the death of De Stoppelaar in 1906, Peltenburg became the sole director of the firm and would remain so until his own death in 1934.

At first his supreme rule was by no means taken for granted. The supervisory directors were of the opinion that two directors constituted a better guarantee of continuity and therefore instructed him to look for a deputy. They even used the argument that a second director was a statutory obligation. Over the years Peltenburg took on several young men as "director in training," but somehow these trainees always disappeared after some time. Peltenburg would not tolerate a second man beside him, and he took the insistence of the supervisory directors personally as a vote of no confidence. They in turn felt obliged to assure the piqued director that they had every confidence in him, and thus the issue of a deputy was gradually erased from the agenda.[13]

Peltenburg was indeed able to manage the company very well under his own steam. During the period preceding the First World War, turnover, profits, capital reserves, and dividends increased year after year. More than sixty people were employed in the print works and the composing room by then, and the total number of employees was around eighty. The year 1911 had been "very profitable" for Brill, the director reported to the Leiden Chamber of Commerce: "The print works constantly had plenty of work, chiefly on account of the increasing network of foreign relations, occasioned by the large extent of the stock of Oriental printing types."[14] In 1913 Brill presented itself at the International Graphics Exhibition in Amsterdam, Peltenburg even taking a seat in the exhibition's general committee. Afterward, he was able to inform the supervisory directors proudly that Brill's exhibit of "Oriental printed editions" had won the highest award, namely the honorary diploma.[15]

The business was running well, or "marching along," to use an expression that in this case should be taken more or less literally. His shattered boyhood dream had left Peltenburg with a military manner, and he cultivated a matching appearance: bolt upright posture, handlebar moustache, penetrating gaze, and a commanding voice with rolling *r*'s. He had the style of an officer in the civilian capacity of a publisher, while in his spare time the publisher acted as commanding officer of the Vigilante Patrol of Oegstgeest. His strict code of honor, too, had a military character; he fully dedicated himself to the company and demanded the same dedication from his subordinates. Peltenburg drilled Brill.

Around 1909 Peltenburg had this decorative "drop vignette" designed by the artist R. W. P. de Vries (1874-1952). The old Luchtmans motto *Tuta sub aegide Pallas* was reinscribed in Brill's new printer's mark. The composition of Pallas Athena and Hermes is derived from the allegorical painting representing the Luchtmans family, which hangs in the offices of Brill (see the illustration at the beginning of the first chapter). The mythological couple in Brill's present logo has the same origin. The drop vignette in *art nouveau* style was in use until the midthirties.

Impending Strike

In his patriarchal way, Peltenburg surely meant well by his workmen, but it did not suit his authoritarian outlook when they organized themselves in trade unions and made demands. In 1913 he was forced to accept the first collective labor agreement between employers and employees in the graphics industry, which was a traumatic experience for him. On the basis of this agreement the working week was fixed at 57 hours, whereas Brill at the time operated on a 60-hour week. In addition, the labor agreement involved a wage increase: the weekly pay for an adult worker would henceforth amount to *f* 13.68, whereas the wages at Brill were still at the same level as in 1890: *f* 9.50 for "ordinary" printers and typesetters, and *f* 12 for those with a qualification in Chinese or Arabic.

The Labor Agreement Act (1907) had created the possibility of such contracts, although they could not be made compulsory for employers. Most graphics enterprises in Leiden had accepted the collective labor agreement over the course of 1913, but the firms of A. W. Sijthoff and E. J. Brill were obstinate and refused to recognize it. When the workers at Sijthoff went on strike and those at Brill threatened to follow suit, Peltenburg finally came around. His greatest grievance was not the increase in labor costs, but the fact that he as director could no longer autonomously decide what his employees would earn.

Peltenburg interpreted the collective labor agreement as an act of disloyalty by the employees, who evidently put more trust in their trade unions than in him. He experienced the course of events as a personal defeat and wished to make clear to his subordinates that he would not be trifled with. The collective labor agreement came into effect on January 1, 1914, and seven weeks later Peltenburg informed his

Three and a half centuries of Dutch ships: J. O. van der Kellen Dzn., *Nederlandsche zeeschepen van ongeveer 1470 tot 1830* (1913). The purpose of this loose-leaf atlas of plates is made clear in the introduction: "The firm of Brill deserves praise for having dared to take the risk of this enterprise . . . by which it contributes to honoring our national reputation." The reproductions, heliotypes made by the Haarlem firm Emrik and Binger, are of very good quality. The planned German and English editions, intended to secure the honor of the national reputation beyond the borders, were never published. ULA

workforce that five of them would be fired. The dismissal was justified by the increase in labor costs and a decline in business. The latter of these arguments was not true: the year 1914 saw the crowning success of the steady growth the company had been undergoing since 1896. The reason for the dismissal was the director's determination to reestablish his authority.[16]

The First World War

It is true that the Netherlands was bypassed by the war, but at Brill the consequences were clearly felt. Owing to the fact that foreign relations were broken off for four years, the contents of the order book dwindled and turnover decreased sharply. Already by August 10, 1914, immediately after the outbreak of the war, working hours at the print works and the composing room were reduced to 45 hours and later even to 42 hours per week. As of September, the regular working week of 57 hours was reintroduced, but until 1918 shorter working hours often remained in place. The decrease in work was in part offset by the mobilization, as a number of employees were conscripted to guard the frontiers. At Brill's, however, relatively many elderly workers were employed: by the end of 1915, twenty-five employees had a record of service of twenty-five years or longer.[17]

Thanks to the financial reserves that had been built up during the profitable years, the company had a solid buffer capacity, but there was now much less money flowing through the business. The balance sheet of 1913 listed liquid assets in the amount of *f* 115,000 and that of 1914, on the eve of the war, recorded the even higher amount of *f* 122,500. About half of this cash was invested, while in addition a considerable amount of capital had been placed over the years in various long-term investments through the so-called reserve funds. The balance sheet of 1917 did not far exceed *f* 60,000, about half the amount of the money flowing through the business before the war.

During the lean years the company cut its clothes according to its cloth, in the hope of being able to spare the capital reserves. This endeavor was successful—during the war years the company even managed to pay off *f* 23,000 on the bond loan of 1896, without drawing on the reserve funds. Actually, the company still made some profit, although considerably less than in the prewar years. In 1917, Brill was one of the last print works in Leiden to replace its steam engine with an electric motor. To cover the purchase cost of *f* 3,000 a few bonds had to be sold off, but these formed part of the invested liquid assets, as opposed to the reserve funds. The same financing method was applied to the premises at Rapenburg 22, which were purchased in 1917 for *f* 17,500. It was intended to house the Oriental antiquarian bookshop there, in the hope that it would be more profitable at that location. The relocation of the bookshop never progressed beyond the planning stage, but the real estate kept its value as an investment.

The First Woman

Basically the company remained sound, but during the war years it had to cope with considerably decreased revenues and sharply increased expenditures. Between 1900 and 1914 Brill published some 450 titles, whereas between 1914 and 1918 no more than about 70 titles were brought out. A large part of the war production was the continuation of previous work, such as the ongoing publications of the Siboga Expedition and new volumes in a few long-term series on Indonesia. A boost was the *Encyclopedie van Nederlandsch Indië* [Encyclopedia of the Dutch East Indies], which came into being during the war years with government funding. On the other hand, *the Encyclopaedia of Islam* had come to a complete standstill: while the first volume had appeared in 1913, the second would not see the light of day until 1927. In view of the work shortage Peltenburg did not hesitate for long, when in 1916 he was offered the opportunity to publish the magazine listing the preaching engagements in the churches of Leiden. In hard times even a trifle of work was not to be despised.

While revenues decreased, expenditures were increasing. The price of paper rose alarmingly, and labor costs also underwent a sharp increase during the war years. At the introduction of the new three-year collective labor agreement in 1917, Peltenburg did not dare to be obstinate as the time before, fearing a strike. It was the year of the Russian Revolution and, in its wake, of the failed revolution in which the socialist leader Pieter Jelles Troelstra tried to provoke in the Netherlands. The workers' fist was clenched in those days, and Peltenburg thought it expedient to act a little less militantly. However, the pay raise that resulted from the new labor agreement did not keep pace with the increase in the cost of living. The prices of necessities rose sharply during the later war years, and wages had to be raised repeatedly in order to prevent labor unrest. In the households of the employees as well as in the management of the company it became increasingly difficult to make ends meet.[18]

Amidst these vicissitudes of war there is also a gratifying piece of news to be mentioned. At the beginning of 1918, the first woman made her entry into the office at Brill, in the person of Miss Catharina Sytsma. At first the old-fashioned Peltenburg had his doubts about a female employee, but this daring innovation turned out much better than he expected: he told the supervisory directors that the lady had "greatly exceeded his expectations, both with regard to her satisfactory performance and her capacity for work."[19]

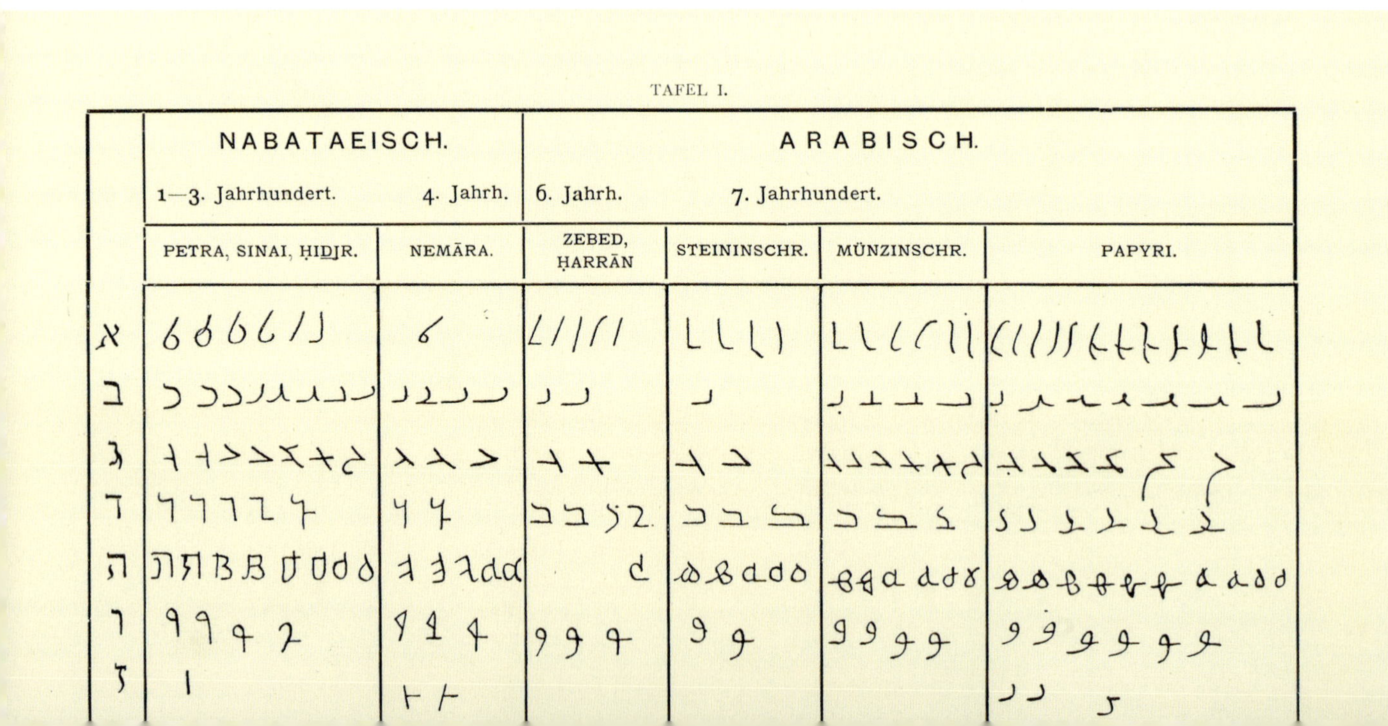

Illustration from the first volume of the first edition of the *Encyclopaedia of Islam* (1913): the development of the Arabic script. ULA

Herman Boerhaave (1668-1738) was the most famous physician of the eighteenth century. Tradition has it that letters with the simple address "Boerhaave, Holland" were delivered without any problem to his residence at No. 31 on the Rapenburg in Leiden. Brill hardly ranked second to Boerhaave: on the basis of this drawing of a pair of glasses (*bril* in Dutch), the postal worker understood that he had to deliver the relevant parcel to the publishing house of Brill on the Oude Rijn. An address featuring only a pair of glasses and the words "Leiden, Holland" is no longer understood by present-day postal workers, as a recent experiment established. The letter was returned to the sender.

Brill Coll.

"Greatness and Decline"

The advent of peace did not mean the automatic restoration of the prewar situation. On the contrary, the difficult circumstances of the later war years lasted into the twenties. The cost of living kept rising, while at the same time the trade unions campaigned for a shorter working week. The main issue was the eight-hour working day, corresponding to a working week of forty-eight hours. After massive demonstrations by the labor movement, this social achievement went into effect on January 1, 1920.

Peltenburg complained to the supervisory directors about the disastrous consequences of these developments for management. His calculations and plans were constantly being disrupted by the "ever-increasing demands of the workers." During these uncertain times it was impossible for him "to be able to work with any prospect of making a profit." The high wages forced up the prices for printing and affected demand adversely. For lack of work, he was unable to keep all the employees busy even after the introduction of the shorter working week. Several employees, including experienced printers and typesetters, were forced to seek their refuge elsewhere. Brill's own bindery was shut down in 1920 because it was no longer profitable. Foreign orders failed to materialize because the guilder was too expensive in relation to the devalued foreign currencies. In particular, the galloping postwar inflation in Germany put an end to orders from that country.[20]

They were not particularly flourishing times, but in these years, too, the company managed to hold its ground without drawing on its capital reserves. According to an article in a union journal, however, the situation at Brill was much worse than it was claimed to be. The author identified himself as "an old Leiden typographer," and his investigation of the company carried the engaging title "Greatness and Decline."[21] His conclusion was that there was little left of the former greatness of Brill and that the firm was on the verge of disaster. The decline was not a result of the circumstances of war but, according to the author, was due to the mismanagement of the director, C. Peltenburg.

Portrait of Peltenburg by Willem Hendrik van der Nat (1864-1929), a well-known Leiden painter. After training in lithography with the lithographer C. Bos, he attended a course at The Hague Academy and became a painter. As a sideline he illustrated books for the publishing house of Bolle in Rotterdam. After he had established himself in Leiden around 1900, he devoted himself entirely to painting. Besides portraits, Van der Nat painted many landscapes, which were very much sought after in England and the United States. In 1923 he made this portrait of Peltenburg on the occasion of his seventieth birthday. Brill Coll.

The anonymous writer took the trouble to send a copy of the journal to Peltenburg himself, who flew into an instant rage. He interpreted the article as an act of revenge by a terminated employee and immediately summoned a special meeting of the supervisory board. These gentlemen tried to placate the frenzied director: he must not take the matter as a personal attack. He should rather consider the article as "an expression of the employees' concern about their future." Peltenburg would have to explain to the workers in a "friendly conversation" that there was no need to worry about the loss of their jobs, and that they could always rely on Brill. By then the supervisory directors had woken up to the fact that in the battle between capital and labor, honey would catch more flies than vinegar.[22]

Cigars from the Boss

A pleasant manner with employees was not Peltenburg's strong point. He rarely showed himself on the work floor but directed operations through the overseers, who received daily instructions from him. Every year the director would deliver a New Year's speech, but for the rest of the year he barricaded himself in his office. His aloofness was reinforced by his realization that the workers could take a hard line, and that they were no longer resigned to their role as subordinates.

At the end of 1923, on the occasion of his seventieth birthday, Peltenburg made an attempt to tear down the walls of rank and class. On a Saturday evening, the entire workforce was invited into his office to celebrate his birthday. Wine was served, and each employee was presented with a box of cigars by the director—let's hope Miss Sytsma was remembered in some other way. By Brill standards this was a highly uncommon event, and the party was still talked about many years afterward.[23] Her Majesty the Queen contributed to the festivity by appointing the host a knight in the Order of Orange-Nassau.

In the same year of 1923, the postwar stagnancy came to an end. International trade picked up, and libraries once again began to buy books on a large scale. The company made a considerable profit, so that within a few years' time the remainder of the bond loan of 1896 could be paid off. After 1925, a period of six unprecedented fat years began, during which shareholders were treated year after year to a superbly generous dividend of 40%. Apparently the director and the supervisory directors did not deem it necessary to invest in the modernization of the company.[24]

The Wonderful World of Brill

In 1927 the journalist M. J. Brusse wrote a series of articles on Dutch publishing houses for the newspaper *Nieuwe Rotterdamsche Courant*. In his wanderings through publishers' territory, he wound up in the former orphanage on the Oude Rijn in Leiden. Brusse had occasionally heard of Brill, and thought he was going to be writing a piece about the umpteenth Dutch publishing house. But things turned out differently, for on this "picturesque little old Dutch canal" he unsuspectingly entered into the wonderful world of Brill. The journalist required a series of three articles to recover from his amazement.[25]

It turned out that Brill published books in languages of which Brusse didn't even know they existed, or had existed. Samaritan, Syriac, Manchurian, Ethiopic—any foreign language or peculiar script you could think of, Brill had published books in it. When the publishing house was offered a manuscript in an exotic script for which the print works had no typefaces available, it had them manufactured. Recently Brill had published a manuscript in Lydian, for which no printing types existed at all. Inscriptions found during excavations were carefully rendered in drawings, on the basis of which matrices were made for Lydian printing types. To Brusse's amazement, it turned out that behind the quaint old-fashioned facade of Brill was hidden an internationally active company. The journalist asked Peltenburg—"the elderly but still *so* youthfully enterprising leader of this classic firm"—about the secret of Brill:

> But how on earth have you managed to run a business, for so many years, on the basis of all of these bulky and expensive folio volumes . . . which are unreadable by the majority of mankind?

Peltenburg explained to him how, over the course of more than fifty years, the firm had built up an international reputation in Orientalia. The present director was reaping

On July 11, 1923, the magazine *Panorama* devoted an article to E. J. Brill Ltd., occasioned by the fact that the company had borne this name for seventy-five years. In this photograph rendered in copperplate, Peltenburg looks considerably younger than in the portrait by Van der Nat, which was made in the same year. *Panorama* had been in existence since 1913 and was published by the Nederlandsche Rotographure Maatschappij in Leiden.

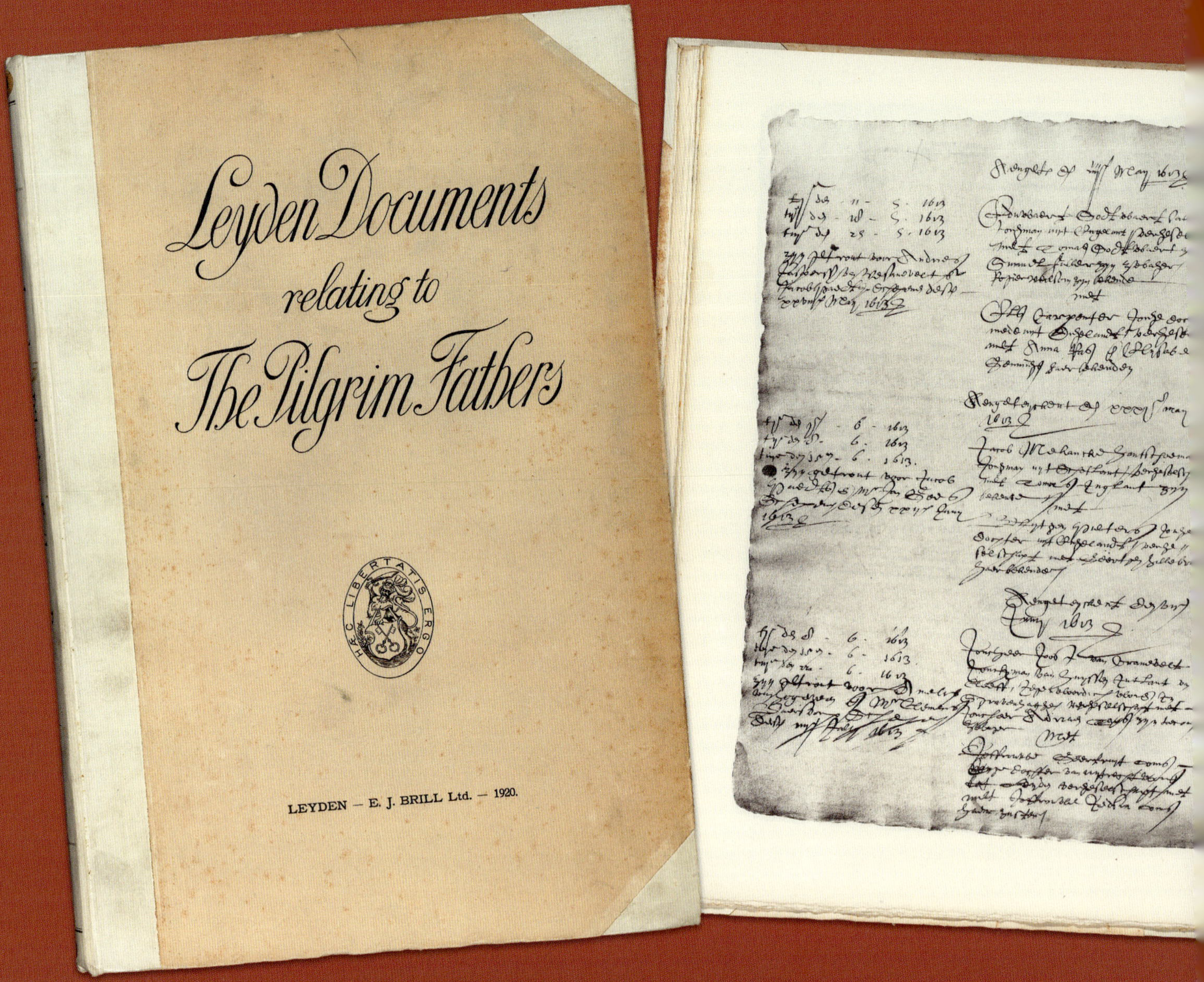

In 1920 Americans and Dutchmen commemorated the third centenary of the crossing of the Pilgrim Fathers from Leiden (via the port of Delfshaven) to America. In 1608 these English Calvinists had sought refuge in Leiden, when Catholic-minded King James I imposed restrictions on the exercise of their religion. In Leiden they decided to found a colony in America where they could live according to their own ideas. They found their Promised Land on the east coast, where they founded the town of Boston. Brill published two books on the occasion of the commemoration: an annotated facsimile edition of the *Leyden Documents relating to the Pilgrim Fathers* and the monograph *The Pilgrim Fathers in Holland (1608–1620)* by J. Irwin Brown. Recently Brill has revitalized the old connection between Leiden and Boston: since 1998 the company has its own "Pilgrims" in the city, in the form of fifteen persons who maintain its American branch. ULA

the harvest sown by his predecessors: Evert Jan Brill, Adriaan van Oordt, and Frans de Stoppelaar. He cherished and respected the tradition of the firm. Brill was not an average publishing house with a peculiar specialty; over time, the business had developed into the hub of an international network in the scholarly world. This web of foreign relations was of vital importance and was maintained with care. Peltenburg corresponded with scholars in several countries, and like De Stoppelaar he was a regular visitor to the International Congresses of Orientalists.

In a continuous development of more than half a century, Brill had acquired a unique position as a publisher of international Oriental studies. Scholars in all quarters of Europe, in Asia, and in America were familiar with the name of Brill and knew the way to the Oude Rijn. On the basis of its reputation, the publishing house was offered all kinds of manuscripts; moreover, as a facilitator of scholarship it also initiated publications by itself. Peltenburg paraded his showpiece in front of the journalist: *the Encyclopaedia of Islam*, the second volume of which was to appear that year in German, French, and English. "In England I sold the publication to Luzac & Co. in London, in Germany to Otto Harrassowitz in Leipzig, in France to Aug. Picard in Paris." The encyclopedia was not just a standard work consulted by all specialists and acquired by all libraries throughout the world. The publication also confirmed the central role of the publisher, for many articles contained references to books that had been or would be published by Brill.

Peltenburg emphasized that Brill specialized in projects requiring a long commitment. An international publisher serving the scholarly world should have the courage to look beyond short-term profits. The books produced by Brill had a much lower turnover rate than publications for the domestic market. Sales were primarily made to libraries and institutions abroad. Often, it took years for a print run to sell out, and only in the long term did investments pay off: "For again and again, a good book on our publishing list turns out to be indispensable in the scholarly world."

The Latter Days of the Patriarch

Brusse had seen Peltenburg in his heyday, but soon afterward dark clouds began to gather on the horizon. The crash of the stock exchange in November 1929 marked the start of a worldwide economic crisis, that would continue into the first half of the thirties. Inevitably, the collapse of the economy affected Brill, too. Whereas for 1931 a substantial profit of *f* 61,000 could still be recorded, by 1933 this had dropped to *f* 24,000. In the intervening years, the turnover of all business segments had decreased alarmingly. In 1934 the printing shop was often at a standstill for lack of work.

Peltenburg was an avowed opponent of mechanized typesetting and had resisted the introduction of typesetting machines for many years. Already before the First World War the Leiden firm of Sijthoff had twelve typesetting machines in operation, but these innovations were banned at Brill: "As long as I live, no typesetting machine in my business," the old gentleman was wont to say.[26] Nevertheless, in order to remain competitive in the early 1930s, Peltenburg could no longer charge the expensive manual typesetting to his customers: he was forced to sell his handmade products for the much lower rate of mechanized typesetting. Eventually he relented, and despite his motto the first typesetting machine made its entrance at Brill at the beginning of 1934.

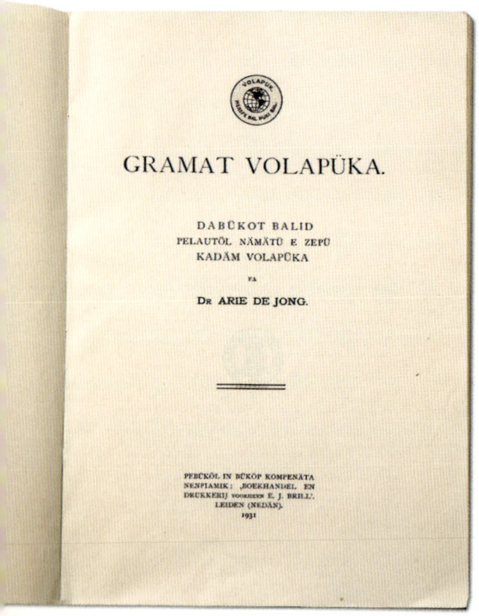

A. de Jong, *Gramat Volapuka* (1931). In 1888 the German priest Johann Martin Schleyer had a dream in which he was ordered by God to devise an international artificial language. He decided to annul the Babylonian confusion of tongues and created Volapük. This first artificial language was not really a success: the number of speakers was small, and the usual quarrels and schisms arose among them. In 1931 Dr. Arie de Jong, with the consent of leading Volapük adepts, wrote a simplified grammar that earned the language some support in the Netherlands and Germany. The Nazis, however, regarded Volapük and Esperanto as tendencies that ran counter to the "Folk" and suppressed the artificial languages. Nowadays it appears that Volapük is still spoken by about twenty people. ULA

But the single machine, long overdue, was an inadequate response to the crisis—it was too little and too late.

On December 28, 1933, Peltenburg celebrated his eightieth birthday with a well-attended reception at Huize Bruyns in Leiden. The man of the hour was honored with presents and speeches. Prominent scholars and publishers came to congratulate him, and the assembled Vigilante Patrol of Oegstgeest turned out to bring a salute to its commanding officer. The guests paid homage to Peltenburg, and the speakers praised the man who at an advanced age was still able to manage a large company. On behalf of the supervisory directors, F. C. Wieder, chairman of the board and librarian of Leiden University, presented him with a divan—perhaps a discreet hint that he should take things a little bit easier. In his speech Snouck Hurgronje conferred on Peltenburg the honorary title of "oldest Orientalist" in the Netherlands, in which category Snouck himself by now ranked second.[27]

After all those accolades, Peltenburg was honorably dismissed as of July 1, 1934. For more than thirty years, he had managed Brill in good times and bad, only to be confronted in his latter days by a decline that was beyond his power to repair. It was intended that the ex-director would stay on as a consultant, but his time had come. Just three months later, on October 7, 1934, Cornelis Peltenburg died after a six-week-long illness. His name lives on at Brill in the Peltenburg Pension Fund, which was established a few years after his death by a considerable bequest from his estate.[28] Posthumously, Peltenburg created a lasting rapprochement between himself and the employees of Brill: to this day the Peltenburg Fund serves as the company's pension plan.

Theunis Folkers: Making the Best of Bad Times, 1934-1945

The Successor

Just as Peltenburg only abandoned his resistance to mechanized typesetting during his final months as director, he also postponed the matter of his succession to the last moment. In all those years he had not succeeded in finding a replacement, so that in May 1934 a suitable candidate was sought outside the company. Consequently, Theunis Folkers succeeded Peltenburg as director on July 1 of that year.[29]

Folkers, born in the northern city of Groningen in 1879, was well prepared for the publishing trade. At the age of seventeen he had gone into service with the firm of Noordhoff in his hometown, where he continued to work until 1914. He then got a job with the publishing house of Martinus Nijhoff in The Hague, where in due course he worked his way up to department head. Folkers, an energetic doer with modern views, took over the management of Brill at its lowest ebb. With his keen eye for new opportunities, he was the right man to put the company back on its feet again.

The new director was a good manager, but he was not entirely free of vanity. He was, for instance, unable to resist the temptation to incorporate his own initials into the publisher's device, which featured the initials "E. J. B." Such a personal appropriation of the name of Brill would have been unthinkable under his predecessor, nor did the thought ever enter the minds of his successors.

Machines and Advertising

Folkers's arrival brought the winds of change to the Oude Rijn. At Brill he encountered a lot of old-fashioned stuffiness, which he could not tolerate very well and which the company could no longer afford in this difficult time. For a start, the new director cleared out the five attic storerooms, where the quantity of books had reached gigantic proportions. He ordered an inventory of the Oriental antiquarian bookshop, which turned out to contain works in as many as eighty-seven different languages. Folkers would have preferred to close down the ailing division, but the supervisory

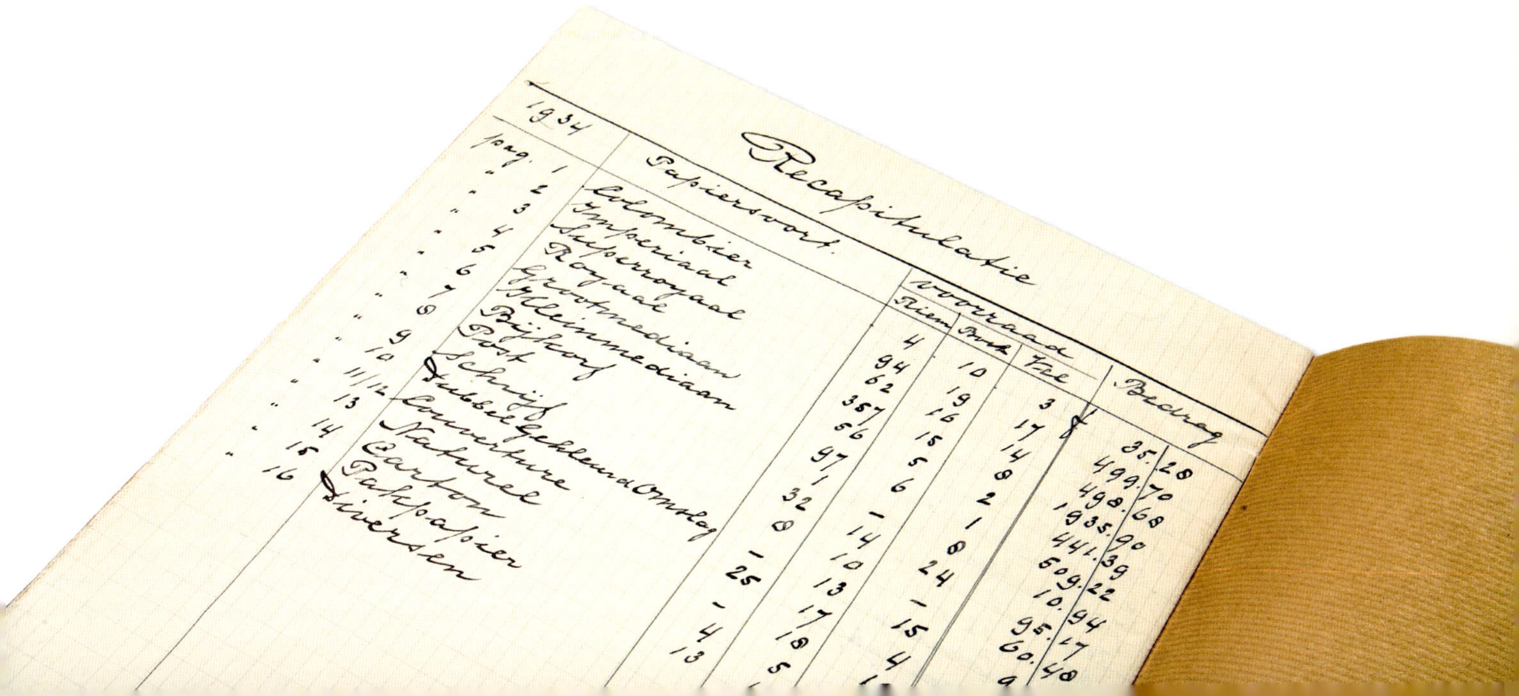

The accounts of Brill's paper stock in 1934: a prosaic aspect of the business enlivened by poetic names such as Colombier, Imperiaal, Grootmediaan, and Bijkorf. BA/ULA

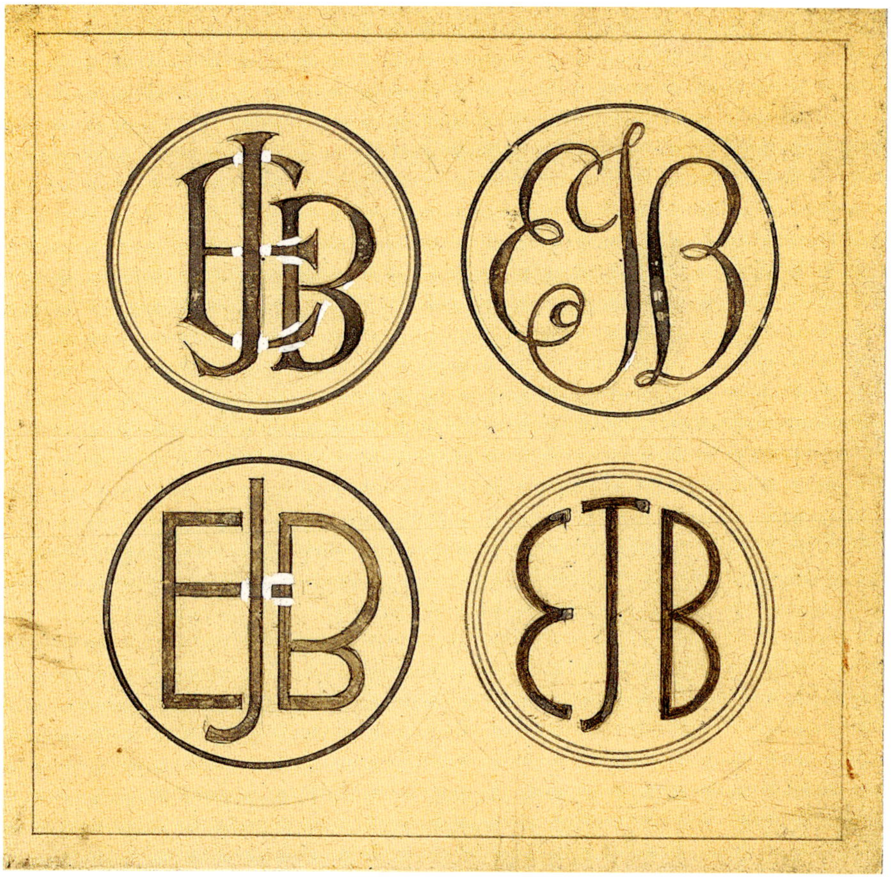

In the process of modernizing the business, Folkers abolished the drop vignette that had been in use since 1909. In 1936 he introduced the succinct "signet ring vignette" with the initials "E. J. B." The artist Jan van Krimpen (1892-1958) designed four versions. The vignette with the flourishes in the top right corner was selected, but the variant in the bottom left was also regularly used. Folkers supplemented these two vignettes with his own initials "T. F.," which were removed after his resignation in 1947. Brill Coll.

board rejected this proposal in 1935. And it was a good thing too, because in 1939 the antiquarian bookshop suddenly justified its existence by selling a collection of books worth *f* 30,000 to a Japanese institution.

The print works and composing room were the greatest sources of concern to Folkers. He solicited bids from other printers for some books printed by Brill, and came to the disagreeable conclusion that printing costs at his own firm were well over a third higher than elsewhere—"indeed, a serious state of affairs." The firm had not kept pace with current market rates for printing because Brill's print works received its orders mainly from its own publishing establishment. The high price level was chiefly due to the high labor costs in the composing room.

In part this was inevitable, for books in unusual languages had to be manually typeset. But Folkers argued that ordinary typesetting should be mechanized as much as possible, in order to reduce the cost of labor. In 1935 he purchased two new typesetting machines, and a year later a third one. The supervisory directors authorized him to spend no less than *f* 60,000 on new machinery, which also enabled him to replace the obsolete equipment of the print works. These investments were possible owing to the fact that in 1934 the share capital of Brill had been raised from *f* 100,000 to *f* 150,000. Folkers wanted to acquire more machines, but the building on the Oude Rijn was unsuitable for further expansion.

Such drastic modernization would not have pleased Peltenburg, but he was no longer around to witness it. Another important innovation was the advertising department created by the new director: "We should not only be able to make a book, but we should also be able to sell it." Folkers was firmly convinced of the need for advertising, which had been neglected at Brill. New as well as older publications should constantly be brought to the notice of the public in order to promote their sale.[30]

Folkers was also the first director to use 1683—the year in which the firm of Luchtmans was founded—as a marketing strategy that emphasized the long history of the publishing house. Thus, in 1937 Brill issued a new and lavishly executed catalog of its Oriental publishing list. The proud title was, in full, *Catalogue de Fonds de la Librairie Orientale E. J. Brill. Maison fondée en 1683*. Henceforth the date of foundation was also mentioned in other publications.

Theunis Folkers behind his desk in the boardroom of Brill (1939).

From the Abyss to the Nile

In 1935 the firm's fortunes took a turn for the better. The worst of the crisis had passed and Folkers's innovations began to pay off. The publishing establishment revived, the print works received more work, and sales also increased perceptibly. The hesitant recovery continued in 1936, and afterward the upward trend was unmistakable. The order quantities were at times so large that employees could hardly cope with the work. A double-shift system was even introduced so that the typesetting machines could be kept in operation from 6 a.m until 8 p.m. (the aim being, according to the pragmatic Folkers, to get the most out of the machines without coming into conflict with the Factory Act).

While turnover in 1934 still amounted to *f* 132,000, by 1939 it had increased to *f* 294,626, more than doubling over six years. The tone of Folkers's reports at the annual shareholders' meeting became more and more jubilant. Year after year he was able to announce increasing results in the establishment known as "The Gilded Turk," where the shareholders traditionally met on a Thursday in June. With the passing of the first generation of shareholders the original shares had changed hands, while in 1934 ten new shares had been issued with a total value of *f* 50,000. Even so, the supervisory directors and shareholders were still old acquaintances of the Brill firm or descendants and relatives of the former directors. Thirty years after the deaths of Van Oordt and De Stoppelaar, their names lived on in the inner circle of Brill's intimates.

The meetings at "The Gilded Turk" must have been pleasant, all the more so as the dividends were high: from 1935 until 1939, 25% was paid out every year. The director would propose the percentage and the supervisory directors, themselves shareholders by definition, had to approve it. Folkers took pains to please his shareholders and evidently wanted to measure up to his predecessor, who had spoiled them for years with high dividends. The figures for 1934, the first year of his management, seem somewhat flattered by the capital-injection of ten new shares; while the company was still suffering from the crisis and turnover stuck at a meagre *f* 132,000, profit was set at *f* 54,000 and dividend at 30%.

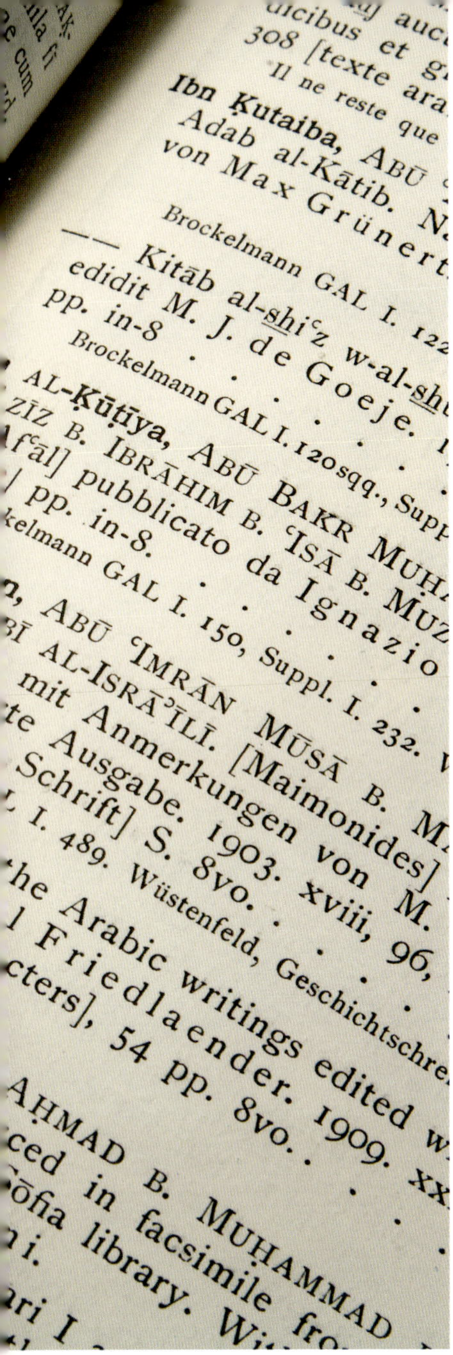

Page from the *Catalogue de Fonds de la Librairie Orientale E. J. Brill. Maison fondée en 1683*. The publishing list of Orientalia (1937) had a cover of blue pseudo-velvet and was illustrated with photographs of scholars from home and abroad. BA/ULA

Brill's business was booming during the last years of the period between the wars. In 1938 the company purchased its first automobile, transporting itself into Modern Times. However, its old reputation remained the most important vehicle of the firm, taking it to faraway Egypt in that same year: the company was commissioned to execute the catalog for a large exhibition that was held in Cairo in 1938. A large number of the titles listed in the catalog had been published by Brill and were on display in book form during the exhibition. This presentation on the banks of the Nile River resulted in an order of royal proportions, as King Farouk I of Egypt decided to purchase all of Brill's publications for his private library.[31]

The Harvest of 1936

Nowadays Brill publishes some six hundred titles annually, apart from well over a hundred learned journals. Before the war, the scope of production was much easier to survey, with an average of about thirty titles a year. A cross section of the year 1936 reveals the program of the publishing house at that time.

In this year the fourth and last volume of the *Encyclopaedia of Islam* was published, a stout volume with 1,200 pages of print. A supplementary volume including a table of contents was in preparation and was scheduled to appear in 1938. By this time Folkers already had concluded an agreement with the publishing house of Kegan Paul in London, in order to bring out an abridged English edition of the encyclopedia.[32] In 1936, the first volume of the *Concordance et indices de la tradition musulmane* was published, initiated by the Leiden Arabist A. J. Wensinck and continued by others; the eighth and last volume of this important series was to appear in 1988. T. Huitema made a contribution to the study of Islam with his *Voorspraak (Shafā'a) in den Islam*. At the same time, preparations were being made for A. Jeffery's *Materials for the History of the Text of the Qur'ān*, the first volume of which would be published in 1937.

In the field of Egyptology W. A. van Leer's *Egyptische Oudheden* was published, while Assyriology was represented by a German study of J. G. Lautner on labor contracts in Ancient Babylon, conserved in clay tablets (*Altbabylonische Personenmiete und Erntearbeiterverträge*). From the Far East came *Japanese Music* by S. Katsumi, while K. S. J. M. de Vreese called attention to the ancient wisdom of Kashmir in his *Nilamata, or the Teachings of Nila*.

The flow of publications resulting from scientific expeditions conducted in the beginning of the century steadily continued in 1936. Two installments of the ongoing saga of Siboga were published (G. Stiasny-Wijnhoff, *Die Polystilifera der Siboga-Expedition*, on sea worms, and L. Döderein, *Die Asteriden der Siboga Expedition*, on starfish). Also, L. F. de Beaufort edited the eighteenth volume of *Nova Guinea: résultats de l'expédition scientifique neérlandaise*. A. A. Beekman stayed closer to home, exploring Dutch geography in his *Lijst der aardrijkskundige namen van Nederland*, while R. Hennig described in his *Terrae Incognitae* the voyages of discovery from the era prior to Columbus.

Antiquity provided two titles in 1936. S. Peppink devoted a philological study to the "The Scholarly Banquet," a dialogue by the second-century c.e. Greek author Athenaeus (*Observationes in Athenaei Deipnosophistas*); in addition, the classical historian R. J. Forbes published a book with the rather intriguing title *Bitumen and Petroleum in Antiquity*. In the field of Dutch history, two books appeared that were somewhat related

R. Hennig, *Terrae incognitae. Eine Zusammenstellung und kritische Bewertung der vorkolumbischen Entdeckungsreisen.* Drawing on all kinds of sources, the historian Hennig described forgotten voyages of discovery in antiquity and the Middle Ages. The work was published in four volumes by Brill between 1936 and 1939 and was reprinted between 1944 and 1956. ULA

with regard to period and subject matter: a study of the impact of Spinoza and Grotius on international law, and a biography of the Amsterdam Jewish heretic Uriël da Costa (respectively J. Coert, *Spinoza en Grotius met betrekking tot het volkenrecht*, and A. M. Vaz Dias, *Uriël da Costa: nieuwe bijdrage tot diens levensgeschiedenis*).

Contemporary history was given its due with J. de Jongh's study of the women's rights movement (*Documentatie van de geschiedenis der vrouw en der vrouwenbeweging*), as did P. L. Dubourcq's treatise on engrained myths about money, as opposed to the hard facts of the stuff (*Schijn en wezen rondom geld*). V. van Wijk operated in the field of the history of religion and described the cult of the Virgin Mary (*De naam Maria: over zijn beteekenis en velerlei vormen, zijn verspreiding en vereering*). Finally, this year saw the ninth impression of a German edition of Goethe's *Faust*. The list of books for the year 1936 is not complete, but it offers a fairly representative sample of Brill's publications during this period.

The Occupation

On May 3, 1940, the supervisory board of Brill assembled in the presence of Folkers. The director presented the figures for the financial year 1939, which once again showed a satisfying increase. The net profit amounted to *f* 76,981.41, on the basis of which he proposed to fix the dividend at 26%. The prospects for 1940 were very favorable, at least in his view. Of course the international situation was tense; Germany had invaded Poland in 1939 and was now at war with England and France. However, due to the neutrality of the Netherlands, the company was able to take advantage of this constellation. German publishers found themselves cut off from their markets in England and France, and wanted to offset this loss by engaging Brill as an intermediary. The Soviet Union, at that time still an ally of Nazi Germany, had to contend with similar difficulties and had requested that Folkers take care of its entire importation of French and English books. He already had established a special export department with a view to these new activities.[33]

A week later the Germans invaded the Netherlands, and all of a sudden the world looked entirely different. This was noticeable at the shareholders' meeting of July 6, 1940,

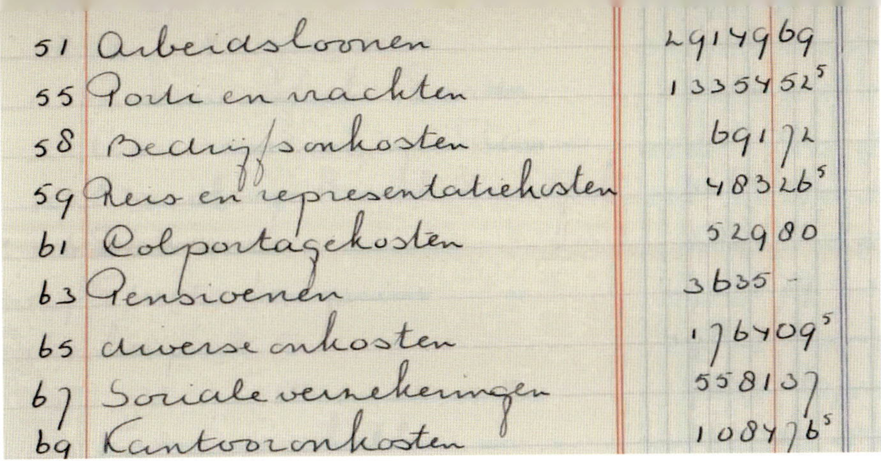

51	Arbeidsloonen	2914969
55	Porti en vrachten	1335452^5
58	Bedrijfsonkosten	69172
59	Reis en representatiekosten	48326^5
61	Colportagekosten	52980
63	Pensioenen	3635 -
65	diverse onkosten	176409^5
67	Sociale verzekeringen	558137
69	Kantooronkosten	108476^5

Entries on the balance sheet of 1940.

BA/ULA

at which Folkers could not help sounding pessimistic notes: "Unfortunately, the war that broke out in May has also hit our company badly, as all exports have been brought to a complete standstill." The promising export department became defunct even before it had been able to prove itself. In these circumstances, the usual dividend could not be paid out and Folkers requested the shareholders to settle for 5%, instead of the 26% he initially had in mind for them. Foreign debtors were unable to pay their invoices, there was no money coming in, and it was of vital importance to keep sufficient cash in the company.[34]

From May until September the company was in a state of acute paralysis, but in the last quarter of the year a hesitant recovery began. Ultimately, the turnover for 1940 amounted to *f* 220,000, about a quarter less than in 1939. In spite of the circumstances of war, however, the turnover rose to *f* 270,000 in 1941. Folkers strained every nerve "to see the company and its full staff ... through these bad times."[35] He started with a series of schoolbooks for the domestic market, in order to compensate for the loss of foreign sales. Thanks to yearbooks and supplemental works, the publishing house was able to achieve its usual production of thirty titles a year. The print works was running at full capacity, while most competitors were forced to introduce a shorter working week.

In 1941 the occupier rationed paper, but Folkers succeeded in expanding the allocation for Brill. He organized a company canteen that daily supplied a hot meal to the workers. The new rulers interfered in the management of the business in all sorts

A. J. de Lorm and G. L. Tichelman, *Beeldende kunst der Bataks* [Art of the Bataks; 1941]. Occasionally, echoes of the war resounded in scholarly publications. "Indeed, the need for a book such as the present one . . . gives rise to joy," stated the introduction by Schrieke, director of the department of ethnography at the Colonial Museum in Amsterdam. He alluded to the fact that in 1941 the Dutch East Indies were still governed in the name of Queen Wilhelmina. His introduction was followed by that of the authors, who sought to find an explanation for the defeat of the Netherlands: "a too strongly intensified individualism has resulted in too strong a differentiation, so that the sense of the unity of life has been lost." This metaphysical diagnosis could hardly have worried the occupier. In a later paragraph, however, the authors spoke about the "French expressionism of the postwar years, inspired by the Negroes' plastic expressions, which we appreciate from an artistic point of view." Rather surprising remarks in a time when expressionism was labeled by the German authorities as "degenerate art," and jazz was banned as decadent "Jewish-Anglo-Saxon Negro music." ULA

of ways—the purchase of lead was subject to restrictions, machines were requisitioned, electricity was only sparsely available, coal for heating could hardly be obtained, and employees were in danger of being called up for the *Arbeitseinsatz* (forced labor) in Germany. To make matters worse, the occupier introduced a tax on profits of 50%, and within the company a representative of the National Labor Front had been appointed as an informant.

Folkers was constantly engaged in parrying these attacks: "Nothing goes smoothly any longer as it did in the past, and everything must be kept going with great effort. Government interference is such that practically everything is under restriction, and one can only achieve something by circumventing these obstacles or by practicing friendly relations."[36] By his own account, Folkers had become rather proficient in that art. It prompted him for instance to make a visit to the *Reichskommissariat* in The Hague, in order to protect his employees from forced labor in Germany.

Steersmanship

Folkers's position was that of what the Dutch call a "wartime mayor": he had to cooperate with the German occupying authorities, but at the same time he used his influence to protect and look after his own people. He had to compromise in order to steer the company through dangerous waters, but it is hard to avoid the impression that on occasion he sailed a little too close to the wind. Traditionally Brill did a lot of business with Germany, and there always had been many German books on the publishing list. From 1941 onwards, with the loss of trading relations with other countries, Germany became more and more important as a market. An additional consequence of the occupation was that the entire territory of "Greater Germany" now belonged to Brill's domestic market.

Folkers occasionally traveled to Germany in order to promote sales and to secure new projects. The contacts he made resulted in publications such as an Indological work commissioned by the University of Marburg and an extremely successful *Handwörterbuch des Islam* (an abridged version of the *Encyclopaedia* of that name). Scholarly publications of this kind formed an extension of Brill's prewar publishing program, and these transactions were unsullied by political factors. Supplying books to German institutions proved to be highly profitable. In some cases, libraries had to be restocked as a result of wartime damage. The bombed-out Bavarian State Library in Munich turned out to be an excellent customer. With a little good will, such deals could be regarded as a pragmatic attempt to make the most of the circumstances. Thanks to the sharply increased demand among German libraries, Brill's antiquarian bookshop experienced golden years.

A souvenir from the war: a bullet found among documents from the occupation period in the Brill Archive. BA/ULA

In some cases, however, Folkers's pragmatism inclined him toward a cynical or perhaps naïve opportunism. For example, he accepted an order from the Interpreters' Bureau in Berlin for a Russian textbook with a print run of 15,000 copies. For the Language Press, also in Berlin, he printed 5,000 copies of a manual which trained German officers to distinguish the insignia and weapons of the Russian army, among other things. The commissioning institutions were directly affiliated with the German government, and indirectly these were orders for the German army. Commissioned by the *Oostinstituut* in occupied Holland, Folkers produced a trilingual dictionary in

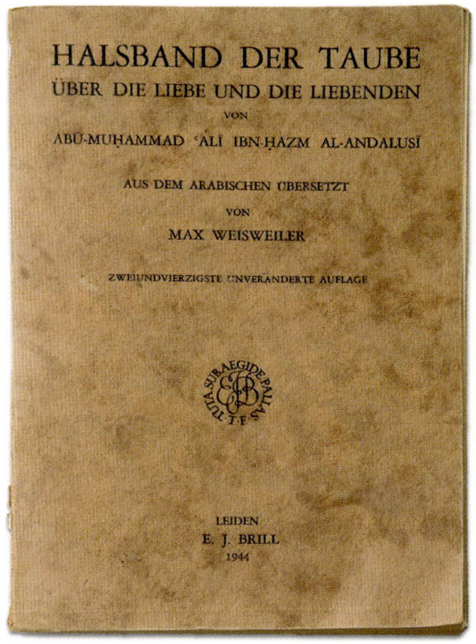

Abu Muhammad 'Ali Ibn Hazim, *Halsband der Taube*. Translated by M. Weisweiler (1944). Not all German scholarly books were ideologically colored under the Third Reich. The Orientalist Weisweiler was especially known as an expert on Arab bookbindings, for which he devised a typology. In addition to fairy tales he translated one of the most famous texts in Arabic literature: the book on love and lovers, the *Tawq al-hamâma*—that is, *The Ring of the Dove*. Not only the content, but also the origin of this book is unique: it is preserved in a single manuscript that was purchased in Istanbul in the middle of the seventeenth century by the Dutch ambassador Levinus Warner. Since 1665 the manuscript has been kept in the Legatum Warnerianum of the Leiden University Library. When the book was first published by Brill in 1942, Folkers had no great expectations. To his surprise it turned out to be the bestseller of the year, and in no time at all 17,000 copies were sold in Germany. The copy shown here is identified on the cover as the "forty-second unchanged edition," but only the last few editions had been published by Brill. ULA

Russian, German, and Dutch with a print run of 10,000 copies, 3,000 of which the publisher was allowed to distribute himself. From the same customer came an order for a multilingual dictionary (Dutch-German-Russian-Ukrainian-Polish) in a print run of 5,500 copies.[37] The *Oostinstituut* was in fact the Nazi authority that sought to recruit "Aryan" farmers in the Netherlands for settlement in the "Slavic East." Folkers remained vague about such customers and referred to the work as "printing for third parties." He did not worry all that much about the moral aspects of collaboration: "Given current circumstances, these will undoubtedly turn out to be bestsellers. I have high hopes for them."[38]

Folkers's efforts resulted in Brill's turnover rising to unprecedented heights during the war years. In 1942 it increased to *f* 447,000 and in 1943 to *f* 579,000, surpassing the magic mark of half a million guilders for the first time in the firm's history. The turnover of 1944 was on the same order of magnitude, doubling the record set in 1939, just before the war. The net profit amounted to *f* 94,956 in 1942, and in 1943 it even totaled *f* 140,000. The shareholders paid tribute to the director, who in spite of bad times had found ways of achieving such brilliant results.[39] The consequence of Folkers's policy, however, was that the liquid assets within the company were to a large extent of German origin. After the liberation this would cause problems, because such funds were then regarded as "enemy money."

Folkers was unable to foresee this, although by the end of 1943 he did foresee that Germany would lose the war. On behalf of the supervisory directors, he wrote a memorandum in which he outlined Brill's postwar development. He envisioned a future in which Brill would act as intermediary between "the Germans and the English." His list of possible projects gave rise to a prediction that the company would become at least three times as big after the war—a forecast that would be realized.[40] As of July 1, 1944, Folkers had been employed for ten years, and his appointment was prolonged for five years. Indeed, he would be sixty-five years old soon, but the supervisory directors requested him to stay on until he had found a successor. Things would turn out quite differently, however.

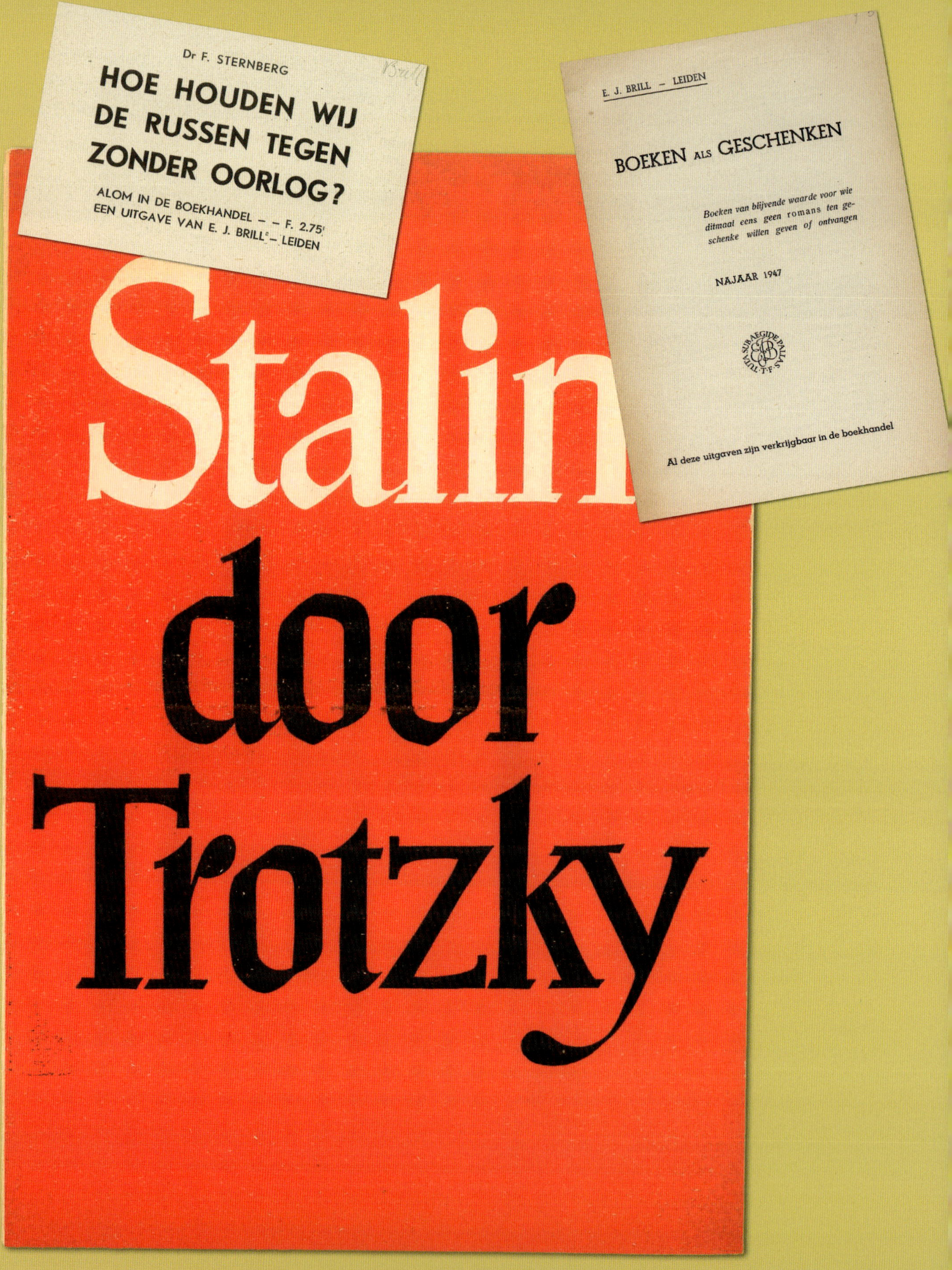
Dr F. STERNBERG
HOE HOUDEN WIJ DE RUSSEN TEGEN ZONDER OORLOG?
ALOM IN DE BOEKHANDEL — — F. 2.75
EEN UITGAVE VAN E. J. BRILL — LEIDEN
E. J. BRILL — LEIDEN
BOEKEN ALS GESCHENKEN
Boeken van blijvende waarde voor wie ditmaal eens geen romans ten geschenke willen geven of ontvangen
NAJAAR 1947
TUTA SUB AEGIDE PALLAS
Al deze uitgaven zijn verkrijgbaar in de boekhandel
Stalin
door
Trotzky

THE EXPANDING UNIVERSE OF BRILL, 1945-2008

Aftermath of War and Reconstruction: Nicolaas Wilhelmus Posthumus, 1947-1958

Exit Folkers

Shortly after the liberation of the Netherlands, a national investigation into political and economic collaboration was initiated. For this purpose special police agencies were created at the local level: the Political Investigation Departments focused on political suspects, and the Political Investigation Departments on Collaboration (PIDCs) targeted economic offenses.

In April 1946 the Leiden PIDC seized Brill's accounts and established the presence of enemy moneys in the company. Folkers's management during the war was regarded by the PIDC as collaboration with the occupier. The matter was considered so serious that in September the director was arrested, a measure that was rather easily carried out in those days. On May 23, 1947, the Purging Board for the Publishing Trade deprived Folkers of the right to hold a managerial post in publishing for a period of two years. Moreover, in addition to this sentence he was fined *f* 10,000. Folkers took the view that the fine should be paid by the company, but it rejected responsibility: the director had been sentenced as a private person and the N.V. Brill was "as such entirely outside the legal proceedings."[1]

On September 23, the sentence of the Purging Board was confirmed by the Central Purging Board for Trade and Industry, three days before Folkers reached the age of sixty-eight. At his own request, he was dismissed as of January 1, 1948; under the circumstances it was not possible to speak of the dismissal as "honorable." By then Folkers had become seriously ill, and he would die three years later. For a man who had committed himself heart and soul to Brill, it was a raw deal to have to finish his career and his life in this way. Undoubtedly he had moved in the twilight zone of collaboration during the war, but the same can be said of a large part of the Dutch business community.

Shades of Gray

To what extent was Folkers "on the wrong side?" According to the criteria of the Special Administration of Criminal Justice, "the printing and/or publishing of German propaganda material and/or National Socialist writings" counted as a criminal offense.[2] Folkers had executed orders for German and pro-German agencies, but dictionaries and grammars did not fall into the proscribed categories. Yet he had indeed "rendered assistance to the enemy while holding a managerial post," as it was formulated in the

Signs of the times from the years shortly after the Second World War. In 1948 Brill published the Dutch translation of Trotsky's biography of Stalin. A controversial book, not only because of its disclosures about Stalin, but also because Trotsky, living in Mexico at the time, was murdered by a henchman of the Russian secret service while writing it. Brill's 1947 flyer in the top right corner is an attempt at a new marketing strategy: "Don't always give a flimsy novel as a present. Try a solid book for a change, which is a joy forever." In 1948 Brill published the Dutch translation of *How to stop the Russians without war* by the American author Fritz Sternberg (flyer in the left corner). According to Sternberg, a united Europe was the best way to stop the Russians and prevent a nuclear war. At the beginning of the fifties this idea would also be the foundation of the European Economic Community, later the European Union. BA/ULA

Decree on the Purging of Trade and Industry of September 3, 1945. According to the same decree, those who had been found guilty of this offense could be deprived of the right to hold a managerial post.[3] On the basis of this general directive, one must conclude that Folkers was duly punished.

Actually, his punishment was made heavier by the stigma of "having been on the wrong side" that accompanied the sentence pronounced by the Purging Board. The shades of gray in the twilight zone of economic collaboration eluded public opinion, which until long after the war phrased its judgments in unambiguous terms of "right" or "wrong." Folkers had committed indiscretions during the occupation, but he was certainly not a war criminal. Membership in the Dutch National Socialist Movement or related organizations was not at issue. His offenses were minor in comparison with other examples of collaboration. In his ambition to make the N.V. Brill great, he had compromised a little too much.

Folkers's attitude during the occupation is not above criticism, but neither is the conduct of the Special Administration of Criminal Justice. The "purging" of the business community in particular was a half-hearted performance. From the start, the exigencies of postwar reconstruction were at odds with the settlement of the war record. Folkers was one of the many who were accused of economic collaboration, given the 30,000 files compiled by the PIDCs within a short time. He was one of the few who were sentenced, since two-thirds of the cases were never settled by the overburdened Purging Boards. The Special Administration of Criminal Justice frequently carried out its work in an arbitrary fashion, while the PIDCs drew much criticism for their amateurish performance. After the peak year of 1947, the purge fizzled out, and in the summer of 1948 the PIDCs were discontinued.[4]

Master typesetter Arie Visser at work. Photograph circa 1950. BA/ULA

To the right of the Leiden Gravensteen is a charming little gate, the former entrance to the home of the headmaster of the Latin School. The gate was constructed in 1613 by the municipal stonemason Willem Claesz van (N)Es. In the tympanum the words *TUTA EST ÆGIDE PALLAS* are chiseled, indicating that Pallas, the goddess of learning, is safe behind her shield. Perhaps this is the origin of the eighteenth-century motto of Luchtmans that was later adopted by Brill.

Professor Publisher

As a replacement for the arrested Folkers, Nicolaas Wilhelmus Posthumus, member of the supervisory board, was appointed interim director on September 16, 1946. Posthumus (1880-1960) was a prominent figure in Dutch intellectual life. He was the pioneer of economic and social history, a new discipline within the domain of historical science, and one of the leading intellectuals of the country during the period between the wars. In 1913 he was appointed the first professor of economic history at the Netherlands Business College in Rotterdam, the precursor of the present Erasmus University; in 1922 he switched over to the University of Amsterdam, where a similar chair was established. His taste for economic history was innate, but it may have been furthered by the historical materialism that he imbued during his Marxist early years. His historical interest was especially focused on Leiden and the textile industry for which the city was famous in the seventeenth and eighteenth centuries. He published both a six-volume collection of sources and a two-volume history on the subject.[5]

Besides being a prolific scholar, Posthumus was an indefatigable organizer, founder of several institutions that are in existence to this day. In 1914 he founded the Netherlands Economic History Archive in The Hague, of which he served as director until 1948 and as chairman of the board of governors until his death in 1960. In 1935 he was the man behind the foundation of the International Institute of Social History in Amsterdam, for which he acquired, among other things, the famous archives of Karl Marx and Friedrich Engels. In 1945 he was involved in the foundation of the National Institute for War Documentation and in 1947, together with the historian Jan Romein, he was among the spiritual fathers of the new Faculty of Political and Social Sciences in Amsterdam. Through his agency, the Institute for the Middle and Far East was formed at the University of Amsterdam in 1956. This last institution ensued from his activity at Brill; in previous years the Arab world had been beyond his scope.

N. W. Posthumus in professorial gown (1947). Portrait by Edgar Fernhout. ULA/SC

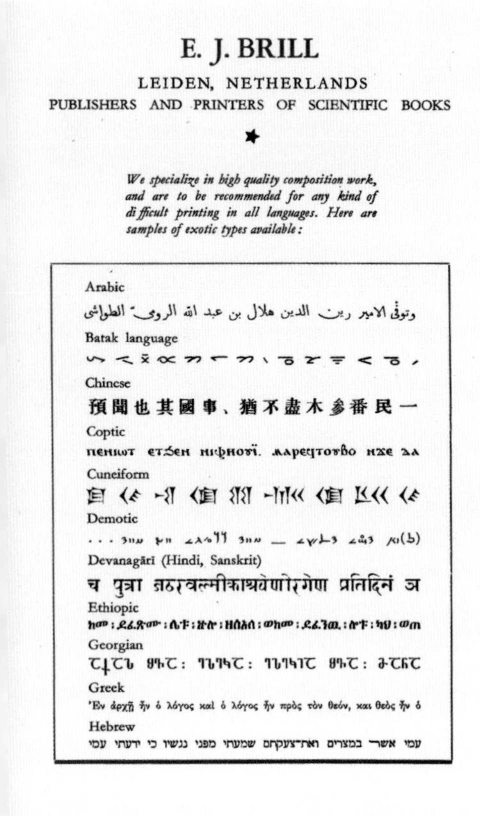

Type samples from Brill in the fifties.

Brill Coll.

Posthumus first got in touch with Brill in the middle of the thirties. He usually published his works with Nijhoff in The Hague, where Folkers was employed as manager until 1934. In 1936, Folkers persuaded him to have the *Yearbook* of the Netherlands Economic History Archive published at Brill henceforth. The *International Review of Social History*, the journal of the new International Institute for Social History, was also placed with Brill in 1936. Posthumus, who during the occupation resigned as professor, published his *History of Commodity Prices in the Netherlands* with Brill in 1943. In the same year he took a seat on the supervisory board of the company, where a vacancy had arisen as a result of the death of F. C. Wieder.

In 1949, shortly before his sixty-ninth birthday, Posthumus was accorded emeritus status as a professor. Almost at the same time, on March 12, 1949, his interim capacity at Brill was converted into a full directorship. Over the past few years the professor had lost his heart to Brill, and he cheerfully began his new career as a publisher. Posthumus was not an unworldly scholar; on the contrary, he had keen business acumen and knew what he wanted. With his prestige and his contacts in the scholarly world, he was just the man to give shape to the postwar reconstruction of Brill. F. C. Wieder Jr., the son of the former chairman of the supervisory board, was appointed deputy director and would succeed him in the future.

In addition to the daily affairs he had to attend to, Posthumus had the intention of committing the history of Brill to paper. He had the sources close at hand, since in those days the company archive was still located in the premises on the Oude Rijn. Brill could not have wished for a more suitable historiographer. Unfortunately, the historian had to give way to the director, who had his hands more than full with the management of the firm.[6]

Aftermath

In the autumn of 1947, Posthumus and Willem van Oordt, since 1943 chairman of the supervisory board, also had to answer to the Purging Board for the Publishing Trade. In their capacity as supervisory directors they were charged with reprehensible negligence—in other words, they should have rapped Folkers over the knuckles when he accepted compromising orders. In the event of their conviction by the Purging Board, they too would have had to resign their positions at Brill. They were able to make a reasonable case that they had known nothing about Folkers's activities and were both acquitted.

At the shareholders' meeting of 1946, Posthumus sought to restore some luster to the besmirched blazon of Brill. He stated that Folkers had cleverly frustrated an attempt by the *Wehrmacht* to use the print works for its publications. Furthermore, he declared, "In many other ways that I am aware of, the Germans were prevented from carrying out plans that were harmful for our N.V." He did not enter into details, but he did mention the supply of money and paper to the resistance.[7]

In 1949 there was an unpleasant aftermath to the Folkers affair. While administering the seized accounts, the Financial Investigation Service found that the former director had failed to declare an amount of some fifty thousand guilders as enemy money. In 1945 a law had come into force obliging businesses to register moneys of German origin. By using bookkeeping tricks, Folkers had tried to launder this money so that it could be retained in the company. At the end of 1944, he had accepted an order from the *Reichsarbeitschaft Turkestan* in Dresden—yet another agency of dubious affiliation—for the production of an atlas. The client had given an advance of nearly *f* 200,000, while Brill's invoice had amounted to no more than *f* 150,000. Either Folkers had neglected to refund the remainder of the advance, or he had conveniently assumed that his client had kicked the bucket during the fall of the Third Reich.

This money was now claimed by the Custody Institute, which was charged with the financial settlement of war issues. Together with other items and a heavy fine of 25%, the initial claim threatened to rise to *f* 78,000. Posthumus lodged a protest against this fine, which was imposed because Brill had been negligent in declaring enemy moneys. His plea was that Folkers had acted on his own initiative at the time, ignoring the supervisory directors; afterwards it had been impossible to make a declaration, since the accounts had been seized by the PIDC. He proceeded to argue that Brill "as a publishing firm enjoys a worldwide reputation, is of high standing, and is generally known throughout the international scholarly world . . . In all of Western Europe there is not a print works and publishing house to be found that is able to print in thirty-three languages as Brill does. It is therefore also a matter of cultural importance for our country itself, that Brill's vitality should not be affected too much by a drastic measure."

The Custody Institute duly acknowledged Brill's high standing and proved itself willing to spare the vitality of the company. The fine was remitted and the final claim was fixed at *f* 57,000. Two-thirds of this amount could be balanced against the company's capital gains tax, which Brill had overpaid in the past few years. A three-year payment plan would take care of the remainder.[8]

"Roll of honor" from 1953, with the names of 18 employees who since 1940 had celebrated their fiftieth, fortieth, or twenty-fifth anniversary at Brill. BA/ULA

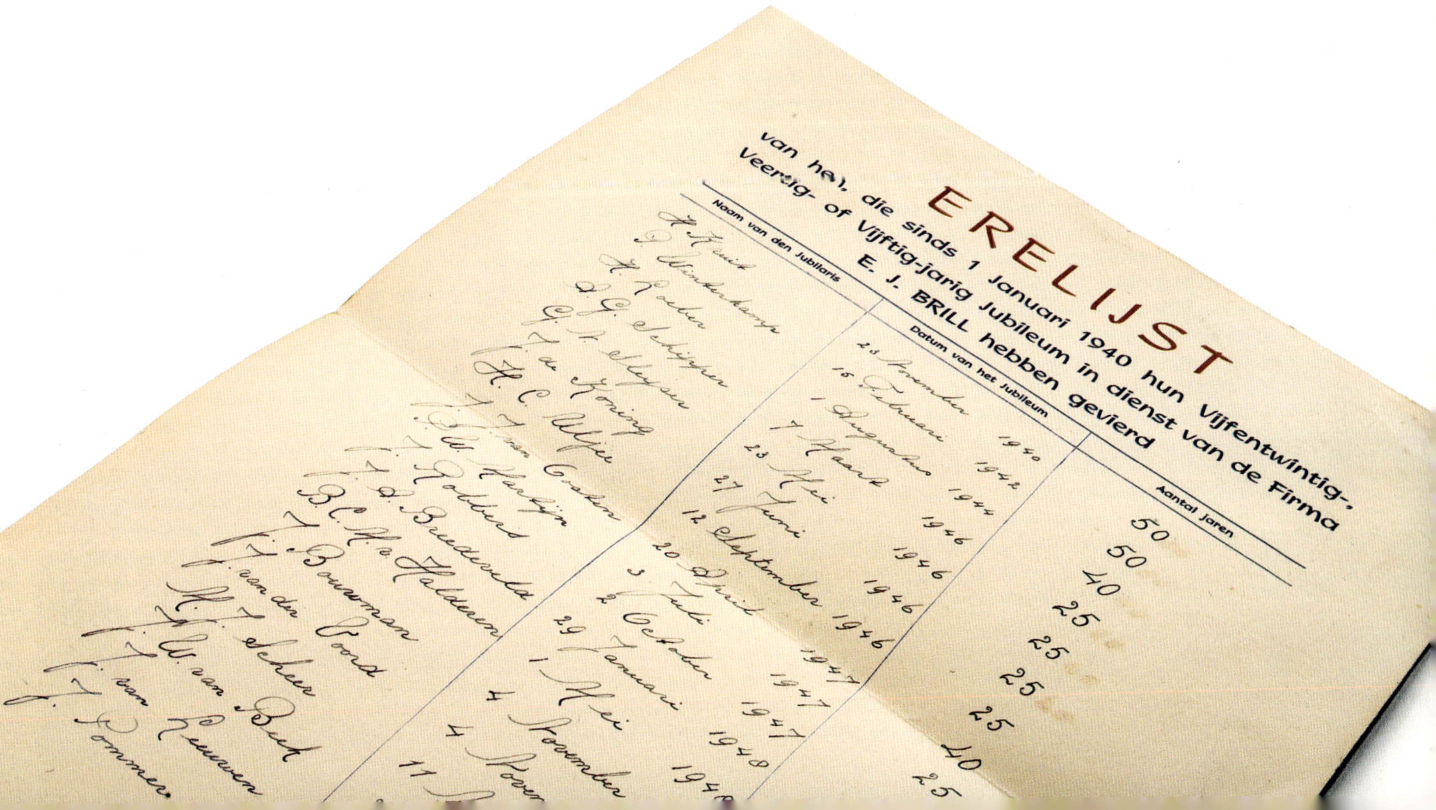

ANTIQUARIAAT
BOEKHANDEL
E J BRILL
2

Lean Years, 1945-1950

After the liberation, the company fared considerably worse than it had during the occupation. Profits sharply declined in comparison to the war years. Whereas in 1947 and 1948 profits of *f* 42,500 and *f* 52,451 could still be recorded, in 1949 the N.V. Brill suffered a substantial loss of nearly *f* 200,000. Dividends were low, and in some years they were only paid out in order to keep up the appearance of prosperity before the public at large. The publishing house succeeded in bringing out the usual thirty to forty titles a year, but sales were slight. The loss of the German market in particular limited sales, while trade with other countries was also hampered. The strict foreign exchange controls constituted a serious impediment for an internationally active company such as Brill.

While sales stagnated, the production costs of the publishing establishment and the print works were increasing. Posthumus estimated in 1948 that these costs were three times as high as they had been before the war. Paper was scarce and expensive, even apart from the difficulty posed by the company's dependence on the State Bureau for Paper for its allotment of this crucial raw material. After the war the machinery was urgently in need of replacement and augmentation, but new machines were hardly available. Moreover, in connection with the scarcity of currency, the company had to apply to the government for a license to purchase new material.

In 1947 Brill requested permission to acquire a Monotype installation for typesetting, consisting of a set of two casting machines and three keyboards. The company was assigned only one casting machine and two keyboards, the result being that the new Monotype could only operate at half power. In 1948 Brill filed an application for an additional keyboard and casting machine, which were installed one year later. The total costs of the new equipment amounted to more than one hundred thousand guilders, including bills for adaptation of the premises. Beams were reinforced and walls were knocked down to make room—even then, every inch of space available on the Oude Rijn had to be utilized.

Lack of space was a reason to rent the premises at Nieuwe Rijn No. 2, where the both the "new" and the antiquarian bookshop were housed in September 1949. In addition, it was hoped that these departments would perform better after the relocation, for both had been losing money since 1945. Apart from falling sales and rising costs, in these years Brill was faced with new taxation measures implemented by the government. A rise in the corporation tax and the introduction of a capital gains tax increased the financial pressure on the company.

Low turnover and high costs contributed to the fact that the company continuously had to contend with problems of liquidity. In order to enlarge its financial capacity, share capital was increased by *f* 100,000 in 1948, but this measure proved inadequate against the scarcity of money. At times the cash on hand amounted to no more than *f* 20,000, far too little for the day-to-day expenses of the company. Posthumus was forced to take emergency measures: he capitalized a large part of the reserve funds and in addition he issued "investment certificates" on the Peltenburg Pension Fund. Issuing more shares, either privately or through the stock exchange, was not a realistic proposition in those lean years. In 1949 Brill applied to the National Reconstruction

Brill's Oriental antiquarian bookshop had been established at No. 2 on the Nieuwe Rijn since 1949. The building with the painted fisherman above the door was popularly called "the Brill shop." Since 1970 the antiquarian bookshop was managed by Rijk Smitskamp, who in 1990 took over the business and operated it under the name "Het Oosters Antiquarium." The quaint old building with its narrow stairways, passages, and bookracks served in 2001 as a setting for the movie *The Discovery of Heaven* by Jeroen Krabbé, based on the book by Harry Mulisch. The shop closed in 2006, on the retirement of Smitskamp. Watercolor by George Boellaard.

ULL Coll.

The first meeting of the editorial committee for the second edition of the *Encyclopaedia of Islam*, held in Leiden in April 1949. None of these gentlemen would live to see the completion of the work. BA/ULA

The Committee of Experts, who, as guests of the Dutch Royal Academy, discussed the coming new edition of the Encyclopaedia of Islām (Leiden, April 1949) (*see p. vii*). Showing from left to right the Professors Johs. Pedersen, E. Lévi-Provençal, E. Garcia Gomez, H. S. Nyberg, H. A. R. Gibb, G. Levi della Vida, H. Massé, J. H. Kramers, and B. A. van Groningen.

Bank for a credit of *f* 200,000. In view of the firm's importance for Dutch exports, the loan was approved. The conditions implied, however, that the Reconstruction Bank controlled Brill's financial policy to a great extent.[9]

German-American Adventure

After the Federal Republic of West Germany was established in 1948, the German market—at any rate the western part—became more or less accessible again. The Dutch government was granted permission in 1949 to export $100,000 worth of books to the Federal Republic, a quota distributed among several publishing houses. Brill was allotted $15,000: a small share compared to the volume of its former trade with Germany, but enough to raise hopes for the future. The prospect of a renewed German market lured the company into a risky adventure.

In the spring of 1948, Posthumus had got in touch with the American historian James William Christopher, a lecturer at the University of Oxford. Christopher offered Posthumus a manuscript on American foreign policy in the Far East, which was published by Brill in 1950.[10] Furthermore, Professor Christopher turned out to own, as a relic from a previous life, a shell company that was registered in Wilmington, North Carolina. Posthumus was extremely interested in Christopher's dormant firm, which he thought he could use as a vehicle to establish Brill in the United States. Consultation with Christopher resulted in the surprising idea that it was also possible to convert the American shell company into an instrument for conquering a market share in West Germany.

Early in 1949, Posthumus and Christopher traveled for a week through the new Federal Republic in order to explore the market in that country. On his return, Posthumus was firmly of the opinion that the time was ripe for a German branch. His younger traveling companion—Christopher was thirty-five at the time—had impressed him favorably: "Sure, he is a little wild, but full of plans and ideas that can be profitable for Brill."[11] Without a murmur the supervisory board agreed to Posthumus's proposal to establish a branch in Heidelberg.

The organizational setup was complex: E. J. Brill Verlag Incorporated in Heidelberg did not fall under the N.V. Brill in Leiden, but under Christopher's company in Wilmington, North Carolina. Brill put up $18,000—equivalent to *f* 60,000 at the time—in the enterprise, corresponding to three-fifths of its capital. Christopher was appointed director of the firm and would, in addition to a nice salary, receive a bonus. Posthumus and Van Oordt, chairman of the supervisory board of Brill, each took a seat on the board of directors of the American company—at least on paper, for between Leiden in South Holland and Wilmington in North Carolina lay the long watery stretch of the Atlantic Ocean. Perhaps the use of the American front also stemmed from a feeling of embarrassment on the part of a Dutch company beginning to operate in Germany directly after the war. Given the prominent American presence in the Federal Republic, the arrangement also offered strategic advantages.

Bogus Brill

As of June 1949, Christopher was engaged in setting up the business. Supervisory director Van Oordt traveled a few times to Heidelberg in 1950 and was greatly surprised: the new branch had thirteen employees and looked tip-top. However, as time went by, doubts began to surface. Christopher did not permit an inspection of his accounts, in spite of repeated requests by Posthumus. Brill-Leiden supplied books to Brill-Heidelberg on a large scale, but the invoices were not paid. It also turned out that Christopher was secretly negotiating with Elsevier to let Brill-Heidelberg act as the German representative of that publishing house. This news did not at all go down well with the gentlemen in Leiden, because in their view Elsevier was "not a proper partner" for Brill.[12] (For the record: this Elsevier bears no relation to the Leiden firm of Elzevier that went out of business in 1712. The publishing house of Elsevier that came into being in Rotterdam towards the end of the nineteenth century had only the name in common with its illustrious predecessor.)

Inquiries in Wilmington revealed that Christopher had not fulfilled his obligations, while all sorts of things were wrong with his corporation. Trust in the American partner had reached its nadir in Leiden, and in July 1950 it was decided to break off cooperation with him. Later that month Posthumus and Wieder left for Heidelberg in order to put things right. To their alarm, it turned out that Christopher had by then established a new firm, which he wanted to have listed in the local trade register as "E. J. Brill Verlag GmbH!" The fact was that in Heidelberg he had gotten acquainted with a certain E. F. J. Brill, who was willing to drop his second initial and lend his name to the new firm. It was rather bewildering for the Dutch visitors to face a homonymic competitor in the publishing business. Obviously the world was not big enough to hold two Brills. By immediately starting summary proceedings, Posthumus and Wieder

Brill's branch office on the Kettengasse in Heidelberg. To the right of the policeman a small sign reading "E. J. Brill" is partly visible. Brill Coll.

were able to torpedo the bogus Brill firm in time. On taking stock of the damage, it turned out that the adventure with Professor Christopher had yielded a painful loss of well over DM 100,000.[13] Brill-Heidelberg continued to exist, but it was converted into a branch office that was a subsidiary of Brill-Leiden (a so-called *Zweigstelle*). As of 1953 the branch office was moved from Heidelberg to Cologne, where the subsidiary company was allowed more autonomy.

Meanwhile, Christopher did not take this lying down; he instituted legal proceedings that dragged on for many years to come. He sued Brill for nonpayment of salary and also submitted a claim for generous compensation. In 1953 his lawyer came forth with a settlement proposal, but Brill was on no account willing to agree to this. A year later, "no change whatsoever had occurred in the state of affairs apropos of Mr. Christopher." In February 1955 Brill was fully vindicated in a court of law. Christopher did not lose heart but appealed to a higher court. In order to rid itself of this nuisance, in 1960 Brill accepted the settlement proposal of $3,000 that he had submitted through his lawyer. Thus did Mr. Christopher disappear for good from the annals of Brill.[14]

Reconstruction, 1950-1958

Indië verloren, rampspoed geboren: "The loss of the Indies is the birth of disaster." This well-known Dutch saying expressed the general view of the time, but for Brill the loss of the Dutch East Indies brought unexpected prosperity. During the 1949 Round Table Conference on the transfer of sovereignty to Indonesia, agreements had also been made on the scientific division of the estate. As a result of these agreements, Brill acquired some lucrative contracts with the new republic for the furnishing of a number of libraries. The chief partner was the Hatta Foundation, named after Indonesia's Vice-President Mohammed Hatta. The large-scale supply of books to this institution provided an unprecedentedly high turnover for a number of years. The antiquarian bookshop, having dwindled away to a vegetative existence after its wartime flourish, once again experienced golden times. Sales of books to the Hatta Foundation generated turnovers of *f* 700,000 and *f* 780,000 in 1950 and 1951.

The composing room of Brill in the fifties. Brill Coll.

The employees of Brill in the fifties. The women sat in the foreground and were clearly in the ascendant.

Brill Coll.

In addition, an agreement was made with the republic's Ministry of Education and Culture. Over a period of four years, shipments of books to three libraries reached a total value of well over *f* 300,000. One of these libraries was equipped on the spot by the anarchist and author Arthur Lehning (1899-2000), a friend of both Posthumus and Hatta.[15] At the insistence of Posthumus he tried to persuade Hatta to continue the importation of books after 1954, but unfortunately the funds were exhausted. In Leiden a Brill-Jakarta was already being dreamed of, but after this disappointment the plans for an Indonesian branch office were postponed indefinitely. Even so, it can be stated without exaggeration that the Republic of Indonesia made an important contribution to the postwar reconstruction of Brill.

The Indonesian "boom" caused the total turnover of the company to rise to record heights of more than one and a half million guilders. After 1952 the sales proceeds from Indonesia diminished, but this decline was offset by the improvement of the European economy. Over the course of the fifties, the turnover gradually rose to two million guilders in 1958. For the same period, the profits showed a corresponding picture of steady growth, rising from *f* 150,000 in 1951 to *f* 200,000 in 1958. On average the profits amounted to 10% of the turnover.

In the fifties Brill was given a new entrance on the world. Sales in the United States became more and more important, and the number of American commissions for the publishing house also increased. Posthumus developed a vast network of productive relations with American universities and publishers.[16] Relations with various European countries, too, were intensified. Brill presented itself at academic congresses and international meetings in France, Germany, Switzerland, and England. Spain came into the picture thanks to a large supply of books to the Instituto Hispano-Árabe in Madrid, a connection that for a while led Posthumus to consider establishing a branch in the Spanish capital. Germany, or at least its western part, was the largest market within Europe: a third of Brill's book sales were realized in the Federal Republic.[17]

"Urge for Expansion"

Year after year Posthumus spoke of "satisfactory progress" in his annual report, although he did not deem it necessary to pay more than a 10% dividend to the shareholders. Besides, things were not all roses, for Brill still had to contend with problems of liquidity. Due to the growth of the business, these problems were becoming bigger rather than smaller—not only did profits rise, but so did the wages of employees and the prices of machines and raw materials.

In his annual report of 1953, Posthumus formulated this paradox as the tension between the firm's "uncomfortably small accommodations" and its "urge for expansion." In a literal sense he was referring to the cramped business premises on the Oude Rijn; figuratively he alluded to the fact that Brill had too little financial power to be able to develop itself. Its equity capital on the basis of shares amounted to well over two hundred and fifty thousand guilders, while according to the director another half million was required to secure the growth of the business. That much capital could not be raised by issuing new shares. In the course of the fifties, the company was forced once again to appeal to the Reconstruction Bank and other banks.

Posthumus also tried to improve liquidity by recruiting outside clients for the print works. In the fifties the Batavian Oil Company, better known as Shell, became a good customer of the printing office. In addition, the publishing house also received commissions from Shell. The oil company sponsored an English edition of its own history by the Utrecht professor C. Gerretson, and as a counterpart a technical history of the company by the previously mentioned oil historian R. J. Forbes.[18]

Bending Floors

Neon lighting and an addressing machine appeared in 1950 as precursors of the new industrial era. Two more Monotypes were acquired, while the mechanization of Arabic and Hebrew typesetting was also under consideration. Old printing presses were replaced by new ones with a larger capacity. Each successive machine, after being turned this way and that, had to be installed in its place in the old building. The attic floors were bending under the weight of the standing type for reprints and the growing stocks of books. Two additional storage facilities had to be rented, Brill spreading itself now over four different locations in Leiden—internal communication required a lot bicycling to and fro.

Another new feature at the publishing house was the employment of academically trained editors. The classicist and Assyriologist B. A. van Proosdij turned out to have business acumen as well, and he would become deputy director in 1958.[19] The Slavist Wap set up a new department for publications in the Slavic languages. Previously, once every few years a single catalog was issued for the entire non-Oriental publishing list, but now it was decided to issue catalogs for each discipline on a more frequent basis. The advertising department established by Folkers dispatched prospectuses and flyers on a large scale to draw the attention of the world to Brill's supply; in 1952, a total of 67,850 "Booklists" and 77,000 "Weekly Lists" were sent out to various countries. Given the quantity of outgoing mail, the increase in postage expenses in 1957 resulted in a substantial cost increase of *f* 7,500. Posthumus loved figures, and he used to calculate such matters carefully.

He also calculated the rate at which investments in Brill's own publications were recovered. He reckoned that owing to the slow turnover rate of academic books, it usually took four years before a break-even point of 75% was reached. The publishing list was marked down by an annual depreciation of 20%, not to mention storage costs, and so it was doubtful whether the last quarter was ever recovered. The unprofitable ratio was a thorn in Posthumus's side, and he aimed at maximum cost-effectiveness during the first year; in other words, for each publication, as many copies as possible had to be sold as soon as it appeared. He developed a mathematical model whereby he could calculate the percentage of its costs earned back by a given publication, which he then used as a measure of its profitability.

"We print and publish in all languages of the world": Brill's booth at the Frankfurt book fair in 1960. Brill Coll.

A company of visiting foreign scholars, probably Indologists, in Brill's boardroom on the Oude Rijn. Seated in the middle is Posthumus and standing behind him, facing the camera with dark-rimmed glasses, his son and secretary J.H. Posthumus. Next to the younger Posthumus, standing to his right, is deputy director and later director F.C. Wieder. In the background, the man with glasses, peeking over the shoulders of others, is B. A. van Proosdij, later deputy director. Photograph circa 1955. Brill Coll.

Work in Progress

In the fifties the publishing house brought out on average sixty titles a year, about twice as many as in the prewar years. The number of journals was well over thirty, including perennials such as *T'oung Pao* and *Mnemosyne*. The composition of the publishing list had not changed substantially. Brill continued along the same lines, exploiting its own past as well as seizing the opportunities offered in the present. The continuity was reflected in the field of Oriental studies, broadly conceived, which remained the trademark of the publishing house. Thanks to a new series of text editions, classical literature was more prominently represented than it had been before. Religious studies had developed into an established segment of the publishing list, and historiography remained an important component.

A new project for the publishing house and for the print works as well was a set of publications in Braille—a fresh set of strange symbols for Brill's typesetters to master. *The Encyclopaedia of Islam* was a legacy from the past, by now ripe for renovation. In 1948 a new edition was talked of for the first time, and a year later the first meeting of the Arabists who would constitute the international editorial staff took place in Leiden. The idea was to produce it in the same format as the prewar edition, namely, four volumes with a supplement. The second edition was to appear in English and French; a German edition was no longer considered viable. The prognosis was that the job could be done within ten years, but this turned out to be pretty optimistic planning. The first installment appeared in 1953, and only in 1960 did the first bound volume see the light of day. Not until 2006 was the second edition of the encyclopedia—in 14 volumes—completed. Once again Brill embarked upon a monumental production with an unanticipated duration of more than half a century. As a spin-off, however, in 1953 *The Shorter Encyclopaedia of Islam* by the Oxford professor H. A. R. Gibb was published, on the basis of a contract that Folkers had approved before the war. The book went through four editions, the latest in 2001 under the title *Concise Encyclopaedia of Islam*.

End of an Era

The orphanage on the Oude Rijn was no longer able to meet the needs of the workforce and the equipment. From 1954 onwards there had been talk of constructing a new home for the print works, which in the long run would also house the publishing establishment. Only a portion of the required capital could be obtained from Brill's own funds, but two banks were prepared to extend credit on the basis of the company's operating results. In autumn 1958, negotiations with the Leiden city council resulted in the purchase of a plot of land measuring nearly two and a half acres on the southern outskirts of the city.

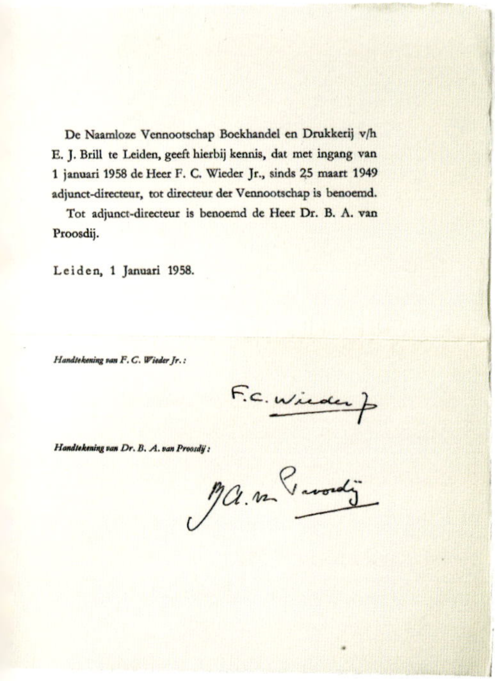

De Naamloze Vennootschap Boekhandel en Drukkerij v/h E. J. Brill te Leiden, geeft hierbij kennis, dat met ingang van 1 januari 1958 de Heer F. C. Wieder Jr., sinds 25 maart 1949 adjunct-directeur, tot directeur der Vennootschap is benoemd.

Tot adjunct-directeur is benoemd de Heer Dr. B. A. van Proosdij.

Leiden, 1 Januari 1958.

Handtekening van F. C. Wieder Jr.:

Handtekening van Dr. B. A. van Proosdij:

Changing of the guard: Brill announces that as of January 1, 1958, F. C. Wieder jr. will be director and B. A. van Proosdij deputy director. BA/ULA

Posthumus made the preparations for the new building, but he left its completion to others. As of April 1, 1958, shortly after his seventy-eighth birthday, he stepped down as director. Unlike other "successions to the throne" at Brill, this time the transition was smooth: F. C. Wieder Jr., deputy director for many years, was appointed in his place, and B. A. van Proosdij was named deputy director. Posthumus, who remained attached to the company as a consultant, intended to devote himself henceforth to historiography. He had found a subject that combined his old love for economic history with the interest in the Oriental world he had gained at Brill. Over the past few years he had initiated a series, *Economic and Social History of the Orient*, that were to comprise some thirty volumes at a rough estimate—an ambitious international project. In preparation for this he founded in 1957 the *Journal of the Economic and Social History of the Orient*, which is still being published by Brill. The same historical perspective was the basis of the Institute for the Middle and Far East at the University of Amsterdam, which Posthumus had instigated in 1956. The institute would be geared towards the history of the East, while Leiden University cultivated instead the linguistic tradition of Arabic studies.

For the time being, the historian did not concentrate on the socioeconomic history of the Arab world, because he wanted to complete the second volume of his *History of Commodity Prices in the Netherlands*. On February 26, 1960, on the occasion of his eightieth birthday, he was presented with the first proofs. Unfortunately, he would not live to see the bound volume. Posthumus died a few months later, on April 18, 1960, and his last work was published posthumously with Brill.[20]

Exuberant Growth: Frederik Casparus Wieder, 1958-1979

No Street for Luchtmans

Like the Dutch economy as a whole, Brill went through a period of great expansion in the 1960s and 1970s.[21] Turnover rose from two million guilders in 1958 to an average of well over twelve million guilders in the second half of the seventies. Individual business segments now generated a much higher turnover than the entire company had in the recent past: for instance, in 1972 the turnover of the publishing establishment alone amounted to nearly 5.5 million guilders, and that of the print works 4.5 million. The profits of the company as a whole rose to between six and seven hundred thousand guilders—unprecedentedly high amounts for Brill, but lower than one might expect on the basis of the sharply increased turnover. During these decades the wage/price spiral had a noticeable effect on the company's profits. In spite of this, the growth of the company was large enough to stay ahead of the inflation rate. In this period the share capital increased from *f* 260,000 to *f* 860,000; in 1965 new shares worth one hundred thousand guilders were issued, and in 1972 a large issue valued at half a million was effected.

In the spring of 1960, the foundation stone was laid for the new print works. When bids were solicited, the original building plan turned out to be too expensive, so that construction had to be skimped on. Building and equipping the print works required

In the spring of 1961 Brill's print works moved to the new building on the Plantijnstraat. In 1985 the publishing house would follow.

Brill Coll.

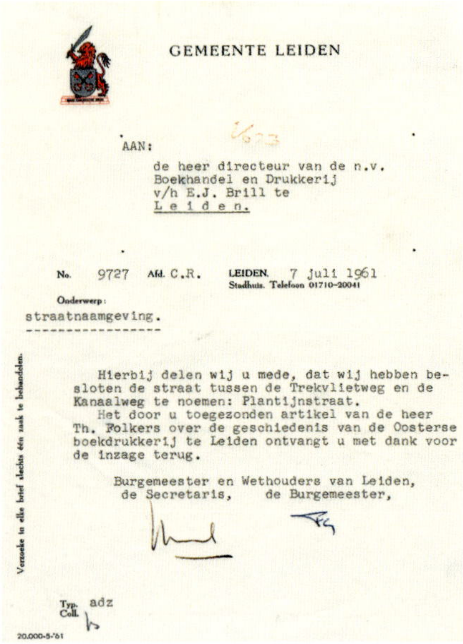

GEMEENTE LEIDEN

AAN:

de heer directeur van de n.v.
Boekhandel en Drukkerij
v/h E.J. Brill te
L e i d e n.

No. 9727 Afd. C.R. LEIDEN. 7 Juli 1961
Stadhuis. Telefoon 01710-20041

Onderwerp:
straatnaamgeving.

Hierbij delen wij u mede, dat wij hebben besloten de straat tussen de Trekvlietweg en de Kanaalweg te noemen: Plantijnstraat.

Het door u toegezonden artikel van de heer Th. Folkers over de geschiedenis van de Oosterse boekdrukkerij te Leiden ontvangt u met dank voor de inzage terug.

Burgemeester en Wethouders van Leiden,
de Secretaris, de Burgemeester,

Verzoeke in elke brief slechts één zaak te behandelen.

Typ. adz
Coll.

20.000-5-'61

Resolution of the city council of Leiden, July 7, 1961, stating that the nameless street between Trekvlietweg and Kanaalweg will be named the "Plantijnstraat." Brill Coll.

a total amount of one million guilders, half of which could be paid from the company's own capital, thanks to reserves built up in previous years. The new building was located in a featureless no-man's-land on a nameless street. Brill suggested a number of possible street names to the city council, all inspired by Leiden's rich book-historical past. Sad to say, in the eyes of the city fathers Luchtmans found no grace as namesake for the new street, which eventually was named after Plantijn, the sixteenth-century Antwerp printer who lived in Leiden for some years. From Brill's point of view, this name contained at least a kernel of historical truth: Plantijn was the great-grandfather of Sara van Musschenbroek, the wife of the firm's founder Jordaan Luchtmans.

The relocation took place in the months of May and June 1961. A year later, plans to extend the new building with storage space and an office for the publishing establishment were postponed indefinitely. For the time being, the publishing house remained on the Oude Rijn, where thanks to the removal of the print works there was enough space. The Chinese composing room initially remained in the old business premises, but in 1964 it also moved to the Plantijnstraat. The available investment scope was used to expand production capacity as much as possible. The publishing house was only able to grow insofar as the printing shop was able to process the rising flow of orders.

Printing in Bombay

In spite of the investments in new equipment, the print works continued to wrestle with backlogs. The greatest problem was the recruitment of qualified personnel, not only owing to a shortage of labor but also as a result of the housing problem. In the sixties the city council was in no hurry to build housing, while typographers from elsewhere were only willing to come to Leiden if they were offered accommodations. By introducing a profit-sharing scheme for the entire workforce in 1961, Brill tried to make the company more attractive to new employees. Even so, the print works and composing room suffered from a permanent shortage of personnel, with paradoxical consequences: in 1965 typesetting machines had to be stopped frequently for lack of manual typesetters, because the machine operators had to catch up with the backlogs of manual typesetting. This reversal of the technological progress was only possible thanks to the fact that the operators of the composing machines had still been trained in the old craft.

Because of Brill's own limited capacity, some printing orders were farmed out to a print works in Nijmegen. Furthermore, the company resorted to Belgian firms that turned out to work at half price, thus yielding a substantial savings. In 1963 an Arabic publication was even farmed out to a print works in Bombay that apparently had the expertise required for this kind of work. Around 1970 the capacity problem caused Wieder to start experimenting with typesetting on a Digiset machine in collaboration with a company in Amsterdam. In this procedure typesetting was reduced to entering data onto punched cards or magnetic tapes, by means of which the printing process was regulated by a mainframe computer. The digital technique was in its infancy and did not as yet constitute an alternative to hot-metal typesetting or offset. Nevertheless, Wieder envisioned a future in which all typesetting would be done by computer, indeed a future in which computers would play a major role in the business as a whole.

This prediction would come true sooner than he expected: already in 1979-1980 Brill acquired five "Compugraphics" for digital photosetting.

Streamlined Tradition

Whereas Brill published about 70 titles a year in the beginning of the sixties, by the second half of the seventies this number had risen to an average of 175. Just like Posthumus and Folkers had done before him, at the annual meeting of shareholders Wieder used to recite the titles of the most important publications of the previous year. In 1970, however, he discontinued this practice—the number of publications had simply become too large. The increase cannot be explained merely by the intrinsic growth of the company and its improved sales opportunities, especially in the United States. Brill was also seeing a continual increase in the number of manuscripts it received, because other publishing houses were less and less interested in specialized works with small print runs. Other publishers' lust for profit during the economic boom had the effect of strengthening Brill's position in its traditional niche market.

Ever since its very beginnings, Brill had a strong scholarly component in its publishing list, but during these two decades the publishing house acquired an exclusively academic character. Many publications appeared in monograph series that remain on the present publishing list, although the names of some series have changed in the meantime. A random selection will suffice: Philosophia Antiqua, Old and New Testament Studies, Documenta et Monumenta Orientis Antiqui, Studies in the History of Religions, Studies in Judaism, Orientalia Rheno-Trajectina, Sinica Leidensia, International Studies in Sociology and Social Anthropology, and so forth—the number of series alone is too large to mention them all. Most of these series were linked to scholarly journals, about thirty during the period in question.

In view of the growing volume of production, the academic staff of the publishing house was also increased. After his retirement as deputy director in 1965, B. A. van Proosdij continued to act as general editor. T. Edridge, who was appointed deputy director in his place, was responsible for the publishing list in classical studies, while F. Th. Dijkema took charge of Arabic studies. In this process of increasing professionalization, Brill's scholarly tradition was stressed. The publishing house converted the most distinctive aspect of its tradition into its core business and capitalized on its past.

Wieder repeatedly indicated that the publishing house should concentrate on "successful series, supplemental works, and standard works." The latter category included the eternal work in progress, the new edition of the *Encyclopaedia of Islam*, four volumes of which were published between 1960 and 1978. Hardly less ambitious in scope was the *Handbuch der Orientalistik* by B. Spuler et al., which has been published since 1952 in eight sections. Another monumental series was the nine-volume history of Arabic literature (*Geschichte des arabischen Schrifttums*: 1967–1984) by the Turkish author Mehmet Fuat Sezgin. In 1969 the seventh and last volume of *Concordance et indices de la tradition musulmane* was published; the project had been started in the thirties by A. J. Wensinck and was completed by the Arabic scholar J. Brugman, who was also a supervisory director at Brill.[22] Reflecting on such enterprises, one can only observe that Brill had a peculiar fondness for projects that other publishers shunned.

In 1959 Mohammad Reza Pahlavi, the shah of Persia, paid a state visit to the Netherlands. During a reception in the royal palace on the Dam in Amsterdam he was presented with a copy, bound in red calf, of the recently published *Archéologie de l'Iran Ancien* (1959; 2nd ed. 1966). From left to right: Shah Mohammad Reza, author L. van den Berghe, director F. C. Wieder Jr., and deputy director B. A. van Proosdij. BA/ULA

Printer at Brill, midsixties. Brill Coll.

Pirated Editions

The *Concordance* is a compilation of the oral tradition of Islam, which for Muslims is almost equally important as the Koran itself. Not surprisingly, in the Arab world there was great interest in the book, which in its original version was very expensive. Already in 1970, barely a year after the completion of the original, a pirated edition of the *Concordance* was brought out in Beirut. As soon as this news made it to Leiden, Joop van der Walle, head of Brill's bookselling firm, boarded a plane to Lebanon. A Leiden Arabist accompanied him to act as interpreter. Van der Walle succeeded in having the edition suppressed by a judge and in buying up the remainder. Yet the whole affair, including the high legal fees, caused a loss of fifty thousand guilders. The seven volumes cost *f* 2,300 at Brill, while the illegal copy sold for a quarter of that price. The Lebanese edition was shipped off to the Netherlands, but it was not destroyed—on the contrary, Brill tried to repair the damage by fobbing off the low-quality pirated version as a cheap "student's edition."

Thanks to the offset technique it was easy for pirates to make photomechanical reprints. In this case legal proceedings were possible, but for works whose copyright had expired after fifty years, the company had no legal recourse. For instance, it was hard for Brill to defend itself against the illegal edition of the *Bibliotheca Geographorum Arabicorum* (1870-1894) by M. J. de Goeje. To prevent others from running off with older works from the publishing list, Brill started of its own accord to reissue some works, likewise in the form of photomechanical reprints. Thus, as a precautionary measure Brill brought out a new edition of the *Annals of* al-Tabari by M. J. de Goeje, which had originally been published in fourteen volumes between 1851 and 1876. The same reasoning motivated the somewhat later reprint of the first edition of the *Encyclopaedia of Islam*, whose copyright would expire in 1986; a pirated edition had already surfaced in the Middle East. Unfortunately, Brill's intervention in Lebanon had little effect in the long run, for according to reports dozens of pirated editions of the *Concordance* are circulating in the Arab world. Reprints were also disadvantageous to the antiquarian bookshop, because old and rare works lost their value.

Flyer for the *Concordance* (1992). This time not a pirated edition, but a reprint by Brill itself. BA/ULA

British Brill

The antiquarian bookshop was the least stable business segment at Brill. Its turnover could amount to one million in one year and drop to half that amount in the next, depending on the market. As a result, the proceeds too fluctuated sharply: in 1976 the shop recorded a loss of more than *f* 50,000, but a year later a profit of nearly *f* 350,000.

The Cologne branch office, the successor to the one in Heidelberg, failed to develop into a distribution center for the German market as intended. Year after year it muddled along with minor losses or minor profits. In 1971 it was discovered that for four years the German manager had been painting a rosy financial picture, because he feared that the subsidiary company would be closed down. The Slavic department proved to be unfeasible in the long run and was given up in 1973. In the same year Brill took over a London bookstore, Bryce, located on Museum Street (W.C.1) near the British Museum. Brill's retail store (the "new bookshop") was in its entirety transferred from Leiden to London.

Henceforth Brill-Leiden consisted of the publishing establishment (Oude Rijn), the print works (Plantijnstraat), the antiquarian bookshop (Nieuwe Rijn), and two storage facilities. Toward the end of the seventies approximately one hundred and twenty people were employed at the parent company, seven at Brill-Cologne, and fifteen at Brill-London.

Brill's Weekly

On September 9, 1967, the thousandth issue of *Brill's Weekly* appeared. Some caution is appropriate here, for it is not entirely clear how this milestone was established. In 1938 Folkers had started producing a "Weekly List of New Books," a one-page flyer that was distributed in a print run of a few hundred copies. During the Second World War the English booklist was discontinued, but from 1946 onwards "Booklists" and "Weekly Lists" were sent into the world in ever increasing numbers to announce new publications. From June 1952 onwards these appeared under the designation *Brill's Weekly*, but strictly speaking it could not have reached its thousandth issue in 1967. Moreover, in spite of its name, the *Weekly* was by no means issued every week. Apparently, all possible predecessors were included in the count so as to reach this milestone.

London Borough of Camden
MUSEUM
STREET WC1
LITTLE RUSSELL
STREET
WC1
publishers E.J.Brill booksellers
E.J.BRILL
E.J.Br

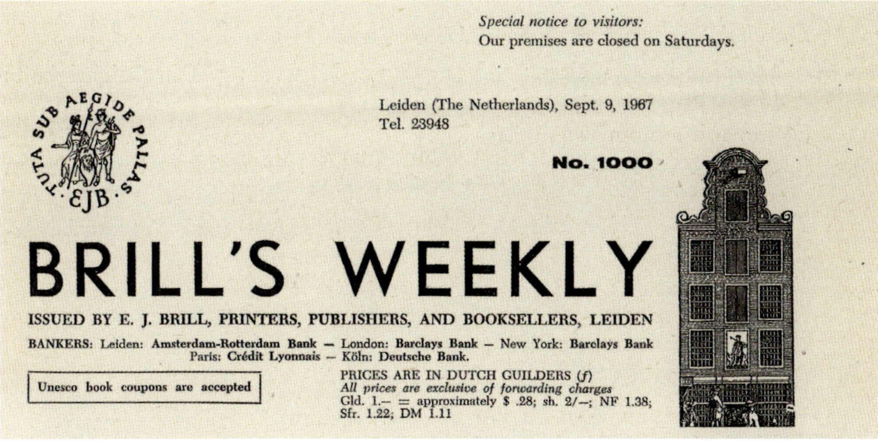
Special notice to visitors:
Our premises are closed on Saturdays.

Leiden (The Netherlands), Sept. 9, 1967
Tel. 23948

No. 1000

BRILL'S WEEKLY

ISSUED BY E. J. BRILL, PRINTERS, PUBLISHERS, AND BOOKSELLERS, LEIDEN

BANKERS: Leiden: Amsterdam-Rotterdam Bank — London: Barclays Bank — New York: Barclays Bank
Paris: Crédit Lyonnais — Köln: Deutsche Bank.

Unesco book coupons are accepted

PRICES ARE IN DUTCH GUILDERS (ƒ)
All prices are exclusive of forwarding charges
Gld. 1.— = approximately $ .28; sh. 2/—; NF 1.38;
Sfr. 1.22; DM 1.11

Brill's Weekly No. 1000. BA/ULA

The first issue was a simple prospectus of Brill's publications, but No. 1000 had considerably more style. In the course of time, the practice developed of devoting each issue to a certain field of study and citing the relevant new literature. The *Weekly* did not only mention Brill's publications on the subject in question, but also those of others. In due course the flyer developed into an internationally esteemed survey of recently published scholarly works. Instead of a prospectus for sales promotion, the *Weekly* was rather a vehicle for Brill's reputation as an academic publishing house. Each issue was meticulously prepared, and indeed months before the publication of an issue, employees were already engaged in collecting titles. The thematically arranged issues provided readers with a convenient tool containing recent bibliographical information.

The magazine went beyond the scope of Brill's direct commercial interest and provided a service to scholarship. It was a costly affair to prepare and distribute the *Weekly*, but this was offset by the fact that Brill derived great honor from the magazine. The digital revolution put a stop to the *Weekly*—the expensive paper production gave way to digital newsletters containing information on new books.

Merger or Takeover?

Brill prospered in the sixties and as a result it became an attractive party for a merger or takeover. In May 1965 M. D. Frank, director and proprietor of the North-Holland Publishing Company, made a proposal to merge his company with Brill. Initially, Wieder rather liked the idea, which was opposed by the supervisory directors. Afterwards, however, the roles were reversed: the supervisory directors were inclined toward a merger, while Wieder increasingly opposed the idea. At a meeting of the board in the beginning of 1967 the issue led to a heated discussion. One of the supervisory directors made the merger a condition of his continued service, while another suggested that Brill would never be able to maintain its position as an independent business in the long run. In his turn, Wieder argued that because of the incompatibility of the two publishing houses a merger would come to nothing, and that the "character of Brill" would be lost in the amalgamation. He stuck to his guns and the supervisory directors backed down.[23]

< The branch office of Brill on Museum Street, London W.C.1. Brill Coll.

Typesetter at the typesetting machine, midsixties. Brill Coll.

It was a period that saw the emergence of the large conglomerates that characterize the present world of publishing in the Netherlands. The firm of Elsevier was taking over one publishing house after another, and it cast eager eyes on Brill as well. Perhaps it was not a coincidence that the same thought occurred to its competitor, Kluwer, who had just incorporated the house of Tjeenk Willink. Thus it could happen that on the same day in January 1969, Wieder was paid a visit by representatives of both publishing houses, although not at the same time. Both gentlemen informed him in guarded terms that their respective bosses were interested in taking over Brill. Wieder refused to commit himself and for the record reported the matter to the supervisory directors. Nothing more was heard from Kluwer, but Elsevier did not lose heart, and at the end of August it submitted a written proposal for the takeover of Brill. Around the same time Elsevier took over the North-Holland Publishing Company, that had wanted to merge with Brill a couple of years before. The acquisition apparently yielded additional information on the sensitivities at Brill about its independence: in a second communication five weeks later there was no longer any mention of a "takeover," but of the incorporation of Brill "into the federative organization of Elsevier's scientific publishing establishments."

One of the more remarkable Brill authors was Robert Hans van Gulik (1910-1967), Sinologist, diplomat and author of the famous detective stories featuring Judge Dee. This bearded magistrate was a sleuth who cleverly solved all kinds of complex crimes in ancient China. Dee was a historical figure who had lived in the seventh century, and who posthumously became the protagonist of an eighteenth-century Chinese crime story. Van Gulik translated it into English and published it in 1949 as *Dee Goong An. An Ancient Chinese Detective Story*. The first Judge Dee was a translation of an existing text, but the plots of the next fourteen novels he invented himself. Van Gulik's interest in criminal history also showed itself in his *T'ang-yin-pi-shih. Parallel Cases from under the Pear-tree. A 13th-century Manual of Jurisprudence and Detection*. This translation of an ancient judicial manuscript was published by Brill in 1956, but Judge Dee was not quite up to the scholarly standards of the firm. Commercially speaking a blunder: Van Gulik's crime novels were translated into twenty-four languages and still are international bestsellers.

For the first Dee story the Japanese publisher wanted illustrations with an erotic tone, in order to promote sales. Van Gulik, a skilled draughtsman, complied with this request and produced some slightly pornographic drawings. One thing led to another, and in 1951 he published at his own cost the *Erotic Colour Prints of the Ming Period*—a beautiful and very rare curiosity, since it was printed by hand in only fifty copies. Apart from a historical study of Chinese pornography, both in English and Chinese, it contained a reproduction of the album *Hua-ying-chin-chen* ("The variegated positions of the Flowery Battle"). Van Gulik explained that he had found the original woodblocks of this Ming-period erotic album in a shady antique shop. A unique discovery, which he now published for the benefit of the learned world. However, to prevent future abuse of these pornographic woodblocks, he had decided to destroy them.

The case of the missing woodblocks has given cause to the rumour that Van Gulik designed some of the erotic prints himself. To say the least, a certain similarity in style may be detected between the woodcuts and Van Gulik's drawings in the Judge Dee novels. His essay on the history of pornography was the forerunner of his *Sexual Life in Ancient* China, which was published by Brill in 1961. The *Erotic Colour Prints of the Ming Period* were reprinted by Brill in 2003.

Left: Judge Dee brooding over a case. Illustration by Robert van Gulik in *The Chinese Maze Murders*, first published in 1950.

Right: The original Judge Dee. Drawing by Van Gulik.

At Brill the proposition led to discussions like those a few years earlier. The supervisory directors thought that the firm's independence would be guaranteed in this arrangement, and they pointed out the advantages of expansion. Wieder resolutely opposed the firm's absorption into a larger organization and again stressed the importance of Brill's identity. He was not convinced that Elsevier would respect Brill's independence, and his doubts were probably not unjustified. This time too he refused to budge on the matter, and once again the supervisory directors backed down. At the 1972 issue, Elsevier acquired a number of Brill shares, apparently with the aim of getting a finger in the pie. However, the interest was too small to permit any manipulation of the shareholders' meeting; also, as a barrier against such threats, Brill had placed a number of priority shares in trusted hands.[24]

In the meantime a merger with the publishing house of Samson in Alphen aan de Rijn had also been turned down (this firm merged with the Leiden-based company Sijthoff afterwards).[25] The chief effect of the internal discussion over a merger or takeover was a reinforcement of Brill's own understanding of its individual character. Moreover, in these years it became increasingly obvious that the company was strong enough to pursue its own course.

Consolidation and Growth, 1979-2008

Jubilee

Wieder, who had managed the expanding company for more than two decades, retired in 1979 at the age of sixty-eight. As in the case of Posthumus's retirement, the changing of the guard proceeded smoothly: Tom Edridge, editor of the publishing list in classical studies and deputy director since 1974, was appointed successor to Wieder. His New Zealand origin required a minor adaptation of the statutes, which stipulated that only a Dutchman could become director of the company. Unfortunately Edridge died suddenly, less than a year after taking over the management of the company.

Wieder returned temporarily, pending the appointment of a new director. Apparently no appropriate candidate could be found within the company, for rather surprisingly the choice fell on the Rotterdam biology teacher Wim Backhuys. He had obtained his doctorate with a thesis on gastropods or snails, which in the parlance of biologists made him a malacologist. He also had a small publishing house with a publishing list in the field of biology and paleontology, which was taken over by Brill as an imprint. In times past Brill had also been active in this field, but around 1980 it had practically disappeared from sight. It was intended that Backhuys would bring the biology section back to life. He devoted much energy to the task, the result being that in time the biology section comprised about a tenth of Brill's publications.

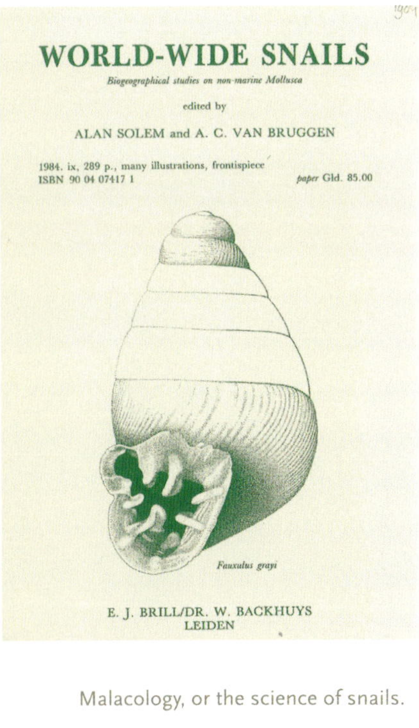

Malacology, or the science of snails.

BA/ULA

Backhuys did not only engage the present; the past also demanded his attention. In 1983 Brill celebrated its tercentenary, counted from 1683, the year in which Jordaan Luchtmans started his bookselling business. The commemoration was accompanied by quite a bit of festivity. In the Leiden Municipal Archive an exhibition on the rich history of Luchtmans and Brill was organized.[26] Six scholars devoted an article apiece to the historical intertwining of their fields of study and the publishing house.

Their contributions constituted a sampling of the most important components of Brill's publishing list: religious studies, Judaica, Assyriology, Egyptology, Arabic studies, Islamic studies, Indology, Sinology, Japanese studies, and classical antiquity. Backhuys wrote an article on Brill's former publications in the field of biology, seizing the opportunity for an *oratio pro domo*.

The contributions were collected in the commemorative publication *Tuta sub aegide Pallas*, of which the first copy was presented to the Minister of Education and Science at a gathering in the Hooglandse Church. On the occasion of the jubilee, Brill also published a *Short-title Catalogue 1683–1983*, listing some five thousand titles and thus giving a picture of the firm's impressive production

Leiden responded to three centuries of affinity with Brill by awarding it the city's gold medal of honor. Mayor C. Goekoop mentioned in his address that Brill "made a great contribution to employment opportunities in Leiden and to the reputation of the city at home and abroad."[27] Finally, mention should be made of the visit that the archbishop of Antioch paid to Brill within the framework of the commemoration. The prelate was presented with a copy of the four-volume *Bible in Aramaic* by A. Sperber.[28] It was a gift that expressed the history of the publishing house in a fitting way: one of the first publications of Jordaan Luchtmans was the *Opus Aramaeum* (1686) by Carolus Schaaf.

The *Short-title Catalogue 1683-1983*, published on the occasion of Brill's third centenary. The owner was very careful about his copy, judging by the handwritten notice: "Don't touch." BA/ULA

Relocation

In the year 1983 another jubilee took place. It was exactly one century earlier that Brill had moved to the former orphanage on the Oude Rijn. This event was commemorated in a different way, with the decision that it was time to move the publishing establishment to the Plantijnstraat as well. The print works were renovated to create sufficient office space. At the same time, it was decided to establish a central warehouse in nearby Zoeterwoude for the stocks of books held in various storage places in Leiden.

In connection with the relocation the old building had to be cleaned out—no minor operation, given the accumulation of stuff over the course of a century. The move was completed in 1985, leaving behind the dismantled business premises, which still feature the name "E. J. Brill" on the facade. The building not only immortalizes the man who gave his name to the company but also serves as a concrete remembrance of Van Oordt and De Stoppelaar, who laid here the foundations for the present-day publishing house. More than that, it is a monument to all those people who committed themselves to Brill for over a century. Their number must run into the thousands—a crowd of Leiden citizens who were attached to the business, often throughout their lives. The empty building echoed the hustle and bustle of the past hundred years in a subdued form; Leiden squatters, who were interested in this vacancy for less poetic reasons, presently took possession of Brill's former accommodations. They established there, among other things, a mushroom nursery and a secondhand clothes shop.

The gold *eerepenning* or medal of honor of the Leiden city council, presented to Brill on the occasion of its third centenary in 1983. Brill Coll.

Hostile Specter

In the same year, 1985, a great panic took possession of Brill. A mysterious investor—of Belgian origin, it was rumored—was buying up shares on a large scale with the intention of taking over the company. It was supposed that by devious means this

In 1985 the publishing house moved to the Plantijnstraat, where Brill's print works had been established since 1961. The premises on the Oude Rijn 33a were cleared out.

Brill Coll.

spectral party had already acquired 70% of the parcel of shares. In order to prevent a hostile takeover, a protective construction under the name "Luchtmans Foundation" was speedily rigged up. In an emergency, the company was given the right to issue a quantity of cumulative preference shares, up to a maximum of 50% of the total capital of shares issued. In the event of an imminent takeover, these preference shares could be transferred to the Luchtmans Foundation, so that this foundation would have sufficient voting rights to keep intruders out.

It was unnecessary for the Luchtmans Foundation to take up arms against the sneak buyer who was supposed to have acquired nearly three-quarters of the Brill shares. Afterwards it turned out that a small miscalculation had occurred. The outsider had not bought full shares of one thousand guilders, but split shares of one hundred. The threat decreased in proportion to this revelation, for the outsider's alleged interest of 70% was in reality no larger than 7%. Even so, the Luchtmans Foundation was a protective construction that would prove its usefulness a few years later.

The exuberant growth of the seventies did not continue into the eighties. Turnover stabilized and was on average a little lower than in the previous decade. In 1981 the company recorded an unexpected loss of two hundred thousand guilders, but this was amply offset by profits of four to five hundred thousand guilders in the following years; in 1984 and 1986 the returns were on the order of a million. Production at the publishing house remained at the same level as in the seventies: approximately two hundred titles a year were brought out, while in addition well over thirty journals were published.

The print works was increasingly becoming the problem child of the company. Rising costs made a profitable exploitation of this division more and more difficult in the eighties. The process of typesetting manualy in metal was only still used for publications in Chinese or Japanese. The Monotype and Intertype machines disappeared from the composing room, because mechanical hot-metal typesetting had become an obsolete technique. The switch was made to photosetting, while the print works chiefly worked with offset. When in 1987 the last Chinese hand-setter retired, the type-metal era came to an end once and for all. Typesetting in Chinese or Japanese was henceforth outsourced to the Far East. In spite of technical innovations and a gradually shrinking workforce, however, the print works continued to post a loss.

Souvenir from the Oude Rijn premises: the sign that showed visitors the way to the upstairs office. BA/ULA

Brill & Brown

During the fiscal year ending in 1987, Brill suffered an unexpected loss of seven hundred thousand guilders. Negative results rarely figured in the annals of the company, and a loss of such magnitude was shocking. In part, the dive into the red was due to macroeconomic forces: the low exchange rate of the dollar was disadvantageous for an internationally operating company such as Brill, the more so because the United States was its largest customer for books. Besides, in those days the publishing establishment was busy with the shift to computerization, which, as elsewhere, was accompanied by large expenditures and unavoidable failures. The print works exacerbated the deficit.

In addition to this, Backhuys's management had a bearing on the loss. The director had planned to create new branch offices abroad for sales promotion, although there were only a few people within the company who recognized the necessity of establishing such branches. The older establishments in Germany and England were hardly profitable, while the new ones in Denmark[29] and the United States only generated costs for the time being. In 1987 Backhuys's penchant for globalization tempted him to acquire a majority interest in the Australian publishing house of Robert Brown, on payment of half a million guilders. According to the director, the subsidiary company "down under" would earn Brill a lot of prestige in New Zealand and Papua New Guinea, a region that was described by him as "a breeding ground of beautiful anthropological and biological literature."[30] The publishing house of Robert Brown turned out to be an utter waste of money: the small business only published travel guides and comprised, apart from Mr. Brown himself, a single employee.

Many people at Brill were of the opinion that Backhuys indulged in his biological hobbies at the expense of the company. Their criticism concerned not only his management,

The Encyclopaedia of Islam
The Key Authority for the Field of Islam
NOW AT AN INCREDIBLE PRICE!
(SEE INSIDE FOR DETAILS)
● Maps
● Illustrations
● Bibliographies
● Bosnia and Herzegovina
● Islamic rule of Palestine
● Oil production
● Islamic law
● Jihad
● Arab women
● And more...
LEIDEN ● BOSTON ● KÖLN
Academic Publishers
BRILL

< Brill's magnum opus: *The Encyclopaedia of Islam*. An entire book could be written on the history of the development of this classic work. Plans were formulated around 1895, but it was not until 1908 that the first fascicle was published, covering the letter *A*. In 1913 the first bound volume was brought out. The first edition, in five volumes, was published in French, English, and German and was eventually completed in 1936. Shortly after the Second World War, Brill conceived a plan for a second edition, this time only in English and French. The idea was to produce four volumes with a supplement, and it was thought that the job could be done within ten years. This proved to be an underestimate: it was not until 2006 that the second edition was completed in twelve volumes plus indices. The reproduced prospectus for the American market shows the work in progress in the year 1996, when eight volumes of the second edition had been completed. Brill is currently producing the third edition, the fourth part of which was published in June 2008. BA/ULA

but also his attitude. The director was under the impression that he had landed in a "picturesque, but archaic museum" of which he had to make a clean sweep.[31] This hardly seems an adequate description of the high-grade company that Wieder had left behind. Backhuys had difficulty in handling the staff, which he regarded as members of the "old guard" who were behind the times and conspired against him. In return, these highly qualified employees were little impressed by the director or the innovations he advocated. Among the rest of the personnel, too, Backhuys's arrogant way of acting created bad blood.

Crisis

The great loss Brill suffered during 1987 brought the simmering tension to a boil. In May 1988 the works council wrote to the director, requesting an explanation for the poor annual figures and the withholding of the employees' bonus. Backhuys hurried to the secretary of the works council, set the letter on fire, and dropped the burning missive on the secretary's desk. The chairman of the works council personally delivered a second communication to the director, who tore it up before the eyes of the bewildered bearer. Such reactions did little to calm the atmosphere in the company.

When the works council subsequently lodged a complaint with the board of supervisory directors, the fat was in the fire. Prof. Dr. E. H. van der Beugel, chairman of the supervisory board for twenty-five years, demanded an independent investigation into Backhuys's management. However, he was unable to convince his fellow supervisory directors of the necessity of this inquiry. Van der Beugel resigned indignantly and was succeeded by R. P. M. de Bok, chairman of the Rotterdam Chamber of Commerce. A few months later, the board of supervisory directors finally came to the conclusion that the management should be subjected to an investigation. The findings of the external expert were so devastating that Backhuys was suspended by the end of November. The director went "on holiday for an indefinite period of time," as the ironic announcement to the personnel ran.

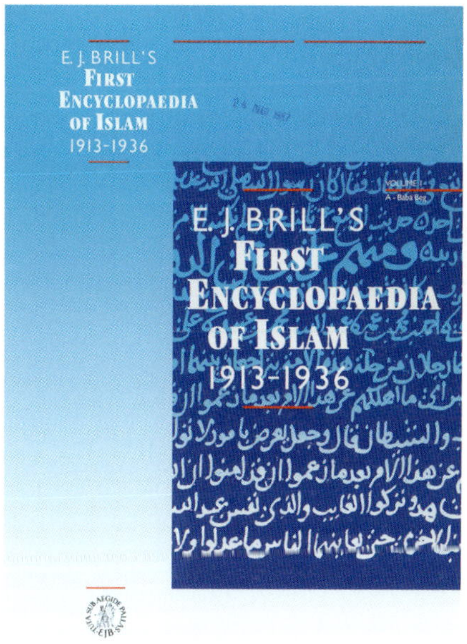

While scholars were was working on the second edition of the *Encyclopaedia of Islam*, a reprint of the first edition (1913-1936) was published in 1987. The reprint was also intended to deter pirated editions, because the copyright expired in 1986. BA/ULA

The end of the type-metal era in the eighties: a typesetter empties the type cases. Manual typesetting, only for works in Chinese and Japanese, continued at Brill until 1987. Brill Coll.

Frans Pruijt, previously employed at the publishing house of Samson-Sijthoff, was appointed interim director as of January 1989. In the following months the figures for the year 1988 became known, which were even more dramatic than those for 1987: Brill had suffered an unprecedented loss of *f* 1,900,000. In addition to employees and supervisory directors, now the shareholders got involved in the matter. Early in March an extraordinary meeting was convened at which the shareholders had to decide on Backhuys's dismissal and termination package. A number of them demanded an explanation of the state of affairs, along with the disclosure of the external expert's report. The supervisory directors refused the latter request, because they had agreed with Backhuys not to wash their dirty linen in public. A large shareholder openly accused them of mismanagement and threatened to bring forward a motion of no confidence. In his opinion, the supervisory directors were trying to disguise the fact that they too were criticized in the report. This time, things did not go beyond threats.

The matter grew more complicated, however, because the "critical" shareholders were old acquaintances of Backhuys or belonged to his in-laws. Jointly they owned a substantial parcel of shares. The dismissal of the director degenerated into a conflict between these shareholders and the supervisory directors, who were supported by the other shareholders and the personnel. In the press, one article after another reported on the difficulties at Brill, hitherto a solid enterprise with an impeccable reputation. In the first half of 1989 the company was flooded with negative publicity. For outsiders, the internal infighting was hard to follow because everybody seemed to be quarreling with everybody else. Brill had plunged deep into the red and was racked by problems: that much was clear. People started to wonder whether the company had any chance of survival at all.

Early in April, supervisory director J. H. Scholte, brother-in-law of Backhuys, suddenly resigned. He made his decision known a day before a second extraordinary meeting of shareholders was to take place. Scholte declared that he disagreed with his fellow supervisory directors over the dismissal of Backhuys and that he was critical of the annual figures of 1988. One can hardly avoid the impression that he knew what was going to happen at the next day's meeting. The fact is that on this occasion the shareholders of the Backhuys faction attempted to seize power by sending the board of supervisory directors packing. The coup failed because the supervisory directors made use of the preference shares of the Luchtmans Foundation, which provided them with a generous majority of votes. With 551 votes for and 1300 against, the Backhuys-sponsored motion of no confidence was rejected.

The use of the protective construction was challenged by the dissatisfied shareholders, who argued that in this case there was no question of a hostile takeover. They instituted summary proceedings in The Hague court of law, but the judge decided against them. An appeal to a higher court was equally in vain; thus the course of events in 1989 gradually put an end to this tragicomedy that had cut deeply into Brill's flesh.

Miniature industrial monuments: matrices from a typesetting machine.
BA/ULA

Reorganization

All of this quarreling concealed a more fundamental problem: the crisis and sharp losses had made it clear that Brill would not be able to continue in its present configuration. Likewise, it was clear which adaptations were required for the firm to survive. Shortly after he had taken up his duties in January 1989, Pruijt wrote a memo in which he outlined the inevitable reorganization. In the first place, all foreign branch offices had to be shut down—not only the ones that had been created by Backhuys, but also the older ones in London and Cologne. The branch offices were unprofitable, and in terms of sales, distribution, and acquisition they hardly served any purpose. With modern means of communication, customers throughout the world could be served from Leiden. Brill's strategic proximity to Schiphol Airport was highly advantageous in this respect, as Pruijt emphasized: "Distribution is achieved through airplane bellies, not through a lot of separate offices."[32]

In the second place, the print works had to be separated from the firm, a decision that was much more painful than closing down the foreign branches. Since 1848 Brill had been a "bookselling firm and printing shop," and the international reputation of the publishing house was based on the unique typographical expertise it had at its command. For Brill to discontinue this glorious tradition was to amputate its own limb, but for many years it had been clear that this business segment was no longer profitable. As early as 1983 Backhuys had become convinced that the print works was a millstone around Brill's neck.[33] The crisis of 1989-1990 brought into sharp focus a problem that had been postponed year after year, precisely because it had only one conceivable remedy.

Pruijt tackled the issue energetically in consultation with the works council and the trade unions. The graphics unions acknowledged that Brill was no longer able to make the print works profitable and accepted the inevitability of the reorganization. What they did demand, however, was that no jobs should be lost in the process. Nor was it Brill's intention to dismiss the well over twenty people who were still employed at the print works. A solution was sought whereby the entire print works would be taken over by another firm and the jobs preserved. The Sigma print works in Zoetermeer agreed to take over Brill's graphics department as of October 1, 1989.

The transaction was effected smoothly, and the employees who went over to Zoetermeer received a job guarantee. In addition, Brill guaranteed that for a period of four years, a share of its publications would be printed by Sigma. In the opinion of all parties concerned, the separation of publishing establishment and print works was arranged under optimal conditions. Through no fault of Brill, the outcome turned out to be tragic after all, for five years later the Sigma print works went bankrupt.

In connection with this reduction in the firm, in 1990 the antiquarian bookshop, too, was closed down—a segment that had been a fixture ever since Brill's very beginnings. The decision did not stem so much from the shop's lack of profitability, but rather from the intention to restrict Brill's activities to the core business of publishing. Moreover, this separation could be arranged without any problems, because Rijk Smitskamp, manager of the antiquarian bookshop since 1970, wanted to continue it as his own business. He changed the name of the shop on the Nieuwe Rijn to "Het Oosters

Director Frans Pruijt in action. Brill Coll.

Antiquarium." Smitskamp's business was a household name in Leiden, and it would continue to be a haunt of booklovers until his retirement in 2006.

Resurrection

After the exodus of the typographers the publishing establishment stayed behind, abandoned in the much too large building on the Plantijnstraat. The printing presses and composing machines also disappeared, so that now there was no reason to complain about lack of space. Following the reorganization sixty people were still employed at Brill, while five years earlier the total workforce, including the foreign branch offices, had amounted to about twice as many. Brill retreated to its core activity, namely publishing. In a way the consolidation marked a return to the past, for the Luchtmanses, too, had been publishers without a print works.

Pruijt summarized his perception of the future in common-sense terms: Brill should "only do those things we're good at."[34] By way of example, he mentioned the traditional strong points of the publishing list—encyclopedias, multivolume standard works, handbooks, and series of monographs in the fields of religious studies, Oriental studies, Arabic studies, classical antiquity, and history. The publishing house did not intend to plunge into new adventures, but rather sought to consolidate and develop its own tradition. In the sixties Wieder had formulated it no differently, but Pruijt had the advantage of a much more easily surveyable company in which to implement the program.

From the crisis was born a "leaner and meaner" Brill, stripped of its dead wood. Thanks to the painful split, Brill was able not only to maintain its continuity, but also to recover its historical identity. The publishing house was able to develop according to the pattern established by its own tradition, no longer encumbered by other business segments. In connection with the reduction of size, the long-winded name "N.V. Boekhandel en Drukkerij voorheen E. J. Brill" was also shortened. The bookselling business and print works had disappeared, and *voorheen* ("formerly") had become an inappropriate anachronism. Henceforth the company was named "E. J. Brill N.V."

As of 1990 Pruijt was appointed tenured director. It was expected that 1989 would also show a loss, but in spite of the costs of the reorganization, a modest profit could be recorded. On the one hand, total turnover decreased to 6.5 million guilders after the print works was split off; on the other hand, the turnover of the publishing house had increased a little thanks to the fact that sales previously made through the foreign branches were now effected through Leiden.

By the beginning of the nineties Brill was gradually recovering. A milestone in its resurrection was the publication of the facsimile and text editions of the Dead Sea Scrolls, at the request of the Israeli government and in cooperation with the Leiden-based company IDC. Because of the unique character of the material this was an extremely honorable commission, apart from the fact that from a commercial point of view it was an interesting project. Brill owed the commission to its earlier production of facsimile and text editions of the Coptic Nag Hammadi codices, which were discovered in the Egyptian desert in 1945.[35] The Dead Sea Scrolls generated a tide of supplemental publications at the publishing house, including a special journal entitled *Dead Sea Discoveries*. The facsimile edition on microfiche was produced by IDC, which specialized in the photographic reproduction of valuable historical documents. The cooperation with IDC contributed to the incorporation of this company as a Brill imprint later on. The facsimile edition of the Dead Sea Scrolls appeared in digitized format on CD-ROM and was published on the Internet in 1999.

Another sign of recovery was the Export Award awarded to Brill by the Ministry of Economic Affairs in 1993. The award was fully justified, as there was no other company in the Netherlands so focused on the foreign market: Brill derived 95% of its turnover from exports and shipped books to 104 countries, all told. Another milestone in the same year was of a sad nature: Frans Pruijt, through whose agency Brill had risen like a phoenix from the ashes, died suddenly at the age of forty-eight. His lighthearted manner was wonderfully suited to the weight of his task. In his early years he had toured the country as a chauffeur with the singer "Drs. P.," famous in Holland for his poetic nonsensical songs, and in a similarly light-footed style he had rescued Brill from the shambles.

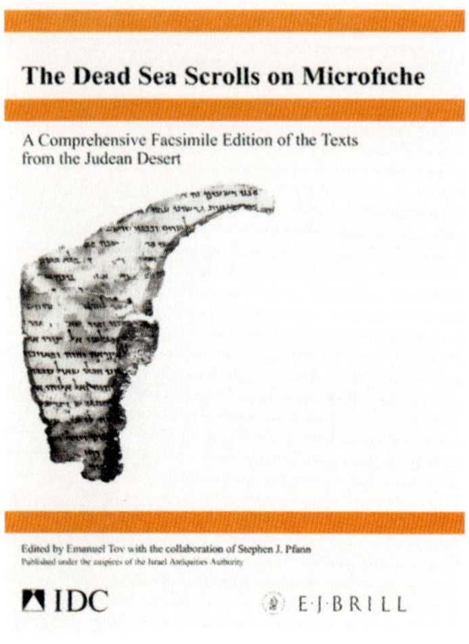

Prospectus for the facsimile edition of the Dead Sea Scrolls. BA/ULA

Expansion

In 1994 Reinout Kasteleijn was appointed director of Brill, after a period of interim management under supervisory director J. Kist. The resurrected phoenix was now really beginning to spread its wings. With a production of two hundred titles, the publishing house realized in 1996 a turnover of 15.8 million guilders and a profit of 1.15 million. The company had never seen such figures in the days when it was still operating as a conglomerate of business segments. Since 1990 fifteen new employees had been taken on, bringing the total workforce to seventy-five people.

An important project for Brill was the publication of the Dead Sea Scrolls in the early nineties. The facsimile edition on microform was a coproduction of Brill and the Leiden-based IDC, which specialized in the reproduction of unique source material. IDC has been an imprint of Brill since 2006. Brill Coll.

In the year 1996 yet another jubilee was celebrated: it was one hundred years ago that Adriaan van Oordt and Frans de Stoppelaar had founded the public limited company. In honor of this centenary, Brill was granted the privilege of bearing the title "royal" (*koninklijk*). The official sobriquet of the publishing house now became "Koninklijke Brill N.V."—old Evert Jan had to sacrifice his time-honored initials for ease of pronunciation. Actually, people at Brill were not much impressed by the new status, as the firm's history went back much farther than 1896. Besides, the royal rank carried little weight in most of the countries that the publishing house did business with. Brill did not deem it necessary to provide its logo with a little crown; Pallas was safe and sound behind her shield and could manage quite well without regalia. Kasteleijn summarized the royal honor rather casually as an acknowledgment that Brill was "a decent company."[36]

A year later the renamed public limited company took the plunge into the stock market. Since its foundation the company had been quoted on the so-called "Unlisted Market," but this old-fashioned sideline of the stock exchange was finally abolished. Thereupon Brill decided in July 1997 to make the switch over to the official stock market. Till then, most shares had been in the hands of a regular clan of Brill adepts—relatives of previous directors, employees, authors, and scholars. In order to prevent Brill from being swallowed up by giants such as Reed-Elsevier or Wolters-Kluwer, precautionary measures were taken. Apart from the Luchtmans Foundation, an additional protective construction was introduced stipulating that new shareholders were allowed to have a maximum interest of 1%. The chief purpose of the stock market flotation was to attract capital for future expansions.[37]

HARE MAJESTEIT DE KONINGIN
HEEFT BIJ HAAR BESCHIKKING VAN
20 mei 1996
HET RECHT TOT HET VOEREN VAN HET PREDIKAAT
KONINKLIJK
VERLEEND
AAN E.J. Brill N.V. te Leiden

DE GROOTMEESTER
VAN HET HUIS
VAN HARE MAJESTEIT DE KONINGIN

In 1996, in honor of the one hundredth anniversary of the public limited company, Her Majesty the Queen bestowed on Brill the right to call itself *koninklijk*—"royal." Brill Coll.

This capital was necessary indeed, for since then Brill has taken an enormous jump forward. While annual production in 1996 was still around two hundred titles, in 2008 it has risen to some six hundred. The number of learned journals published is now well over a hundred. Correspondingly the number of employees has risen from 75 in 1996 to 130 in 2008. During the past few years several small publishers' lists have been taken over, all fitting the niche market served by Brill: Humanities Press (1998), VSP (academic journals, 1999), Styx (history and archaeology of the Near East, 2001), the *Index Islamicus* (2001), Gieben (Greek, 2006), and Hotei (Japanese art, 2006). Larger takeovers were the previously mentioned IDC (2006) and Martinus Nijhoff Publishers (2003). The latter is a prominent publisher in the field of international law, international relations, and human rights, whereby Brill acquired a strong positioning in the academic market for these fields. VSP, Nijhoff, IDC, and Hotei are published as imprints of Brill.

Brill makes increasing use of the opportunities provided by the Internet, for instance by cooperating with Google. Information on new publications is distributed electronically and the present publication portfolio includes several digital publications. Contacts with Russia and especially with China have been intensified, and these countries are also emerging distribution markets. The production of books is to an ever greater degree taking place abroad, both with regard to printing and layout. Brill is not only a strongly growing company, it is also a company that is greatly changing.

In spite of all this, Brill continues to exist by virtue of the traditional book, and this will not be any different in the foreseeable future. The second edition of *the Encyclopaedia of Islam*, completed in 2006, can also be consulted in digital format, and the same applies to the third edition the publishing house is now working on. The digital publications derive their authority from the physical substrate of the fourteen volumes of the second edition and the as yet unknown number of volumes of the third. A mammoth

First quotation of the Brill share on the Amsterdam Stock Exchange, July 1997. Brill Coll.

production like the twenty-volume *Brill's New Pauly: Encyclopaedia of the Ancient World* (since 2002, twelve volumes have been published) will also be available in print and electronic editions.

Brill has taken Pruijt's advice to heart: the company has continued to do what it's good at and has taken advantage of opportunities as they present themselves. The lines set out in the past have been extended into the present. Not only has Brill continued to do what it's good at, Brill is doing well, as its strong growth attests. Since its introduction, Brill's stock ranks among the fast climbers on the exchange, and on the basis of its growth figures it has been nominated for the "Gazelle Award" several times already.

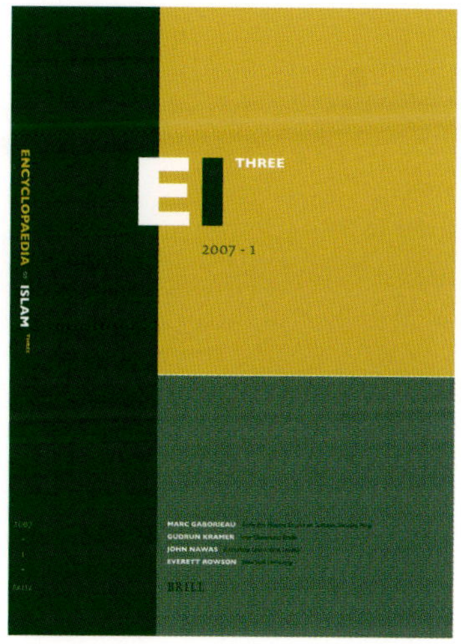

Cover of the first volume of the third edition of the *Encyclopaedia of Islam*. By now the publication enjoys such renown that the abbreviation *EI* suffices on the cover. Brill Coll.

Continuity

The history of a company is a description of the changes it has undergone over the course of time. In conclusion, two recent changes are recorded here: in 2005 Brill relocated once more, this time to a new building on the Plantijnstraat that is entirely suited to the requirements of the publishing house. The older building, dating from the early 1960s and the pride of the company at the time, has been demolished. That is the way things go—at any rate, with buildings that do not enjoy a monumental status such as the former orphanage on the Oude Rijn. As for the second change, which occurred a year earlier: in March 2004 Reinout Kasteleijn stepped down as director and was succeeded by Herman Pabbruwe, since 1683 the eighteenth director in succession. With him we leave the past and enter the present. In the last chapter of this book his vision of the future will be presented.

Luchtmans in 1683 and Brill in 2008: the differences are great, but so are the similarities. The company first saw the light of day as a scholarly publishing house, and through all of its metamorphoses it has retained this character. Between the six books a year of Jordaan Luchtmans and the six hundred of Brill there is a continuing line, with striking constants such as the Syriaca. Yet this continuity is by no means something to be taken for granted, as has already been mentioned at the beginning of this book. A company does not have a built-in mechanism enabling it to survive the vicissitudes of time and market trends. It would have been more in the order of things for Luchtmans or Brill to have come to grief at some point in the course of those 325 years. That the opposite is the case may be called a miracle. To put it in a less metaphysical way, chance and circumstance have played a major role in the firm's continued existence over such a long period of time.

While the workings of chance cannot be evaded, in part they are counterbalanced by other factors. The quality of a book is not the result of luck, but of goal-oriented human action. A company that pollutes the world with inferior products has no right to exist in the long run. Quality, on the other hand, and the reputation founded on it, have a preserving effect on a firm's continued existence. And the people who over the course of time have given shape to the company—they too resist the whims of fortune, trying to anticipate the future and striving to turn chance to their advantage.

Inevitably in this brief history the emphasis has been on prominent figures, ignoring the many anonymous people who made Brill great. It is precisely these people who, in the relay of successive generations, are the chief driving force of continuity. Not only is craftsmanship passed down from generation to generation, but so is the sense of solidarity within the company. It is hard to put a name on the guiding spirit of this tradition—professional pride, loyalty, a sense of partnership in an unique company. Call it a Brill feeling, cherished by its employees and other stakeholders. At the same time, this Brill feeling transcends the local context thanks to the international character of the publishing house. Anyone who has dealings with Brill knows that he or she is connected to a world that is much larger than Leiden.

Without the devotion of all of its associates, Brill could not have developed into a publishing house of global reputation. The flood of books, some twenty thousand titles since 1683, not only stems from commercial or academic motives, but just as much from Brill's special company culture.

The new Brill building on the Plantijnstraat. Brill Coll.

BRILL
PARKEERPLAATS
BRILL

Heroes of the grand pacification

Kuniyoshi's *Taiheiki eiyū den*

BRILL: PRESENT AND FUTURE

Under the Fax

"In 2015 we will live in a different world. America and Japan will be next door. We can transmit ourselves by fax machine, so to speak." This remark by director Frans Pruijt in 1989 shows how fast the world, in particular the world of publishing, is changing.[1] Barely twenty years later, Japan has been superseded by China as an economic power, and Pruijt's metaphor is outdated: hardly anyone uses the fax machine any longer, because we transmit ourselves via the Internet and e-mail. Amid fundamental changes in society, the economy, and technology, Brill seeks to chart a course that is realistic and feasible.

In this process the company's own history is a source of inspiration for present-day Brill. The reorganization of 1989-1990 and the closing down of unprofitable business segments enabled the publishing house to reinvent itself. Henceforth Brill restricted itself to its core activity of publishing, thus emphasizing its own tradition. Going by the numbers, the company has made a quantum leap in the past two decades: approximately six hundred titles a year, more than one hundred journals, and a turnover of € 26,000,000 were inconceivable figures around 1990.

Although the company can justifiably be proud of such results, in comparison with the big publishing firms in the global market, it is a relatively minor player. Nevertheless, it can be stated without exaggeration that Brill ranks among the top scholarly publishers worldwide. Whereas large international publishing houses seek to distinguish themselves by offering a broad range of titles in science, education, and professional training, Brill mainly serves niches of the scholarly research markets in the humanities and law. Given its orientation, the company is more closely related to an academic publishing house such as Oxford University Press than to a company such as Reed-Elsevier.

Flexibility and Keeping Pace with the Times

Globalization, digitization, and the demands of new generations of readers are developments that need to be taken seriously by a publisher. No internationally operating company can afford to shrink from such changes, if it does not want to run the risk of jeopardizing its own survival. Taking advantage of these changes, however, demands more than just the survival strategies taught by the struggle to compete on an international level. It also requires the art of combining the opportunities of the present with the reputation and status gained in the past.

A history spanning more than three centuries testifies that Brill has always succeeded in adapting itself and making choices, which remains a significant talent in 2008. This does not mean that every new development merits a response: some developments are incompatible with Brill's own character. Choosing between what matches Brill's

In the literal as well as the figurative sense, the recently acquired Hotei publishing list adds color to Brill's Asian Studies. The imprint is an established name in the study of Japanese printmaking.

profile and what doesn't requires an energetic approach and a strict watch over the company's own identity. Passive assimilation to external realities is a form of mimicry that only works in the short run, until the next change in the outside world forces the adoption of yet another color. A company that is only riding on the waves of time becomes the plaything of market trends; to put it in terms of Brill's logo, mere opportunism will result in too much Hermes and too little Pallas.

Thousands of Titles

The same line of reasoning applies to the technological challenges facing the company now and in the near future. Not every new technology will in itself be decisive for the future of Brill or guarantee its lasting prosperity. Equally important is the way in which the organization succeeds in integrating and applying technological advancements. Here too it is not just a matter of the company's capacity to adapt to external circumstances, but also its ability to adjust the possibilities of the digital age to its own tradition. Digitization for the sake of digitization alone is not necessarily a guarantee of survival in the twenty-first century. The question, then, is whether Brill will be able to secure its continuity by identifying and adopting the new technologies that are best suited to its historically evolved identity.

Evidently Brill is fully capable of adapting to the new era. Judging by developments from the middle of the nineties onwards, the Brill tradition is highly compatible with the computer and the Internet. The strong growth of the publishing house during the past decade has been facilitated by its adoption of appropriate digital possibilities. Even in a literal sense the company is digitizing its past: older titles from the publishing list are being brought back to life by making it possible to search their contents on the Internet.

Technology and history also go hand in hand in the compilation of a digital publishing list of all titles published since 1683 under the imprint of Luchtmans, and from 1848 onwards under that of Brill. Given the magnitude of this task it is still a work in progress, in which Internet users are asked to join the search for unknown publications by Brill. The Luchtmans titles have been fairly completely recorded within the framework of the Short Title Catalogue of the Netherlands (STCN). The publishing list of Luchtmans for the years 1683-1800 can also be consulted at Brill's website.[2] Including the period 1800-1848, the Luchtmans publishing list comprises around 2,500 titles in all. Add to that figure the ongoing production of Brill, and the result is a staggering quantity of books that no individual can survey: the counter has already passed 20,000. The end is not yet in sight, but the conclusion is justified that during its long existence the publishing house has made a major contribution to the intellectual heritage of the world.

Pallas and Hermes

Apart from technology, other issues play a role in the book market, such as the publisher's reputation and the quality of his products. A strong share in a particular segment of the market also contributes to the stability of the company. In both respects Brill can count itself fortunate. Furthermore, the human factor is of vital importance to the company. The publishing house could not exist without the commitment of highly

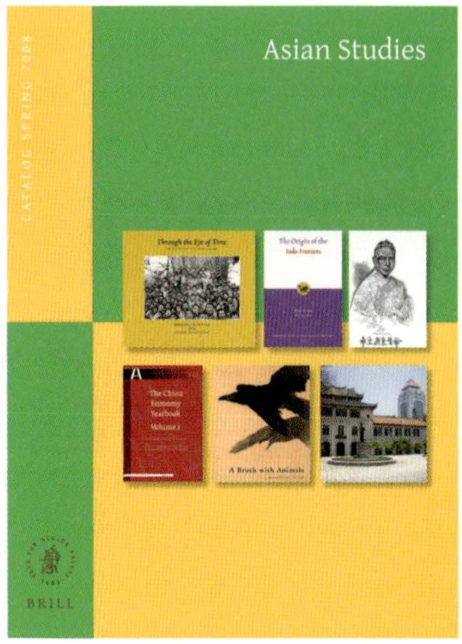

Once or twice a year, catalogs in a large number of disciplines are published. In addition to traditionally extensive domains such as Asian Studies, Biblical & Religious Studies, and Middle East & Islamic Studies, there are new developments such as African Studies. All of the promotional material features the same house style and is instantly recognizable. Catalogs are increasingly downloaded from www.brill.nl

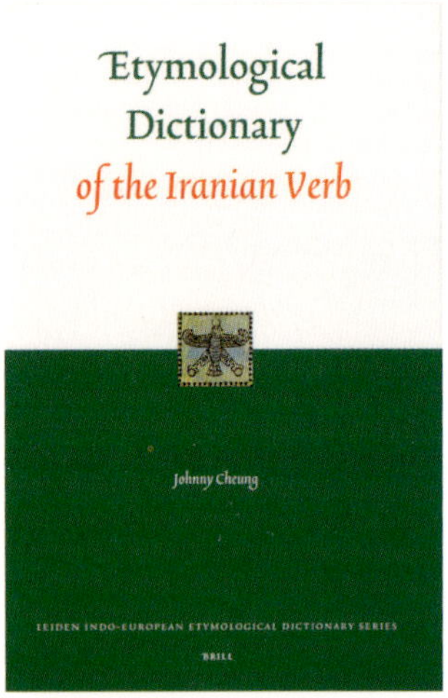

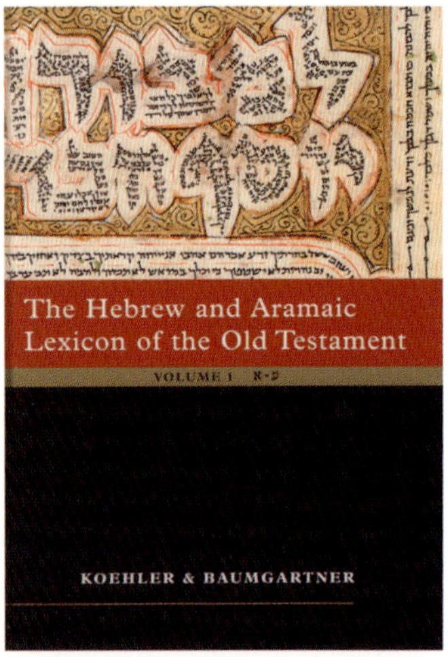

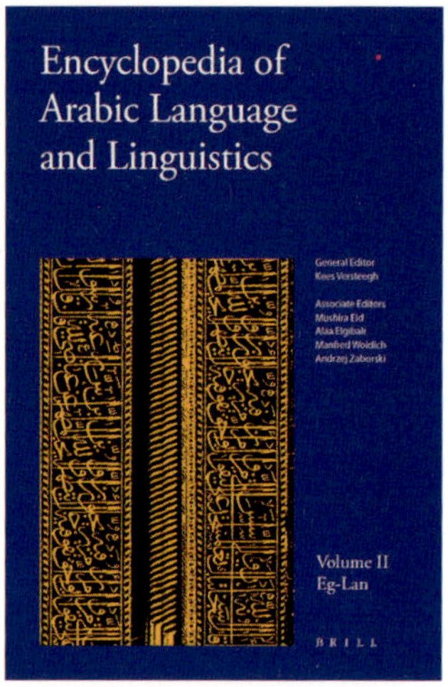

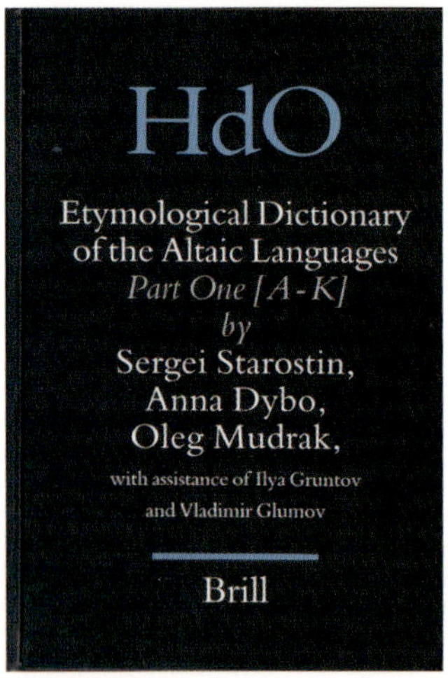

In the past Brill did not have a special publishing program for languages or linguistics. Publications in this field were classed among Oriental studies, religious studies, or history. When an inventory of language publications was drawn up across all publishing lists, it turned out that there was a perfectly sound basis for a separate program geared to minor, endangered, and ancient languages. Thanks to the past, Language and Linguistics made a flying start. On the basis of the existing publishing list, catalogs have also been compiled for Slavic & Eurasian Studies, Philosophy and Art, and Architecture & Archeology. They highlight Brill's latent strength in these fields and promote the sales of older titles. The acquisition of IDC has accelerated plans for Slavic studies and art history. The takeover of Hotei stimulated a plan to develop an art-historical publishing list within the portfolio of Asian Studies.

CATALOG 2008
Language &
Linguistics
BRILL

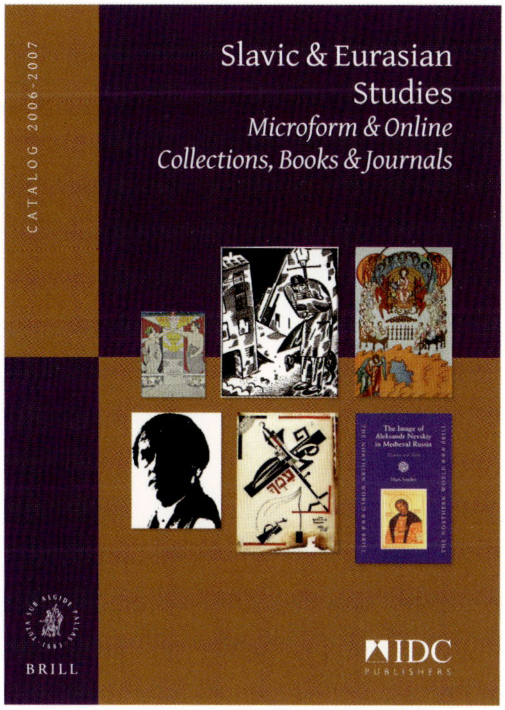
CATALOG 2006-2007
Slavic & Eurasian
Studies
Microform & Online
Collections, Books & Journals
BRILL
IDC
PUBLISHERS

CATALOG 2008
Philosophy
BRILL

CATALOG 2008
Art, Architecture
& Archeology
BRILL

The Hotei Encyclopedia of
Japanese Woodblock Prints
I
Amy Reigle Newland
General Editor

中国出土瓷器全集
COMPLETE COLLECTION OF CERAMIC ART UNEARTHED IN CHINA
1
北京
BEIJING
BRILL
科学出版社
www.sciencep.com

От Коммунистического ун-та
Нац. Мен. Запада
им. Ю.Ю. Мархлевского.
XV
ЛЕТИЕ
Московского государственного
еврейского театра.
„Король
Лир."
1919–1934

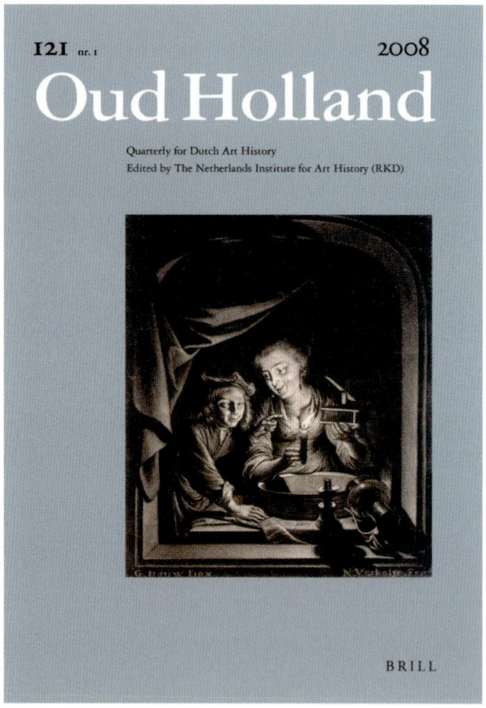
121 nr. 1
2008
Oud Holland
Quarterly for Dutch Art History
Edited by The Netherlands Institute for Art History (RKD)
BRILL

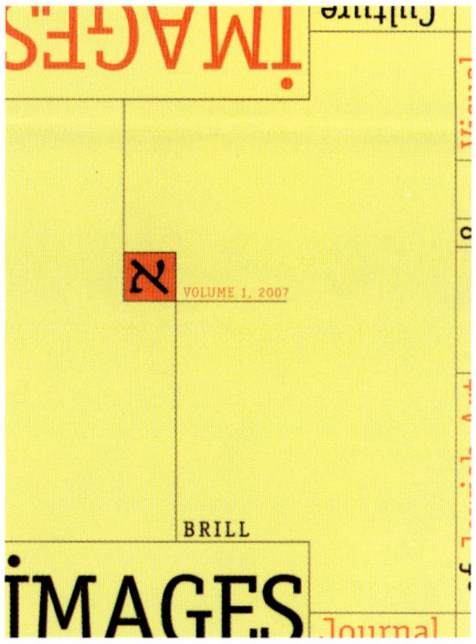

A search of Brill's publishing lists yielded a large number of titles that are relevant for a catalog on art history and archaeology. Both the takeover of Hotei and cooperation with Sciences Press in China have accelerated the development of a Visual Arts program within Asian Studies. IDC supplied the basis for a strong art-historical component within Slavic Studies. Moreover, the acquisition of IDC gave Brill the opportunity to make documentary collections of source material for Western art history available online, such as the *Art Sales Catalogues, 1600–1900* and the *Répertoire des catalogues de ventes publiques* by Frits Lugt. Contacts with the Netherlands Institute for Art History in The Hague resulted in the contract for *Oud Holland*, which is published by Brill as of 2008. *Oud Holland* is an internationally renowned journal for the study of Dutch art and the oldest surviving art-historical periodical in the world.

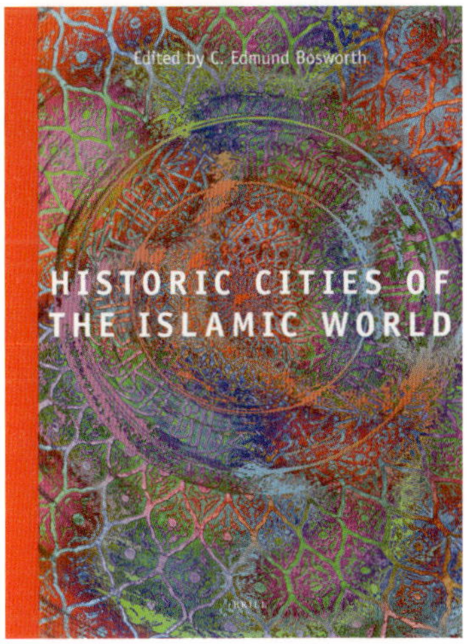

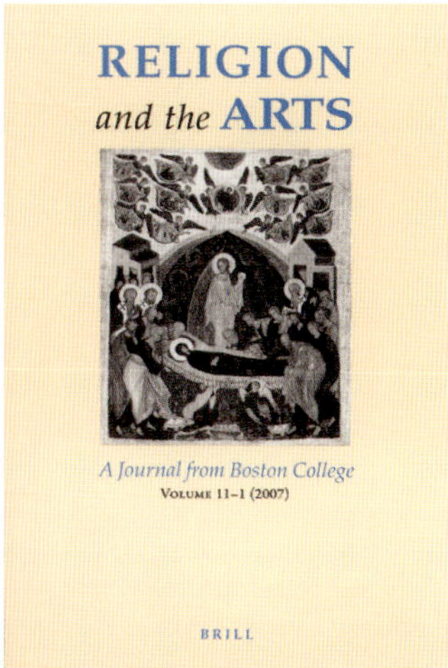

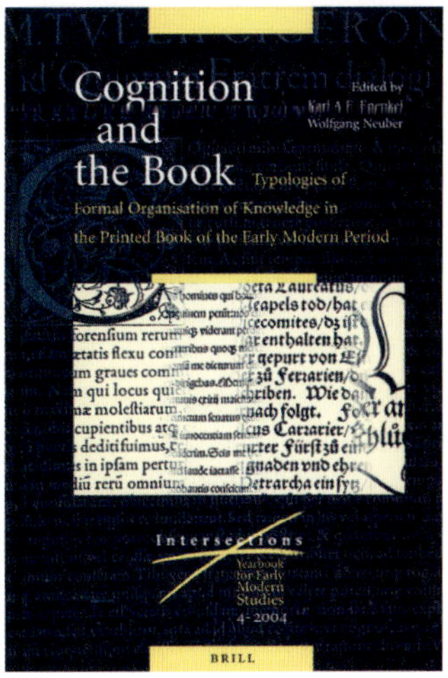

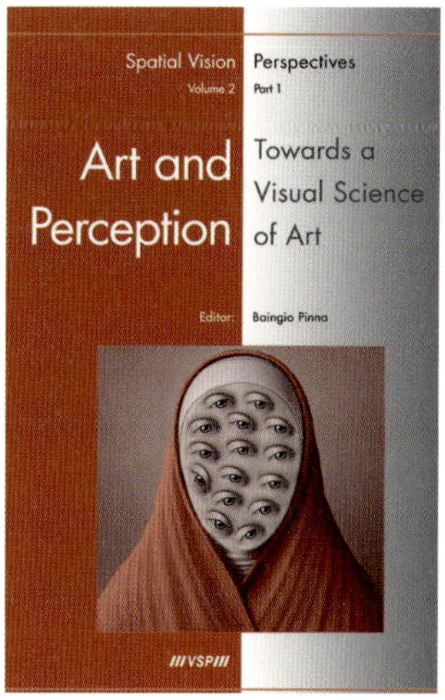

educated and well-motivated staff, who maintain a network of worldwide contacts and are on the lookout for new academic research. This means that upholding and refining standards of quality are basic strategic principles for healthy growth.

Following in its own tradition, the publishing house seeks to achieve the right balance between commerce and learning. Pallas Athena, the goddess of learning, and Hermes, the god of commerce, appear beside one another in Brill's logo. Their joint contribution is the best guarantee of the company's prosperity. The cooperating gods do not only embody a corporate vision, but also a worldview that emphasizes social responsibility and sustainable economic growth. A socially conscious outlook in business not only signals an attitude of respect for the public at large, but also contributes to a healthy work climate within the organization.

Brill's portfolio is, in almost all respects, well diversified. The publishing list is evenly divided among disciplines and product forms, sales run through various distribution channels, and the proportion of turnover from recent and older titles is well balanced. Brill makes sure that it does not get involved in too many different and unconnected disciplines. Growth is sought through product development and through acquisitions that fit into the company's historically evolved program, which means a strong emphasis on the humanities. Through the recent acquisition of the Nijhoff imprint, Brill has gained a strong position in international law as well. The strategy of the publishing house is to follow the development of research within a specific field of study. The primary target group always consists of participants in a particular scholarly discourse, a circle of professionals to which both the authors and the customers of Brill belong.

Authors and the texts they supply are naturally of vital importance for the publishing house. A network of scholars assesses submissions before they are published. This peer review process guarantees the academic quality of Brill's products and also ensures the independence of the publishing house.

Dynamic Heritage

Traditionally Brill has distinguished itself from other publishing houses by its specialization in "peculiar" languages. Luchtmans's publishing list already contained several publications in Syriac, Arabic, and Hebrew. Around 1825 Arabic studies expanded enormously, owing to the systematic publication of manuscripts from the Legatum Warnerianum of Leiden University. Until 1848 this series of publications appeared under the name of Luchtmans, but it was in fact a co-production including Johannes and Evert Jan Brill. After the latter took over the firm, he continued the tradition of publishing Arabic books.

The man for whom the present publishing house is named had a penchant for strange characters, and he ventured to publish books in Sanskrit, Japanese, and the hieratic script of ancient Egypt. In the last quarter of the nineteenth century, exotic languages became the most distinguishing feature of the publishing house, especially in the field of Orientalia. Brill published books in more than thirty languages, whereby the firm acquired an international reputation. To quote the proud slogan used by the publishing house at the Frankfurt book fair in 1960: "We print and publish in all languages of the world."

Thanks to the takeover of Martinus Nijhoff Publishers in 2003, Brill acquired a leading position in the field of international law. A year later The Hague Academy of International Law awarded the publishing contract for its *Recueil des Cours* or *Collected Courses* once again to Nijhoff. Since the beginning of 2008 this important and voluminous collection is also offered online. All of Brill's publications in International Law and Human Rights carry the established imprint "Martinus Nijhoff Publishers."

In the past few decades Brill has published relatively few titles in the field of unique, endangered, or dead languages. Recently the publishing house decided to reestablish this old specialty by creating the list segment Languages and Linguistics. The planned publications require that the expertise for which Brill was traditionally known, namely the typography of exotic characters, must once again be cultivated.

Back in the type-metal era, when the publishing house brought out a book in an unknown script such as Lydian or Estrangelo, special typefaces were manufactured for this purpose. Books in such languages were set manually by the most experienced typesetters of the firm. At an early age they had become familiar with typesetting in strange characters, and they in turn passed down their craftsmanship to the next generation of typesetters. They were the master typesetters who composed Brill's typographic elite. It was only by virtue of these craftsmen that the publishing house could boast that it was able to publish "in all languages of the world." In 1987 the last master typesetter retired, as a result of which this manual tradition came to an end. Until that time, works in Chinese and Japanese were still manually typeset.

For publications in the new list segment Languages and Linguistics, the necessary exotic characters are now being designed by computer, in accordance with the Unicode standard. A traditional handiwork, formerly a key element in the firm's reputation, makes it way back to the present in a digital form. Brill's adoption of computer design for outlandish scripts is a striking example of the way in which the company matches the possibilities of the present to its own tradition. Because this new publishing practice requires some six thousand unusual characters, the company is designing its own typeface. This so-called "Brill Text" converts digital codes in clear letters and signs, both in print and on the monitor. The usual typefaces do not meet Brill's need for special signs.

Digital Times

Undoubtedly, digitization has been the most important development for Brill in the past decade. The publishing house is taking advantage of the many developments that have presented themselves in recent years, ranging from online monographs and journal archives to concordances, encyclopedias, and everything in between. The addition of new electronic components to traditional print publications and the creation of hybrid products go hand in hand with the development of purely electronic publications. For instance, in connection with the list segment Languages and Linguistics, it is feasible to publish sound material and music of threatened languages, both as a means of conservation and as a tool for researchers. The traditional monopoly of written or printed sources is losing ground, and the demand for audiovisual material for research purposes is steadily increasing.[3]

Moreover, the technology of the Internet has greatly improved Brill's efficiency in the field of marketing, especially owing to the use of e-bulletins and targeted e-mailing. The firm also closely cooperates with Google. As of 2005 most Brill books are being digitized and incorporated into the Google Book Search program. The publishing backlist is also made accessible in this way, which means that older titles become visible again and are given a second life. A title that is still available can be ordered by the customer from the publishing house, a bookstore, or Amazon.com. The technology

For fifty years now, IDC has specialized in the photography of fragile and unique source material. This is not done at random, but according to a meticulous plan whereby geographically diverse sources are brought together in coherent research collections. The subjects of IDC fit almost perfectly within the domains in which Brill already occupies a strong position. The first cooperation resulted in the publication of the Dead Sea Scrolls in the 1990s. The Waldenses collection shows that IDC is cooperating with the *crème de la crème* of libraries at home and abroad.

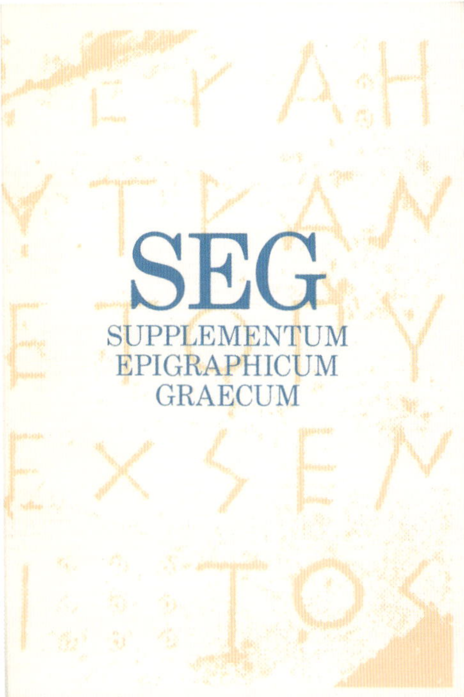

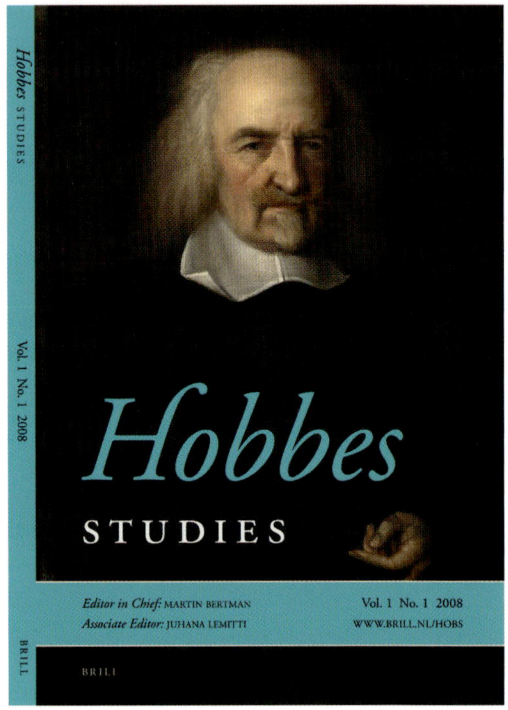

Acquisitions are only made if they will contribute to returns in the foreseeable future and offer particular strategic benefits. Most of the activities taken over are continued under the imprint of Brill. The takeover of Gieben Publishers reinforced Brill's Classical Studies portfolio with the voluminous series *Supplementum Epigraphicum Graecum*. Thanks to Van Gorcum Publishers, Brill acquired new publications in the fields of religious studies, Judaica, history, and philosophy. The journal *Hobbes Studies* forms a welcome addition to Brill's own publishing list. Transnational Publishers reinforced Nijhoff's program with post-graduate textbooks and standard works such as the *Ocean Yearbook*, whose twenty-second edition has now been published.

of the Internet supports the publishing house in one of its chief missions toward authors: the advertisement and distribution of each publication on the widest possible scale.

If a certain book is no longer available, the publisher may decide to issue a reprint if there is sufficient demand. Moreover, it is possible to print additional copies of nearly all of the more recent publications by using "print on demand" technology. Thus, in the near future it will be possible to supply an enormous diversity of titles without having to maintain large stocks.

Brill seeks worldwide distribution for its products, both books and electronic publications. To preserve them for the future, printed texts are stored in several archives. Electronic publications are preserved in the digital depository (the e-Depot) of the Royal Library in The Hague. This national library has the expertise necessary to ensure long-term access to the digital publications, as new modes of rendition technology become standard.

Brill generally develops its publications at its own expense and at its own risk. Moreover, in the case of large reference works, authors and editors are often invited and contracted by the publisher. For this reason discussion of "open access" policies, whereby the author or the author's academic institution pays the publisher for its services, does not yet play a major role in the company's considerations. At Brill, it is chiefly the favor of the customer and the reader that must be won. If scholarly independence can be guaranteed, however, and the publishing house is clearly able to provide added value, Brill is prepared to employ other payment models as well, such as those that make academic publications available to readers for free.

Brill and the World

Since the days of Luchtmans, the publishing house has had an international character. In the seventeenth and eighteenth centuries, Leiden was Europe's "city of books," a meeting place for authors, scholars, and publishers. As described previously, the Luchtmanses regularly traveled abroad and maintained a network of international contacts. The same applies to the nineteenth-century directors of Brill, who traveled all over Europe to visit international congresses where they played a role as brokers of knowledge. They developed the publishing house as the hub of an international scholarly network, especially in the fields of Arabic studies and Oriental studies.

Today, Brill continues this tradition and maintains contacts with all important centers of academic research throughout the world. Brill has traditionally been closely attached to Leiden University, although no longer in the capacity of academic printer, an office the company held for a century and a half. Particularly in Islamic studies, Arabic studies, Sinology, and archaeology, Leiden academics are well represented among Brill's authors.

In time, Asia will become an emerging market for Brill and will perhaps be just as important as the United States. As more funds become available for academic research and education in China, the demand for specialist literature will strongly increase. In recent years Brill has entered into cooperative agreements with several publishing houses in China, including Peking University Press. This publishing house is especially geared to the humanities, a domain in which Brill has traditionally excelled.

At the Beijing International Bookfair in 2007, Brill concluded important cooperative agreements with some Chinese publishing houses. On one day a contract was made with the Social Sciences Academic Press of the Chinese Academy of Social Sciences, and on the next with Peking University Press. Brill has its own website for the Chinese market and even has its own name in Chinese, phonetically corresponding to "Brill." The first two characters form the words *Bo Rui*, signifying "rich knowledge or source" and "broad outlook and profound wisdom" respectively. The following characters indicate that Brill is a scholarly publisher. The signs have been calligraphed by SHU Zhongru (Loudi, Hunan province).

For the time being, cooperation is limited to the exchange of staff and know-how and the launch of joint projects.

A strategic cooperative agreement has also been concluded with the Social Science Academic Press of the Chinese Academy of Social Sciences. These and other cooperative partnerships are facilitating the English translation of Chinese publications, and vice versa. Brill has the ambition of becoming one of the most important publishers in and on China. The feasibility of a Chinese branch will be given serious consideration in the long run. Meanwhile, Brill has adopted a Chinese identity and publisher's name and maintains a Chinese website of its own.

Brill made its entry into the Russian market thanks to the acquisition of IDC, which offers various products in the field of Russian history. Certain segments of Brill's publishing list are perfectly suited to a publishing list in Russian Studies. With a view to growth in this area, the publishing house has compiled a survey of publications that will be the basis for a multimedia Slavic and Eurasian Studies program.

Brill USA

North America continues to be an important market for Brill. The American market share was around 25 percent, which has now increased to well over 40 percent. Brill's original offices in the United States were established in 1986, in the W. S. Heinemann bookstore in Manhattan. At that time, Brill was using bookstores as part of its distribution strategy. During the reorganization of 1989-1990 initiated by Frans Pruijt, the Manhattan office and bookstore were closed and the company moved its U.S. operations to Kinderhook, a small town near Albany in upstate New York. All other functions, including editorial, production, finance, and distribution, continued to be based in Leiden.

In 1998, under the leadership of Managing Director Reinout Kasteleijn, Brill N.V. established a permanent base of operations in Boston. Given the strategic importance of the U.S. market, the potential for growth in the United States, and the large number of major universities in the area, Boston was a logical choice. Originally, two legal companies were established within the Boston office at 112 Water Street: Brill Academic Publishers, a publishing company and imprint; and Brill USA, a company providing sales, marketing, and distribution services in the United States on behalf of the parent company, Brill N.V. During the early 2000s, Brill Academic Publishers (Boston) published paperback reprints of Brill N.V. titles for the North American market and continued to issue Humanities Press journals and book series, following the acquisition of parts of the Humanities Press list in 1999. The company also published a few new titles, primarily in Religious Studies.

In order to further capitalize on the sales growth potential in the United States, Brill decided to provide local customer service as well as fulfillment and distribution services to the American market. In June 2000, Brill appointed Books International, Inc., a Virginia corporation with warehouse facilities in Dulles, to provide complete book fulfillment services to customers in the Americas. The strategy proved to be successful. Customers in the United States and Canada now received orders more promptly and enjoyed faster customer service. Consequently, book sales continued to improve in the Americas.

博睿學術出版社

In March 2003, after the acquisition of Martinus Nijhoff Publishers, the company moved to larger offices on the sixth floor of the Water Street facility in order to accommodate more staff. When Herman Pabbruwe was appointed managing director of Brill N.V. in 2004, greater emphasis was placed on the Boston organization, and Brill began a new period of growth and expansion in the United States. Following the launch of Brill Online major reference products and the acquisition of IDC primary source material in microfiche and electronic formats, the North American sales and marketing organization was considerably expanded in order to provide coverage for the key trade channel accounts, as well as more direct representation to libraries and library consortia. The Brill Academic Publishers (Boston) publishing program was integrated into Brill N.V., and the imprint was retired. At the same time, new publishing activities were launched within the Boston organization, including programs in Jewish Studies and Modern China Studies. The program in International Law resulted from the acquisition of Transnational Publishers of New York in 2006. A publishing program in Latin American Studies is also under consideration. These studies reflect an active research base in North America.

During 2006, Brill USA and Brill Academic Publishers, the original companies formed as part of the move to Boston, formally merged into one corporation: Brill USA, Inc. The growing organization, which includes publishing, production, marketing, and sales staff totaling fifteen employees, required more office space. In February 2007, Brill USA moved a short distance away to larger premises at 153 Milk Street. Brill USA has developed into a fully fledged department of Brill's integrated global organization offering editorial, operational, and commercial services.

The exterior of 153 Milk Street in downtown Boston, home of Brill's Boston office since early 2007. Boston's Custom House Tower as seen from the office's interior.

The Archives of Brill and Luchtmans

In 2006 Brill gave its company archive on loan to the Library of the Book Trade, which is housed in the Department of Special Collections of the University of Amsterdam Library. Under a commission from Brill, the archive of forty-five linear meters is being inventoried, arranged, and made accessible to scholars. This archival material was used for the first time in the present publication; it not only covers the history of Brill but also provides information on the publishing trade in general.

The Luchtmans archive—eleven linear meters covering the period between 1683 and 1848—had previously found a home among the Special Collections of the University of Amsterdam Library, as described in the first chapter of this book. In combination with the Brill archive, which spans the period from 1848 to 1991, it is possible to form an almost complete picture of the development of the firm.[4] Covering a continuous period of more than three centuries, the two archives constitute a unique source for Dutch book history and a cultural and historical monument of the first order. A supplementary archive is housed in Leiden: in 2007 Rijk Smitskamp, the owner of "Het Oosters Antiquarium" (formerly Brill's antiquarian bookshop), donated his archive to the Leiden University Library. It comprises correspondence between 1970 and 2004, a large collection of annotated sales catalogs dating from around 1930 to 2005, special files, photographs, and nearly a hundred drawers of index cards recording titles of books sold.

Since 2006 Brill has been funding the stay of one or two "Brill Fellows" at the Scaliger Institute of the Leiden University Library. The Scaliger Institute was established in 2000 with the purpose of promoting and supporting the Special Collections of the Leiden University Library. The institute initiates research projects, organizes lectures and symposia, publishes research results, and grants scholarships to researchers and guest researchers. For a short period of time, a Brill Fellow examines the sources in the Special Collections that correspond to the publishing areas of Brill. With these fellowships Brill underscores the traditional alliance between the publishing house and Leiden University.

The World of Brill

Brill continues to develop itself in a dynamic set of relationships that includes authors, readers, customers, suppliers, shareholders, staff, and its immediate surroundings. Naturally, a concern for economic growth and returns plays a major role in a company listed on the stock exchange. Brill's commercial goals, however, are selected in a way that makes a sustainable long-term strategy possible. To achieve that purpose, care must be taken to maintain a healthy balance, in the literal and the figurative sense, and the various interests of all parties concerned must be considered. Brill's evolving perception of its role as an organization committed to corporate social responsibility keeps the shareholder's interest in view and provides a lasting foundation for the pursuit of harmony between Pallas and Hermes.

6 IV 2005

MD
CL
XXX
III
2008

DIRECTORS OF THE FIRMS OF LUCHTMANS AND OF BRILL, 1683-2008

Jordaan Luchtmans	1683 - 1708
Samuel I Luchtmans	1708 - 1755
Samuel II Luchtmans	1755 - 1780
Johannes Luchtmans	1755 - 1809
Samuel III Luchtmans	1809 - 1812
(Johannes Brill, manager a.i	1812 - 1821)
Johannes Tiberius Bodel Nijenhuis	1821 - 1848
Evert Jan Brill	1848 - 1871
Adriaan Pieter Marie van Oordt	1872 - 1903
Frans de Stoppelaar	1872 - 1906
Cornelis Peltenburg	1906 - 1934
Theunis Folkers	1934 - 1947
Nicolaas Wilhelmus Posthumus	1946 - 1958
Frederik Casparus Wieder jr.	1958 - 1979
Tom A. Edridge	1979 - 1980
(Frederik Casparus Wieder jr., a.i.	1980 - 1981)
Willem Backhuys	1981 - 1989
Frans H. Pruijt	1989 - 1993
(Joost Kist, a.i.	1993 - 1994)
Reinout J. Kasteleijn	1994 - 2004
Herman A. Pabbruwe	2004-

For four years now, the company has produced little notebooks with colorful covers that replicate the illustrations on Brill's annual reports and corporate brochures. The notebooks are distributed at book fairs and academic congresses as promotional gifts, in numbers exceeding ten thousand a year and are very much in demand among authors and librarians. The first three notebooks have been printed with characters, ciphers, and punctuation marks using Unicode. They are a reminder of the specialization in exotic languages to which Brill owes its reputation, and they underscore the fact that this tradition is continued in the digital present.

SUPERVISORY DIRECTORS OF BRILL, SINCE THE FOUNDATION OF THE PUBLIC LIMITED COMPANY IN 1896 *

Prof. dr. M.J. de Goeje	1896 - 1909
W.H. van Oordt	1896 - 1904
Dr. W. Pleyte	1896 - 1903
J. de Stoppelaar	1896 - 1911
Prof. dr. A.C. Vreede	1896 - 1908
D. van Oordt	1905 - 1934
Mr. Th.B. Pleyte	1909 - 1913
W.P. van Stockum jr.	1911 - 1927
Mr. D.W.K. de Roo de la Faille	1914 - 1948
Dr. F.C. Wieder sr.	1928 - 1943
W.H. van Oordt	1934 - 1954
Prof. mr. dr. N.W. Posthumus	1943 - 1949
Ir. L.W.G. de Roo de la Faille	1949 - 1969
Ir. J.J. van den Broek	1957 - 1967
Mr. J.L. Heldring	1961 - 1989
Prof. dr. E.H. van der Beugel	1964 - 1988
Prof. dr. A. Kraal	1969 - 1987
Prof. dr. mr. J. Brugman	1969 - 1995
F.C. Wieder jr.	1979 - 1987
Drs. J.H. Scholte	1984 - 1989
Mr. R.P.M. de Bok	1988 - 1999
Mr. N.J. Westdijk	1989 - 1993
Mr. J. Kist	1990 - 2001
Prof. dr. P.J. Idenburg	1993 - 2007
Jhr. Mr. H.A. van Karnebeek	1998 - 2008
Drs. ing. H.P. Spruijt	2000-
Mr. R.E. Rogaar	2007-
Mr. A.R. Baron van Heemstra	2008-

* (The designation of Dutch (academic) titles has been retained for practical reasons)

NOTES

I In Olden Times. The House of Luchtmans and the House of Brill, 1683-1848

1 ULA/Spec. Coll., Luchtmans Archive BVA 71-44 a/b. As described in the last section of this chapter, the Luchtmans Archive is housed in the University of Amsterdam Library, Department of Special Collections (henceforth abbreviated as "ULA/SC").

2 De Clercq, *At the Sign of the Oriental Lamp: The Musschenbroek Workshop in Leiden.*

3 ULA/SC, Luchtmans Archive F.21, "Balance" of Samuel Luchtmans I, dated August 1, 1714.

4 Hoftijzer, "Veilig achter Minerva's schild," in Bouwman et al., *Stad van Boeken*, pp. 200-201; Van Vliet, *Elie Luzac*, pp. 52-53.

5 Blaak, *Geletterde levens*, p. 270; Goinga, *Alom te bekomen*, p. 64; *Bibliopolis*, pp. 71-72.

6 Ophuijsen, *Three Centuries of Scholarly Publishing*, pp. 12-14.

7 Samuel Luchtmans I estimated his share in this partnership in 1714 at nearly *f* 7,000 (see n. 3). The participation of Joh. Enschedé is mentioned by Muller, "Bodel Nijenhuis. Brill," pp. II, III.

8 Hoftijzer, *Pieter van der Aa*, pp. 21-25.

9 Van Eeghen, "Archief Luchtmans," p. 132.

10 ULA/SC, Luchtmans Archive F.21 and 26, balance sheets of Samuel Luchtmans I of August 1714 and October 1747.

11 Van Vliet, *Elie Luzac*, p. 51.

12 ULA/SC, Luchtmans Archive F.21, *Catalogus librorum quos Samuel Luchtmans vel ipse typis mandavit, vel quorum major ipsi copia suppetit*. Lugduni Batavorum, 1714.

13 J. Israel, *Radical Enlightenment* (Oxford, 2002), pp. 278-279; W. P. C. Knuttel, *Verboden boeken in de Republiek der Vereenigde Nederlanden* (The Hague, 1914), pp. 110-111, 115-116. In the Spinozist roman à clef *Vervolg van 't Leven van Philopater* (1697) by J. Duijkerius, reference is made on pp. 194-197 to the *Rechtsinnige Theologant*; cf. G. Maréchal (ed.), *Het leven van Philopater en Vervolg van 't Leven van Philopater* (Amsterdam, 1991; also at www.dbnl).

14 Hoftijzer, *Van der Aa*, pp. 26-32.

15 Folkers, "Oostersche boekdrukkerij te Leiden," pp. 63-64.

16 Ophuijsen, *Three Centuries of Scholarly Publishing*, p. 19.

17 G. Schwetschke, *Codex nundinarius Germaniae literatae bisecularis. Meß-Jahrbücher des Deutschen Buchhandels* (Halle, 1850). Jordaan Luchtmans is recorded under the years 1686, 1691, and 1699; Samuel I is nowhere mentioned. Perhaps he is to be identified with the anonymous bookseller from Leiden who is mentioned under 1722.

18 ULA/SC, Luchtmans Archive H.1-5; Kruseman, *Aanteekeningen betreffende den Boekhandel*, pp. 606-622.

19 Cf. Hoftijzer and Van Waterschoot (eds.), *Johannes Luchtmans. Reis naar Engeland in 1772*; Van Waterschoot, "Samuel Luchtmans, een reislustig boekhandelaar."

20 Van Vliet, *Elie Luzac*, pp. 177-197.

21 ULA/SC, Luchtmans Archive H.1.

22 Ibid., F.1, F.29-32.

23 J. T. Bodel Nijenhuis, *Dissertatio historico-juridica, de juribus typographorum et bibliopolarum in regno Belgico*. Lugduni Batavorum, apud S. et J. Luchtmans, Academiae typographos. MDCCCXIX. The work also appeared in a Dutch translation.

24 ULA/SC, Luchtmans Archive, uncatalogued.

25 Muller, "Bodel Nijenhuis. Brill," p. III.

26 See also Van Eeghen, "Het archief van de Leidse boekverkopers Luchtmans."

27 Cf. Blaak, *Geletterde Levens*, pp. 270-274; Smilde, "Lezers bij Luchtmans."

28 ULA/SC, Luchtmans Archive F.21, "Balance" of Samuel Luchtmans, dated August 1, 1714.

29 Du Rieu, "Levensschets Bodel Nijenhuis," p. 260.

30 Regional Archive Leiden, section Notarial Deeds (notary H. Obreen), testament of J. T. Bodel Nijenhuis, June 22, 1866; M. Storms, "Dit waarlijk vorstelijk legaat," in idem et al., *De verzamelingen van Bodel Nijenhuis*, pp. 9-24.

31 Muller, "Bodel Nijenhuis. Brill," p. I.

32 ULA/SC, KVB Archive 1886/14, J. L. Bienfait to the Board of the Association, December 11, 1885 (courtesy of Martine van den Burg); Hoftijzer and Lankhorst, *Drukkers, boekverkopers en lezers tijdens de Republiek*, pp. 12-28: "De periode van de bouwstoffen."

33 ULA/SC, KVB Archive 1886/14, A. C. Kruseman, L. D. Petit and R. W. P. de Vries as members of the historical commission to the Board of the Association, March 3, 1886; ibid., Verslagen van het Bestuur (1852-1915), "Verslag der werkzaamheden... over het Vereenigingsjaar 1885-1886," pp. 9-10, 14.

II The Firm of E. J. Brill, 1848-1896

1 For this chapter and the following ones, extensive use has been made of the Brill Archive. Like the Luchtmans Archive it is preserved in the Library of the Book Trade, housed in the Department of Special Collections of the Library of the University of Amsterdam. The definitive inventory has not yet been established, and so references are given with some reservation.

2 ULA/SC, Brill Archive fv.139, I-IV, *Catalogus van eene uitgebreide and zeer belangrijke verzameling Hebreeuwsche, Grieksche, Latijnsche, Nederlandsche en Fransche*

ongebonden boeken, zijnde de kopijen en een zeer belangrijk assortiment toebehoorende aan de firma S. en J. Luchtmans, August 20, 1849, and following days; in the fourth copy of the catalog a settlement and a letter from Brill to Bodel Nijenhuis, dated August 5, 1850; *Nieuwsblad voor den Boekhandel*, No. 33 (August 17, 1849) and No. 40 (October 4, 1849); Kruseman, *Bouwstoffen*, vol. 1, pp. 635-637.

3 Details on Brill's publications in various scholarly areas in Lebram et al., *Tuta sub aegide Pallas: E. J. Brill and the World of Learning*.

4 ULA/SC, Brill Archive fv.233.I, *Catalogus eener belangrijke verzameling ongebonden boeken, aangekocht en uitgegeven door E. J. Brill te Leiden* (1871).

5 N.N., "Adriaan P.M. van Oordt."

6 ULA/SC, Brill Archive, Company History 01, deed of sale of the firm, dated January 21, 1872.

7 F. de Stoppelaar and G. J. Dozy, *Proza en Poëzie. Leesboek ten gebruike van de laagste klassen der gymnasiën en hoogere burgerscholen*. The book was published by Van Looy in Tiel and reached its eleventh edition in 1906. See also De Goeje, "Frans de Stoppelaar"; Vreede, "Frans de Stoppelaar"; www.destoppelaar.com/genealogy.htm.

8 ULA/SC, Brill Archive, Company History 01, deed of partnership, dated October 17, 1872.

9 *Catalogue des collections étendues historiques et artistiques formées et délaissées par feu Mr. Bodel Nijenhuis* (3 vols., Leiden-Amsterdam, 1873-1874); A. van der Lem, "Verzamelaar en schenker van boeken: de bibliotheek van Bodel Nijenhuis," in Storms et al., *De verzamelingen van Bodel Nijenhuis*, pp. 62-86.

10 In full: *Annales quos scripsit Abu Djafar Mohammed Ibn Djarir at-Tabari*. Cum aliis. Edidit M. J. de Goeje (Leiden, 1879-1901).

11 ULA/SC, Brill Archive, Company History 03; contract dated May 21, 1875. The Ministry of Colonial Affairs was the owner of the printing types and had given them on loan to Leiden University.

12 M. J. Brusse, "De uitgeverij," *Nieuwe Rotterdamsche Courant*, January 5, 1927; E. Zürcher, "East Asian Studies," in Lebram et al., *Tuta sub aegide Pallas*, p. 62.

13 Wolters, "De firma Brill in hare nieuwe woning"; Regional Archive Leiden 519/4762, *Verslag van de verbouwing van het Heilige Geest of Arme Wees- en Kinderhuis*, with lithographs by the architect J. Bijtel (Leiden, 1882).

14 *Verslag omtrent het onderzoek, ingesteld door de Derde Afdeeling der Staat-commissie van Arbeids-enquête* (The Hague, 1894), pp. 201-202 (courtesy of dr. Berry Dongelmans).

15 ULA/SC, Brill Archive N.26, copy of the notarial deed, dated January 23, 1881.

16 *Catalogue de Manuscrits arabes provenant d'une bibliothèque privée à Medina et appartenant à la maison E. J. Brill*. Edited by C. Landberg (Leiden, 1883); Witkam, "Verzamelingen van Arabische handschriften," p. 26. Afterwards, al-Madani and Landberg sold three more collections of manuscripts to Brill, which found their way to Berlin and Princeton (courtesy of Dr. A. J. M. Vrolijk, head of the Eastern Collections of the University of Leiden Library).

17 C. Snouck Hurgronje, *Het Leidsche Oriëntalistencongres. Indrukken van een Arabisch Congreslid* (Leiden, 1883).

18 Ibid., p. 54.

19 *Verslag omtrent het onderzoek, ingesteld door de Derde Afdeeling der Staat-commissie van Arbeids-enquête, benoemd krachtens de Wet van 19 Januari 1890* (The Hague, 1894), pp. 201-204; 223-226 (courtesy of dr. Berry Dongelmans).

20 B. Dongelmans, "Industrialisatie, emancipatie en technologische vernieuwing," in: Bouwman et al., *Stad van Boeken*, p. 346.

21 According to the *Verslag over den toestand van handel en nijverheid in de Gemeente Leiden* of the Chamber of Commerce (Leiden, 1891), in 1890 there were 44 persons above the age of sixteen and 5 persons below that age employed at Brill in the print works and the composing room. Together with the staff of the shop, the antiquarian bookshop, and the office, the figure of 60 employees is a reasonable estimate.

III The N.V. Bookselling and Printing Firm, Formerly E. J. Brill, 1896-1945

1 ULA/SC, Brill Archive, Company History 01, deed of foundation of the N.V. (public limited company). After the deed had been executed on March 21, 1896 before the Amsterdam notary C. J. Pouw, the company was registered on the Stock Market on March 24. The royal decree approving the association was dated March 2. The deed of foundation and the royal decree were published in the supplement of the *Nederlandsche Staatscourant* of April 22, 1896.

2 ULA/SC, Brill Archive 1.2-1, Minute Books of the Meetings of the Supervisory Board (SB) and of the General Meetings of Shareholders (GMS), 1896-1945.

3 Ibid. 1.2-1, SB January 28, 1896; June 3, 1897; June 19, 1902; June 19, 1903; June 21, 1904; November 22, 1907; February 2, 1909; March 31, 1911.

4 Ibid. 1.2-1, SB December 30, 1896 and June 3, 1897; 1.2-2, GMS June 19, 1902; B. Dongelmans, "Aanbieders en aanbod," in: Bouwman et al., *Stad van Boeken*, pp. 362-364.

5 Ibid. 1.2-1, SB June 3, 1897; June 9, 1898; June 15, 1899; November 22, 1907.

6 Ibid. 1.2-1, SB June 19, 1903.

7 B. Dongelmans, "Aanbieders en aanbod," in: Bouwman et al., *Stad van Boeken*, p. 402.

8 Krom, "Levensbericht van C.M. Pleyte Wzn.," p. 9.

9 ULA/SC, Brill Archive 1.2-1, SB April 1, 1898; June 15, 1899; March 20, 1900. Later on, his brother Th. B. Pleyte was a supervisory director at Brill for some years, until he was appointed Minister of Colonial Affairs in 1913.

10 Ibid. 1.2-1, SB June 9, 1898; GMS June 9, 1898.

11 Ibid. SB June 21, 1900.

12 Wieder, "Peltenburg," p. 174.

13 ULA/SC, Brill Archive 1.2-1, SB September 11, 1908; October 19, 1911; December 29, 1911.

14 *Verslag van den toestand van handel en nijverheid in de gemeente Leiden over 1911*. Report by the Chamber of Commerce and Factories to the city council of Leiden (Leiden, 1912), p. 30. Courtesy of dr. Berry Dongelmans.

15 ULA/SC, Brill Archive 1.2-1, SB September 30, 1913; B. Dongelmans, "Aanbieders en aanbod," in Bouwman et al., *Stad van Boeken*, p. 373.

16 Ibid. 1.2-1, SB December 31, 1912 and April 9, 1914; ibid., Company History 02, "Enige herinneringen aan de heer C. Peltenburg," undated manuscript by master typesetter P. W. Martijn Sr.
17 Ibid. 1.2-1, SB December 30, 1915.
18 Ibid. 1.2-1, SB and 1.2-2, GMS, both over the years 1914-1918.
19 Ibid. 1.2-1, SB May 25, 1918.
20 Ibid. 1.2-1, SB 1919-1920.
21 *Bondsorgaan van den Nederlandschen Grafischen Bond* (vol. 7, no. 2), April 15, 1920.
22 ULA/SC, Brill Archive 1.2-1, SB April 23, 1920.
23 Ibid. Company History 02, "Enige herinneringen aan de heer C. Peltenburg," undated manuscript by master typesetter P. W. Martijn Sr.
24 Ibid. 1.2-1, SB 1923-1932.
25 Brusse, "Onder de Menschen: De uitgeverij" (X-XII), *Nieuwe Rotterdamsche Courant*, January 5, 12 and 19, 1927.
26 ULA/SC, Brill Archive, Company History 02, "Enige herinneringen aan de heer C. Peltenburg," undated manuscript by master typesetter P. W. Martijn Sr.
27 *Nieuwsblad voor den Boekhandel,* December 30, 1933.
28 ULA/SC, Brill Archive 1.2-1, SB April 13, 1938; 1.2-2, GMS June 4, 1938. The promise of a bequest of *f* 20,000 by Peltenburg's widow instigated the Peltenburg Pension Fund. It was exclusively intended for the office personnel of Brill; the retirement funds of the typographers were administered by the trade unions by then.
29 Ibid. 1.2-1, SB May 12, 1934.
30 Ibid. 1.2-1, SB 1934-39.
31 Ibid. 1.2-2, GMS 1934-1939.
32 Ibid. 1.2-1, SB October 10, 1935.
33 Ibid. 1.2-1, SB May 3, 1940. The new export department was previously discussed on October 20 and November 24, 1939.
34 Ibid. 1.2-2, GMS July 6, 1940.
35 Ibid. 1.2-2, GMS June 26, 1943.
36 Ibid. 1.2-2, GMS July 22, 1944.
37 G. Groeneveld, *Zwaard van de geest. Het bruine boek in Nederland 1921-1945* (Nijmegen, 2001), p. 222. Reference courtesy of dr. Berry Dongelmans.
38 ULA/SC, Brill Archive 1.2-1, SB April 28, 1943.
39 Ibid. 1.2-2, GMS June 26, 1943.
40 Ibid. 1.2-1, SB October 10, 1943; also as typescript "Overzicht voor nà den oorlog" (Outline for after the war) in Company History 10.03.

IV The Expanding Universe of Brill, 1945-2008

1 *Nederlandse Staatscourant*, October 3, 1947; *Nieuwsblad van de Boekhandel*, October 9, 1947; ULA/SC, Brill Archive 1.2-3, SB January 6, 1948.
2 J. Meihuizen, *Noodzakelijk kwaad. De bestraffing van economische collaboratie na de Tweede Wereldoorlog* (Amsterdam, 2003), p. 695.
3 Ibid., p. 226-227.
4 Ibid., p. 739-750. Meihuizen (see note 2) does not mention Folkers in his work. Nor does A. Venema pay any attention to the affair in his work on collaboration among writers and publishers (*Schrijvers, uitgevers en hun collaboratie*; 4 vols., Amsterdam, 1988-1992).
5 N.W. Posthumus, *Bronnen tot de geschiedenis van de Leidsche textielnijverheid* (a publication of source material in six volumes, The Hague, 1910-1922) and *Geschiedenis van de Leidsche lakenindustrie*, vol. 1 (The Hague, 1908; also his dissertation), and vol. 2 (The Hague, 1939).
6 ULA/SC, Brill Archive 1.2-3, SB November 11, 1949.
7 Ibid. 1.2-11, GMS 1946, annual report of Posthumus for 1945.
8 Ibid. 1.2-3, SB March 1, 1949; August 5, 1949; November 11, 1949; ibid. 10.03, Posthumus to the Beheersinstituut, September 30, 1949.
9 Ibid. 1.2-3, SB and 1.2-11, GMS, both over the years 1945-1949.
10 Ibid. 1.2-3, SB April 4, 1948 and August 19, 1948; J. W. Christopher, *Conflict in the Far East: American Diplomacy in China from 1928-1933* (Leiden, 1950).
11 Ibid. 1.2-3, SB March 1, 1949.
12 Ibid. 1.2-3, SB May 16, 1950; Company History 03, Christopher to Brill, June 8 and 9, 1950.
13 Ibid. 1.2-3, SB Jan.-Aug. 1950; 1.2-11, GMS 1951 (annual report of Posthumus for 1950).
14 Ibid. 1.2-3, SB February 12, 1953; January 18, 1954; February 14, 1955; May 9, 1955; March 7, 1960.
15 Arhur Lehning also published with Brill five books (1965-1977) on his hero, the anarchist godfather Mikhail Bakunin, and seven volumes in the series *Archives Bakounine* (1961-1981).
16 ULA/SC, Brill Archive N.23, undated memo by Posthumus on his American relations on behalf of his successor F. C. Wieder.
17 This section and the following ones are based on the minutes of the supervisory board (SB) and the general meeting of shareholders (GMS) over the years 1950-1958 (ULA/SC, Brill Archive 1.2-3 and 1.2-11 respectively).
18 F. C. Gerretson, *History of the Royal Dutch* (4 vols., 1953-1957), previously published as *Geschiedenis van de Koninklijke* (4 vols., 1932-1941); R. J. Forbes, *The Technical Development of the Royal Dutch/Shell (1890-1940)* (1957). Brill also published Forbes's *Studies in Ancient Technology* (9 vols., 1955-1964).
19 His Ph.D. thesis was published by Brill in 1952: B. A. van Proosdij, *Babylonian Magic and Sorcery: Being "The prayers of the lifting of the hand."*
20 The second volume of Posthumus's *Nederlandse Prijsgeschiedenis* was published with some delay in 1964. In 1971 Brill also published his *Uitvoer van Amsterdam, 1543-1545*.
21 This section and the following ones are based on the minutes of the supervisory board (1958-1975), those of the general meeting of shareholders (1958-1979), and the accompanying annual reports by F. C. Wieder (ULA/SC, Brill Archive 1.2-3, 1.2-11, 1.2-19 respectively).
22 In 1988 a supplementary eighth volume by W. Raven and J. J. Witkam was published.
23 ULA/SC, Brill Archive 1.2-3, SB May 24, 1965; December 2, 1966; January 13, 1967.
24 Ibid. 1.2-3, SB January 15, 1969; October 15, 1969.
25 Ibid. 1.2-3, SB July 7, 1970.
26 *Luchtmans & Brill: driehonderd jaar uitgevers en drukkers in Leiden, 1683-1983*. Compilers of the catalog and the exhibition were M. Castenmiller, J. M. van Ophuijsen, and R. Smitskamp.

27 "Erepenning voor jubilerende drukkerij Brill," *Leidse Courant*, October 3, 1983.

28 A. Sperber, *The Bible in Aramaic* (4 parts in 5 volumes). The first edition appeared between 1959-1973, the second in 1992, and the third in 2004.

29 In 1984 Brill bought the Scandinavian Science Press in the Danish Klampenborg. Its publishing list specialized in biology.

30 H. Kops, "Opwaaiend stof. De tragi-komische bestuurscrisis bij E. J. Brill," *Elsevier*, April 22, 1989.

31 Ibid.

32 P. de Waard, "Platvoerse ruzie onder professoren bij uitgever Brill," *Volkskrant*, May 6, 1989.

33 B. Büch, "Brill, werelduitgever. Driehonderd jaar uitgeven in oplagen van 500 exemplaren of minder," *Vrij Nederland*, October 22, 1983.

34 J. Nijsen, "E. J. Brill wil zich uit de rode cijfers tillen," *Boekblad* 39, September 29, 1989.

35 *The Facsimile Edition of the Nag Hammadi Codices*, ed. F. Shafik (13 vols., 1972-1984). Between 1984 and 1996 Brill published a text edition with translation (*Nag Hammadi Codices*, 11 vols.); second edition under the title *The Coptic Gnostic Library* (5 vols., 2000).

36 G. Stroucken, "Beursdebutant Brill koestert professorale werkwijze," *Parool*, July 30, 1997.

37 J. Alberts, "Uitgever Dode Zeerollen gaat niet voor snel geld," *NRC/Handelsblad*, July 20, 1997.

V Brill: Present and Future

1 J. Nijsen, "E.J. Brill wil zich uit de rode cijfers tillen," *Boekblad* 39, September 29, 1989.

2 See www.brill.nl.

3 *De Telegraaf*, July 15, 2008, interview with CEO Herman Pabbruwe.

4 The contents of both the Luchtmans and the Brill archives can be consulted in the near future at bc.uba.uva.nl/bbc.collectie-beschrijvingen.

BIBLIOGRAPHY

Blaak, J., *Geletterde levens. Dagelijks leven en schrijven in de vroegmoderne tijd in Nederland 1624-1770* (Hilversum, 2004)

Bodel Nijenhuis, J. T., "Luchtmans, Jordaan; Samuel (I); Samuel (II) en Johannes; Samuel (III)," in: A. J. van der Aa, *Biographisch Woordenboek der Nederlanden*, vol. IV (Haarlem, 1852), pp. 214-215

Bodel Nijenhuis, J. T., "Die Buchhändler-Familie Luchtmans in Leyden," in: H. Lempertz, *Bilderhefte zur Geschichte des Bücherhandels*, vol. IV (Cologne, 1856)

Bouwman, A., B. Dongelmans, P. Hoftijzer, E. van der Vlist and C. Vogelaar, *Stad van Boeken. Handschrift en druk in Leiden 1260-2000* (Leiden, 2008)

Brugman, J., "De Arabische Studiën in Nederland," in: N. van Dam et al., *Nederland en de Arabische Wereld van Middeleeuwen tot Twintigste Eeuw* (Lochem-Ghent), pp. 9-18

Brugmans, H. J., "Bodel Nijenhuis (Mr. Johannes Tiberius)," in: *Nieuw Nederlandsch Biografisch Woordenboek*, vol. IV (Leiden, 1918)

Brugmans, I .J., "N. W. Posthumus," *Economisch Historisch Jaarboek* 28 (1961), pp. 281-287

Brusse, M. J., "Onder de menschen. De uitgeverij," (fasc. X-XII: "N.V. Boekhandel en Drukkerij v.h. E. J. Brill"), *Nieuwe Rotterdamsche Courant*, January 5, 12 en 19, 1927

Castenmiller, M., J. M. van Ophuijsen and R. Smitskamp, *Luchtmans & Brill: driehonderd jaar uitgevers en drukkers in Leiden, 1683-1983. Catalogus van de tentoonstelling gehouden van 1 september tot 1 oktober in het Gemeente-archief te Leiden* (Leiden, 1983)

Clercq, P. R. de, *At the sign of the oriental lamp. The Musschenbroek workshop in Leiden, 1660-1750* (Rotterdam, 1997)

Deahl, J. G., "1683 – E. J. Brill – 1983," in: *Short-title Catalogue E. J. Brill, 1683-1983* (Leiden, 1983)

Deahl, J. G., "E. J. Brill's role in Arabic and Islamic studies," *New Books Quarterly on Islam & the Muslim world*, vol. I, nos.4-5 (London, 1981), pp. 11-13

Deahl, J. G., *Brill Leiden* (Leiden, 1991)

Delft, M. van, and C. de Wolf (eds.), *Bibliopolis. Geschiedenis van het gedrukte boek in Nederland* (Zwolle/The Hague, 2003)

Dillen, J. G. van, "Ter gedachtenis aan Nicolaas Wilhelmus Posthumus, een ondernemend historicus," *Tijdschrift voor Geschiedenis* 73 (1960), pp. 337-339

Dongelmans, B. P. M., P. G. Hoftijzer and O. S. Lankhorst, *Boekverkopers van Europa. Het zeventiende-eeuwse Nederlandse uitgevershuis Elzevier* (Zutphen, 2000)

Eeghen, I. H. van, "Het archief van de Leidse boekverkopers Luchtmans," in: *De Amsterdamse Boekhandel 1680-1725*, vol. V.I (Amsterdam, 1978), pp. 131-177

Eeghen, I. H. van, "De uitgeverij Luchtmans en enkele andere uitgeverijen uit de 18de eeuw," *Documentatieblad Werkgroep 18de Eeuw* (1977), pp. 5-8

Folkers, Th., "De geschiedenis van de Oostersche boekdrukkerij te Leiden," *Cultureel Indië* (vol. 3, 1941), pp. 53-68; also published in: *Cultureel Indië. Bloemlezing uit de eerste zes jaargangen 1939-1945* (Leiden, 1948), pp. 280-295

Goeje, M. J. de, "Levensbericht van F. de Stoppelaar," *Levensberichten der afgestorvene medeleden van de Maatschappij der Nederlandsche Letterkunde, 1905-1906* (Leiden, 1906), pp. 187-194

Goinga, H. van, *"Alom te bekomen." Veranderingen in de boekdistributie in de Republiek 1720-1800* (Amsterdam, 1999)

Hoftijzer, P. G., *Pieter van der Aa (1659-1733). Leids drukker en boekverkoper* (Hilversum, 1999)

Hoftijzer, P. G., and J. van Waterschoot (eds.), *Johannes Luchtmans. Reis naar Engeland in 1772* (Leiden, 1995)

Hoftijzer, P. G., and O. S. Lankhorst, *Drukkers, Boekverkopers en lezers tijdens de Republiek. Een historiografische en bibliografische handleiding* (The Hague, 2000[2])

Jansma, T. S., "Nicolaas Wilhelmus Posthumus," *Jaarboek van de Maatschappij van Nederlandse Letterkunde* (1961), pp. 126-133

Kerling, J. B. J., "C. Peltenburg Pzn., 1852-1934," *Leidsch jaarboekje 1935* (Leiden, 1935)

Krom, N. J., "Levensbericht van C. M. Pleyte Wzn.," *Jaarboek van de Maatschappij der Nederlandsche Letterkunde* (1919), pp. 5-25

Kruseman, A. C., *Bouwstoffen voor een geschiedenis van den Nederlandsche boekhandel, gedurende de halve eeuw 1830-1880* (2 vols.; Amsterdam, 1886-1887)

Kruseman, A. C., *Aantekeningen betreffende den boekhandel van Noord-Nederland, in de 17e en 18e eeuw* (Amsterdam, 1893)

Lebram, J. C. H. et al., *Tuta sub aegide Pallas. E. J. Brill and the world of learning* (Leiden, 1983)

Masurel, G. J. ""Door die zucht geleid, waarvan u 't harte brandt." Johannes Tiberius Bodel Nijenhuis (1797-1872)," *De Boekenwereld*, vol 8 (1991-1992), pp. 70-74

Molhuysen, P. C. "De Academie-drukkers," *Pallas Leidensis MCMXXV* (Leiden, 1925), pp. 305-322

Muller, F., "Mr. J. T. Bodel Nijenhuis. E. J. Brill," *Algemeen Adresboek voor den Nederlandschen boekhandel* 19 (Amsterdam, 1873), pp. I-VI; also published in *Bijdragen tot de geschiedenis van den Nederlandschen Boekhandel*, vol. I (Amsterdam, 1884), pp. 174-182

Muller, F., "De feestgave der firma E. J. Brill, bij het derde jubileum der Leidsche Hoogeschool - Leiden, vóór 300 jaren en thans," *Nieuwsblad voor den Boekhandel* (1875), pp. 79-80

N. N., "N.V. Boekhandel en Drukkerij voorheen E. J. Brill, 1848-1923, en S. en J. Luchtmans, 1683-1923," *Nieuwsblad voor den Boekhandel* (1923), pp. 631-634

N. N., "Adriaan P. M. van Oordt," *Leidsch Jaarboekje 1905* (Leiden, 1905), pp. 13-17

Ophuijsen, J. M. van, *E. J. Brill. Three centuries of scholarly publishing* (Leiden, 1994)

Otterspeer, W., *Groepsportret met dame*. Vol. II, *De vesting van de macht. De Leidse universiteit 1673-1775* (Amsterdam, 2001); vol. III, *De werken van de wetenschap. De Leidse universiteit 1776-1876* (Amsterdam, 2005)

Proosdij, B. A. van, *250 jaar Tuta sub aegide Pallas, adagium van Luchtmans en Brill* (Leiden, 1971); also published as article in *De Antiquaar*, vol. II, no. 4 (1971), pp. 81-92

Rieu, W. N. du, "Levensschets van Mr. Johannes Tiberius Bodel Nijenhuis," *Levensberichten der afgestorvene medeleden van de Maatschappij der Nederlandsche Letterkunde 1873* (Leiden, 1873), pp. 247-288

Smilde, A., "Lezers bij Luchtmans," *De Negentiende Eeuw*, vol. 14 (1990), pp. 147-158

Storms, M. et al., *De verzamelingen van Bodel Nijenhuis. Kaarten, portretten en boeken van een pionier in de historische cartografie* (Leiden, 2008)

Tersteeg, J., "Het 75-jarig bestaan van de N.V. Boekhandel en drukkerij v.h. E. J. Brill te Leiden, 1 juli 1848 - 1 juli 1923," *De uitgever*, vol. 6, no. 7 (Leiden, 1923), pp. 79-81

Vliet, R. van, "Nederlandse boekverkopers op de Buchmesse te Leipzig in de achttiende eeuw," *Jaarboek voor Nederlandse boekgeschiedenis* vol. 9 (2002), pp. 89-109

Vliet, R. van, *Elie Luzac (1721-1796). Boekverkoper van de Verlichting* (Nijmegen, 2005)

Vreede, A. C., "Frans de Stoppelaar," *Leidsch Jaarboekje 1907* (Leiden, 1907), pp. 1-8

Warendorf, S. jr., "Frans de Stoppelaar 1841-1906," *Adresboek van den Nederlandschen Boekhandel*, vol. 53 (Leiden, 1907), pp. 1-8

Waterschoot, J. van, "Samuel Luchtmans, een reislustig boekhandelaar," *De Boekenwereld*, vol. 15 (1998-99), pp. 298-306

Wieder, F. C. sr., "C. Peltenburg Pzn.," *Handelingen en levensberichten van de Maatschappij der Nederlandsche Letterkunde, jaarboek 1934-1935* (Leiden, 1935), pp. 174-178

Wieder, F. C. sr., "C. Peltenburg Pzn.," *Tijdschrift Koninklijk Nederlandsch Aardrijkskundig Genootschap*, vol. 51 (Leiden, 1934), pp. 647-648

Wieder, F. C. jr., "*Tuta sub aegide Pallas* in former times," *Catalogue No 505. E.J. Brill Antiquarian Booksellers* (Leiden, 1979), pp. 1-2

Witkam, J. J., "Verzamelingen van Arabische handschriften en boeken in Nederland," in: N. van Dam et al., *Nederland en de Arabische Wereld van Middeleeuwen tot Twintigste Eeuw* (Lochem-Ghent), pp. 19-29

Witkam, J. J., "De sluiting van Het Oosters Antiquarium van Rijk Smitskamp," *De Boekenwereld*, vol. 23 (2006-2007), pp. 207-214

Wolters, W. P., "De firma E.J. Brill in hare nieuwe woning," *Eigen Haard* (1883), pp. 356-360

Wijnmalen, T. L. C., "Ter nagedachtenis van Mr. J. T. Bodel Nijenhuis," *De Nederlandsche Spectator* 18-1-1872

ABBREVIATIONS USED IN CAPTIONS AND NOTES

BA	Brill Archive, in ULA/SC
Brill Coll.	Brill Collection, Leiden
KVB	Collection of the Koninklijke Vereniging van het Boekenvak [Royal Society of the Book Trade], in ULA/SC
LA	Luchtmans Archive, in ULA/SC
RAL	Regional Archive Leiden
SML	Stedelijk Museum De Lakenhal, Leiden
St. Mus. Leipzig	Stadtgeschichtliches Museum Leipzig
ULA	University of Amsterdam Library
ULA/SC	University of Amsterdam Library, Special Collections
ULL	University of Leiden Library

NOTES ON CONTRIBUTORS

Dr. Paul Dijstelberge (1956) took his doctoral degree in 2007 with the thesis *De beer is los!*, a study of seventeenth-century ornamental typographical material as an aid to the identification of anonymously produced printing. He is deputy curator at the Department of Special Collections of the University of Amsterdam and lecturer in book history at the Department of Book Studies and Codicology. His bibliographical research on Brill's publishing list is reflected in the captions of several illustrations in this book.

Mirte D. Groskamp (1982) completed her studies at the Reinwardt Academy for Museology. Since 2006 she has been working at the Department of Special Collections of the University of Amsterdam on the inventorization, arrangement, and access of the Brill Archive. The information she extracted from the archive and the draft texts she supplied form a substantial contribution to this book.

Nynke Leistra (1951) translated the Dutch version of this book into English. She had been long employed in the antiquarian book trade before she joined the cataloguing team of the Short-Title Catalogue of the Netherlands (STCN). She is also a freelance translator, occasionally providing translations for *Quærendo, A Quarterly Journal from the Low Countries Devoted to Manuscripts and Printed Books,* which is published by Brill.

Drs. Kasper van Ommen (1964) is art historian and coordinator of the Scaliger Institute at the University Library of Leiden. He regularly publishes on book-historical subjects and library history. He wrote the last chapter on the basis of interviews with CEO Herman Pabbruwe and supplied a number of texts for the captions of the illustrations.

Dr. Sytze van der Veen (1952) is historian and publicist. He wrote the text of this publication and was responsible for its final editing as well as the editing of the visual material. In 2007 he published a biography of John William, Duke of Ripperda (1682-1737), a Dutch adventurer who became prime minister of Spain and ended his days as corsair in Morocco. He is presently working on a book about the relations between the Netherlands and Latin America at the beginning of the nineteenth century.

COLOPHON

First published in Dutch as *Brill 325 jaar uitgeven voor de wetenschap* (2008)

Text
Dr. Sytze van der Veen, with contributions by Dr. Paul Dijstelberge, Mirte D. Groskamp, and Drs. Kasper van Ommen

Translation into English
Nynke Leistra

English language copy editor
Gene McGarry, Ph.D.

Design
André van de Waal and Remco Mulckhuyse, Coördesign, Leiden

Cover design
André van de Waal, Coördesign, Leiden

Photography
Joost Kolkman
University Library of Amsterdam, Special Collections
University Library of Leiden, Special Collections
Municipal Museum De Lakenhal, Leiden

Typeface
Scala

Paper
Arctic Volume White 130gr/m², internal pages
Arctic Volume White 150gr/m², covering pages
Arctic Volume White paper has a FSC mixed sources certificate. The wood used in its production originates from plantations and other controlled sources.
Cover made of sulphate cardboard, 240gr/m²
Grafisch Papier Andelst

Printing
Drukkerij Groen, Leiden

Binder
Jansenbinders, Leiden

ISBN 978 90 04 17032 2

www.brill.nl
www.brillusa.com

SPES ALIT AGRICOLAS